For Val e Neil

best wishes

$\mathcal{B}$RIAN

on the

$\mathcal{B}$RAHMAPUTRA

DAVID FLETCHER

BRIAN

on the

BRAHMAPUTRA

(WITH SUJAN IN THE SUNDARBANS)

Matador
9 Priory Business Park,
Wistow Road, Kibworth Beauchamp,
Leicestershire. LE8 0RX
Tel: (+44) 116 279 2299
Fax: (+44) 116 279 2277
Email: books@troubador.co.uk
Web: www.troubador.co.uk/matador

ISBN 978 1780884 547

British Library Cataloguing in Publication Data.
A catalogue record for this book is available from the British Library.

Printed and bound in the UK by TJ International, Padstow, Cornwall
Typeset in 11pt Bembo by Troubador Publishing Ltd, Leicester, UK

Matador is an imprint of Troubador Publishing Ltd

MIX
Paper from
responsible sources
FSC® C013056

For Sue

2009

1.

here was another dimension. It was the only explanation. There were the three standard ones: the up and down, the to and fro, and the side to side. And here in Jorhat, there was a fourth. No, not time, but another quite remarkable and entirely new dimension – in space. Or there again, perhaps it wasn't new. Perhaps it was just the modern manifestation of that fourth space dimension they'd used for the Indian rope trick. Only now they were using it to skim inches off the sides of buses and whisk entire rickshaws into non-existence. How else, Brian asked himself, could it possibly be happening?

Sandra had chosen to sit directly behind the driver, which meant Brian, in the seat next to her, had an unimpaired view through the windscreen of the minibus. That's to say he had an unimpaired view of a never-ending series of countless moving-traffic miracles, which could only ever be explained by his new hypothesis on a further space dimension, a dimension of which even Stephen Hawking was still ignorant. Assuming that is, that Mr Hawking hadn't ever ventured into the east of Assam.

'And shit, look at this one!'

It was a red, blue and green "public carrier" – with a horrible list. One of the countless pre-historic lorries seemingly constructed from dented cast iron and wooden off-cuts, which lumbered around the roads of Assam and, most significantly, had pre-eminence on these roads. Public carriers trumped buses, buses trumped minibuses, minibuses trumped 4x4s, 4x4s trumped cars, cars trumped rickshaws, and rickshaws trumped bicycles. Pedestrians were somewhere below bicycles, but Brian was not yet clear as to how they ranked in relation to cows, goats and dogs. And anyway, the status of pedestrians vis-à-vis that of the four-legged furniture of the thoroughfares was not now at the forefront of his mind. No, that place was currently occupied by the prospect of the moving metal equivalent of a brick shithouse bearing down on their insubstantial minibus and the unavoidable conclusion that there was about to be an unavoidable collision. Both vehicles were steaming past rickshaws and cycles as though the road ahead was clear – when it clearly wasn't. When it was clearly far too thin and far too cluttered to allow the two vehicles to pass each other without there being a seriously destructive encounter.

Brian gripped his seat-belt. This time their driver had got it wrong.

'And God! Look at that bloody cyclist! There's no way...'

A cyclist had just emerged from behind a lorry, which might have been making a delivery or which might have been abandoned sometime in the Sixties. It was difficult to tell. But it was easy to tell what was about to happen to the cyclist. He was about to be squashed between a red, blue and green public carrier and a minibus carrying a dozen "Nature-seekers", their agreeable guide, Sujan, and a blind or stupid driver.

Brian's eyes widened to cartoon proportions. He couldn't not watch. It was just about to happen...

Then the cyclist disappeared. Past the near-side front corner of the minibus straight into that novel dimension – followed quickly by a six-inch slice of the bus itself (complete with its rear-view mirror) as it slid effortlessly past the side of the oncoming lorry. The two vehicles hadn't even slowed. Such is the efficacy of this fourth dimension and people's confidence in its use. Only Brits two days out of Brit-land would have had any doubts.

Brian was stunned. Although he was no scientist, he had, many years ago, graduated in chemistry from the University of Birmingham. The course had included quantum mechanics and something equally impenetrable called solid-state chemistry. All he could remember from the quantum mechanics was the image of a one-dimensional box with a potential of infinity inside and a potential of zero outside (which had served to convince him he was not a natural for the subject) and from his solid-state chemistry lectures, all he could recollect was that within the theories studied was the proof that there were only twenty-seven basic designs for wallpaper. But he could also remember that in neither of these rather challenging disciplines was there even a hint of a fourth dimension in space. Not in Birmingham and certainly not here in the cacophony of humanity that went by the name of Jorhat. It shouldn't exist. But it did. And to reinforce its existence beyond any remaining doubt, it swallowed up a rickshaw. Right before Brian's eyes, a slow-moving rickshaw travelling in the same direction as the minibus and about to be mangled under its wheels, instead glided by its side where there was simply no room for it to do so, but where obviously there was a convenient corridor of that "Indian fourth space".

Brian took a small plastic bottle from between his legs. Perhaps a refreshing drink of water would help him come to terms with his new knowledge of the universe. He unscrewed its cap – and made his second new discovery about space in India: that they don't leave any of it at the top of their water bottles. It was full right up to the rim. Or at least it was before Brian spilt the top inch or so of its contents over his binoculars.

'Shit!'

'What's up now?' demanded Sandra. 'And why have you poured water over your binocs?'

'I haven't. It was the bottle. It was too full.'

'Oh, naughty bottle. Why didn't you stop it? Why did you let it do that?'

Brian looked at his wife. He was just about to deliver a suitably clever retort to her sarcastic observations when it slipped away to be lost in the depths of that blasted fourth dimension. Or that's what he thought. The truth, of course, was that he was simply distracted by the moistened state of his Swarovskis. This was just the start of the holiday. He hardly wanted to screw up his wonderful binocs before he'd even used them.

'Here's a tissue,' announced Sandra in the middle of his distraction. 'Although I hardly think a little bit of water is going to hurt them.'

It was true. Modern binoculars, and especially binoculars requiring a Northern Rock-scale mortgage to acquire, were hardly going to dissolve in a teaspoon-full of water.

'Thanks,' managed Brian. And he took the tissue and applied it to the dampened surface of his precious eyepieces. He felt mildly ridiculous. But so what? He often felt mildly ridiculous. It was almost his default state of mind. And furthermore, he had a new distraction. Not someone else's moistened binoculars, but a change of scenery. Yes, finally Jorhat was behind them. They had made it through the metropolis with their minibus and their limbs intact (thanks to that magic new dimension) and they were now into open country.

Well, "open country" might not be the most accurate description of the sort of landscape through which they were now driving. Indeed, in a court of law, even the most incompetent of advocates would have successfully challenged the use of this terminology and would easily have convinced a jury that a more appropriate phrase might be "non-urban, ribbon despoilment" or just possibly "a bit of a bloody mess".

Brian wanted to be charitable. This was a poor country. It couldn't afford the credit-supported niceties of Britain, and it had the concerns of daily survival to contend with, not the challenges of winning the forthcoming "Britain in Bloom" competition. But really, it was all a bit grim. Everywhere seemed to be falling down, or standing up only because it didn't have the energy to fall down. And it was all so ugly; decrepit (possibly) abandoned factories, buildings painted before paint had even been invented – and litter, litter all over the place. And not even "modern" litter. Some of it had the air of antiquity about it. Brian felt that he could have sifted through some of those piles of detritus and learnt how the Empress of India had enjoyed her recent honeymoon. Although would they have reported that in the "*Times of India*"? Brian wasn't sure.

However, being unsure was the stable-mate of feeling mildly ridiculous, and soon Brian had dismissed all thoughts of rural ugliness from his mind, along with all that fourth dimension stuff. Because now the minibus was in tea country…

'It's flat,' he informed his wife. 'And well, you know, you think of tea in Assam, and you think of hills, don't you? Not flat stuff like this.'

'Mmm…' responded Sandra. 'But I suppose they'd need hills for that, wouldn't they?'

Sandra's tone was somewhere between dismissive and inscrutable, and her comment left Brian struggling. Was his wife being sarcastic again or thoughtful or pedantic? Or was she suffering from their ultra-early start to the day? They had risen at 4.30 in the morning, had left the boat at 5.30, and after their journey from the river, through Jorhat, through the fourth dimension and through bucolic squalor, it was still only a little before seven. And who, thought Brian, other than a traditional French baker or maybe Margaret Thatcher, would operate lucidly and efficiently at such an alarmingly early hour?

Brian therefore decided not to express any further thoughts on the rather horizontal topography of Assamese tea-plantations and instead merely examined their nature in a studied silence. They were very neat. That was what one could not fail to notice (after one had first taken note of their flatness) – and they appeared to be unbounded. There were no hedges, no fences, nothing which appeared to mark one spread of tea plants from the next, and therefore nothing to guide the pickers. How, thought Brian, do they know which bit they've picked and which bit they haven't? How do they even know where they were the previous day and where they should kick off again on the new shift? And what if one of them leaves his Tiffin can by mistake? How could he ever find it again? Or maybe *her* Tiffin can. Maybe all the pickers are women.

Brian stared into space. It was always a source of wonderment to him that he could be so ignorant about so many things. He often thought that too many people thought they "knew it all", that they had an answer for everything and that they had nothing else to learn. Brian, on the other hand, knew more than many, but he also knew that he knew very little. He knew that there was a whole mountain of knowledge out there and that he hadn't even begun to scale it, not even after sixty years on this Earth. And as much as he observed, and as much as he listened, and as much as he read, he knew he'd still not get more than a couple of yards up its slope. Even though he now knew that Assamese tea plantations were not hilly – and that they were studded with trees – to provide a bit of shade by the looks of it. And as he took in these trees he became aware of a lot more trees – on the left hand side of the bus – and then of the bus slowing. 'This must be it,' he thought. 'The gibbon sanctuary. We've finally arrived. We've got here.'

'Malayan giant squirrel,' pronounced Sujan. 'Top of trees. Everybody out!'

'Wow,' thought Brian. 'A giant squirrel. I wonder how giant.'

Well, when he saw it, he didn't think "very". It was a bit of a monster, but for a squirrel to be a giant squirrel, Brian would have required something the size of Ronnie Corbett, and this chap wasn't anywhere near as big as that. That said, it was still a good spot. Hell, it was the first time in his life that he had seen one of these animals. And they were pretty rare. 'So forget the "giant" disappointment,' he told himself. 'And just relish the experience. Make the most of it.'

He did. He followed the movements of the squirrel for as long as it was in sight, and then he found a bird: a green-billed malkoha. It was fabulous, and it gave Brian his first chance to do a bit of active co-birding with his fellow Nature-seekers – and to start sorting them out in his mind.

This was not going to be easy. The boat, back on the Brahmaputra, accommodated twenty-four guests, and had been chartered for the exclusive use of Brian and his fellow nature-nuts. There were therefore twenty-three people in the party, eleven couples and a single traveller. Brian's minibus held twelve of them, but there was a second minibus, now drawn up behind his own, which held another eleven. These had been disgorged from this bus and were now mingling with Brian's dozen to make a perplexing mêlée of individuals whom he still hardly recognised and whose names were still a mystery. No matter, he'd have a go. And why not with this lady here?

'Have you seen it?'

'Yes, I got a really good shot.'

The lady he'd addressed, whom he later learnt was Pauline, the wife of Dennis, was now showing him the digital screen thing on her camera, the sort of camera Brian associated with photographers at football matches – when long ago he'd still had an interest in that sort of stuff. It had an enormous lens on it, and on the screen, an enormous picture of the green-billed malkoha. While Brian had been feeling smug that he had managed to clock this remarkable bird as it flitted between the branches, not only with his eyes but with his binoculars as well, Pauline had managed to take a bloody photo of it – and a photo that filled the whole of that screen thing. Brian felt suitably deflated – and mildly ridiculous again.

'Wow,' he said, but it was a wow without conviction. It was just as well his first encounter with Pauline was about to be drawn to an abrupt conclusion. It was time to re-board the buses. They had arrived at the gibbon sanctuary, but only at its edge. There was still a little way to go to the entrance, so it was back on the wheels again. And thankfully Pauline was on the other vehicle. It would give Brian more time to gather himself and develop a more cautious approach to his breaking-the-ice programme for the rest of the party. Like he'd take a good look at their cameras to start with…

Within fifteen minutes both minibuses were parked in the sanctuary forest and the first of what would become a regular custom of the expedition to North-east India was underway: the early-morning mass-relief session.

This was a fairly rapid affair for the gentlemen in the party as they were granted peeing rights within the forest. For the ladies, of course, it was a very different matter. The minibuses were parked next to a "rest house", within which apparently there was a "rest room". But only one. And with so many ladies, most of whom were wrapped around with webbing, camera-straps, binoculars and other safari-type paraphernalia which, for all Brian knew, might have to be loosened or even detached before things could get under way, the process of their discharging their rest room responsibilities was interminable. Had it taken much longer, Brian would have suggested some improvised device of some sort. But, no, maybe he wouldn't have. He'd have just thought about it and said nothing… And anyway, the enforced wait had given him all the time he needed to secure himself against leeches…

They had all been warned about these little blighters the previous evening. So Brian had already swathed his feet in two pairs of socks. He had no great desire to repeat his experience in Madagascar. There, he had been well and truly sucked – and despite his spending an hour in a forest doing little more than studying his boots as he walked along, and being no less than meticulous in removing the leeches with his fingers as they arrived on his footwear, rolling them up, and then flicking them off. He still got sucked on his thigh. Which wasn't quite as bad as Sandra's suck. Hers was on her stomach. In neither case did they find the leech.

But this was Assam, and Brian was very well girded and very alert. He had his Rohan trousers tucked firmly into his two pairs of socks and he had his mind tucked firmly into the avoidance of leeches. This time they wouldn't get through. Even if it meant missing the odd glimpse of a gibbon in the distance. Oh, and he'd keep in the middle of the party as it strolled through the forest. Apparently the leeches went for the leaders and the stragglers, and those in between were rarely troubled...

It worked. There were leeches about, but not too many. And a bonus: an easily visible family of gibbons – in what appeared to be a leech-free zone of the forest. Brian was even able to take some photos of them as they peered down on the strangers beneath them. They were western hoolock gibbons; two black males and a fawn coloured female with a young one in her arms. They were charming. Although he doubted they had the same opinion of their observers. They probably thought they were just rather odd, and that the tall one down there hadn't even got a good covering of fur on his head. 'He must be very old or very ill. And how does he attract a mate?'

Brian was suffering from a little bout of anthropomorphism, which probably meant he was hungry. It was just as well that the party was now retracing its steps and returning to the rest house for some breakfast.

This was quite a production. Another bus had arrived while they'd been away, and this had brought from the boat its catering staff and all the comestibles needed for a hearty, late-morning feed. A crescent of chairs had been arranged in front of the rest house and food preparation was already underway in a well-equipped field kitchen. Brian was impressed, as was everybody else. And despite the growing heat of the day there was no shortage of customers for the fry-ups on offer.

Brian served himself with some bacon and fried bread and then queued for his egg choice.

'One egg, please. Fried both sides.'

He accompanied this request with the internationally recognised hand signal for the "both-sides" treatment of the single egg, and observed immediately that in India, "one egg" means "two". It had happened in Kolkata on their first morning in the country. There he had made an identical request, and as now, he had ended up with double his requirements. He knew he mumbled a bit, but he had pronounced his order with the clarity of a seasoned newsreader (as one tended to do in foreign parts) and he could only conclude that this duplication approach was a standard part of Indian egg cuisine. Presumably if one asked for two eggs, one would get four, and so on. Or was it just eggs? If a wife expressed a desire for two children in India was that taken by her husband as four? A sort of pleasing generosity of spirit that had now got out of hand. Well, there were an awful lot of children everywhere…

Brian chided himself. That was a terrible thought not worthy of a true Nature-seeker. All they were doing was trying to feed him properly, and here he was being mean and spiteful. He felt properly ashamed. So much so that he didn't enjoy his breakfast. He ate it but he felt guilty and a little miserable, his mood picking up only at its conclusion when he discovered on his ankle an enormously engorged leech. It had clearly found no trouble at all in reaching his blood supply through two layers of socks as he'd been sitting there eating his eggs. Something had moved in mysterious ways and the world had been put to rights. Through the agency of a small sucking animal, justice had been delivered swiftly and proportionately. He picked the leech off his ankle, laid it carefully on the grass and smiled. Sandra said she thought he was mad.

She also said that she thought he should now wear his hat. The sun was getting higher in the sky, the temperature was rocketing, and the party was now about to embark on a proper walk. This wouldn't be just a pre-breakfast stroll, this would be a two to three hour hike, much of it along an old road through the sanctuary, where the sun was free to beat down on unprotected heads and beat down with intensity on heads without a good covering of fur on them. But Brian hated hats. And if he made use of all the shade – or of what shade there was…

So nearly three hours later he'd seen some capped langur monkeys, any number of new birds, including a Jerdon's baza and a pale-chinned flycatcher, passed a few words with other members of the party – and he was beginning to feel entirely exhausted. However, so were most of the others, and now they could re-board their buses and relax on the way home. Or they could have if all that manic traffic had disappeared. And Jorhat had been removed. And there wasn't more of that fourth dimension nonsense. And if their bus's horn had gone on the blink… Brian had been conscious of a more than enthusiastic use of the horn by the driver on the outward journey. But now, on the way back, he was conscious only of those rare interludes when it wasn't being used.

India's traffic must be the noisiest in the world. Horns are used constantly to announce one's presence to other road users. And with the roads packed full of road users, that means virtually all the time. If some other vehicle isn't blaring a warning at you, you're blaring a warning at it. And for all Brian knew, this constant use of horns was also an essential part of conjuring up all that fourth dimensional space out there.

Eventually, however, the purgatory of the roads was over, and the two minibuses pulled up to the muddy bank of the Brahmaputra. To be precise, they pulled up to the muddy, south bank of the Brahmaputra. Which wasn't ideal, as their mother boat, the MV Sukapha, was moored half a mile away on the north bank. There was therefore a final stage to the homeward journey: a short ride in the Sukapha's "country boat", a small enclosed tender that was used to ship its passengers from shore to ship and ship to shore whenever it was moored on the wrong side of the river – which, as it transpired, was always.

This final leg of the journey took an age. First, twenty-three Nature-seekers, keen to spot that last new bird for the day, or to capture that last special image on their Nikon, had to be rounded up and kitted out with their garish orange life-jackets – of which more later. Then, when all were aboard, there was a further delay due to an impromptu performance of a pantomime on the bank of the river. A driver of a local minibus had been loading his vehicle onto a fat, black cargo boat – by driving it across two strategically placed gang-planks – when the strategy failed. His vehicle was now stranded on the planks, three wheels still on the planks – but one not. At the left front corner of the minibus it was not rubber resting on the woodwork but axle. And he was well and truly stuck.

Clearly entertainment on this scale could not be ignored, and the Sukapha's tender only pulled away when it became clear that the pantomime's plot line had nowhere to go. The minibus was stuck and would probably remain stuck for the foreseeable future. So there was nothing more to see.

Now, the trip across the river could have taken no more

than fifteen minutes. But for Brian, this trans-river trip seemed to take as long as a Neil Kinnock speech. And this was because Brian had developed a big problem. Yes, an early start to the day, all those hours on the road, that double egg for breakfast and then a walk in the sun, had all conspired to generate for this particular Nature-seeker what could only be described as an urgent evacuational event situation. If he didn't get to a lavatory very, very soon, there would be a very personal but very public disaster.

It was a close run(s) thing, but he managed it. He made it to the privacy of his en-suite privy just in time, and there he relieved himself mightily. And this relief would have been unbounded if he hadn't then realised that this was just the start. That his problem wasn't merely a touch of the sun and too many eggs – but also something a little more bacterial. And that for the next twenty-four hours at least his closest friend would be the closet on which he was now sitting. Nature-seeking would have to go on hold for a while. He would have to stay on board the Sukapha – and close to this loo.

For the third time today, he felt mildly ridiculous.

2.

*B*rian resorted to a diet of bananas. What it lacked in variety it more than made up for in its digestibility and its "intestinal integrity". That is to say that the bananas, even when chewed, seemed to remain reasonably solid as they passed through his gut. And, at least, this allowed him to sleep through the night, without his having to make repeated visits to what he now regarded as his porcelain haven.

The morning, however, was not so good. Even bananas, it seemed, had their limits. And on several occasions Brian was once again reduced to the pose of "*The Thinker*", and Sandra, in the cabin outside the door, was forced to try not to listen. But there again, that's what being married is all about, isn't it? One party to the marriage coping with the unspeakable bodily functions of the other party – whilst at the same time trying not to display too much in the way of intrusive interest in their loved one's discomfort. After all, it could be her turn next...

There are, of course, also limits to this sort of intimacy, and eventually Sandra decided to leave him on his own – to conduct the next movement of his sufferings in splendid isolation and without an audience of even one. She had decided she would take herself to the sundeck, and there take in the splendour of the Brahmaputra and enjoy her own isolation. Because all the other Nature-seekers had left the boat some time ago to visit a nearby temple and absorb some local culture, and she would thus have the sundeck to herself.

So Brian was now on his own – in bed. Propped up against a couple of pillows, he was staring at the shape of his body beneath the bed-clothes and he was feeling sorry for himself in a way only a man could feel sorry. And why not? Hell, he'd spent all that money to get to Assam, and now he was here he was out of action. And not only had he got a full-blown belly-ache, but he also had a pretty awful headache, and on top of that, an awful lingering taste of stale bananas in his mouth. It just wasn't fair. Especially when everybody else was out there soaking up new experiences. Or just relaxing on the sundeck without even a hint of any ailments. Life was such a bitch…

But no, this was being far too negative, even for Brian. If he was stuck here for now he should use the time as best he could. And to start with, why not take in the delights of the cabin? After all, it was a pretty nice cabin, and it even had an extra window. Yes, the Sukapha, on its upper deck, housed twelve cabins, six either side of a central corridor. But the end cabins, one of which was now in the possession of Brian and Sandra, had not just a window looking out of the side of the vessel, but another equally expansive window looking out of the stern of the vessel. This was a real treat, the sort of treat normally afforded to well-connected people or the members of quangos, and very rarely to the likes of Brian, who were normally grateful to get any sort of window at all – or even a reasonably large bed. And yes, that was OK as well. In fact, it was more than OK. It was easily large enough to accommodate Brian's six-foot-two-ish frame, his appreciably smaller wife, his night-time excursions around the mattress, and now, even his emaciated husk of a body as it lay slumped like a cadaver…

'Oh, come on,' he said out loud. 'This isn't good enough at all. I think it's about time I had some air.'

And with that, he eased himself out of bed and then he eased himself into the shower. This worked wonders, and within a quarter of an hour he was emerging onto the sundeck of the Sukapha and squinting along its length to locate the whereabouts of his temporarily estranged wife. It didn't take him long. The sundeck was more or less the size of the whole boat, but it was fitted out with only enough sun-loungers and cane chairs to serve the needs of its two dozen passengers. Other than this furniture there was just a small wheelhouse, a small bar, a cabinet containing a selection of local handicrafts and three postcards and, at the far end of the deck (over the blunt end), a row of pots containing plants, most of which were either in the process of recuperation or in the process of expiring. It was difficult to tell which.

He approached Sandra and announced his presence.

'Hi. I'm up.'

'Have you got the key? You haven't locked it in the room, have you?'

Brian blinked. He hadn't quite prepared himself for the warmth of this greeting. And worse, he now couldn't remember what he'd done with the key. He mumbled something even he didn't understand, and as he mumbled he fumbled. Somewhere in one of his pockets he must have the key.

He did. He withdrew it with a dramatic flourish and presented it to his wife.

'Amazing,' she observed, as she took it from his hand. 'I suppose I shouldn't have left it...'

She was sitting in one of the cane chairs with a book in her lap and now a smile on her face. And there was real concern there as well.

'And I suppose I should ask how you are. And how your stomach is.'

'Well, I'm feeling much better, thanks. And I think my stomach is as well. At least, I haven't heard from it for a while. And that can't be bad.'

'Good. And what are you going to do now?'

'Nothing. And I hope my stomach has the same idea. And then, who knows? I might even have some lunch.'

Sandra regarded her husband with a look that suggested she might be considering the effect on his bowels of a new delivery of Indian fuel. But all she said was: 'Well, don't sit in the sun'.

He didn't. He sat in another cane chair in the shade of the sundeck awning – and he thought about getting entirely well again – and about what was still in store…

He and Sandra had booked this trip as soon as they had seen it advertised. Assam was essentially a tourist-free zone, and was only now being opened up at all following the easing of the separatist problems that had plagued this remote part of India for years. Furthermore, as well as an absence of tourists there was an abundance of wildlife in this area, and many species of animals and birds that Sandra and he would never have seen before. And to clinch it, they would be able to visit this area with a group of like-minded people and with some more than competent guides – and *on a boat!* Yes, rather than slogging around from lodge to lodge and camp to camp (as they'd done in many other "challenging" parts of the world) they would be able to glide down the mighty Brahmaputra on what was nothing less than a floating hotel. No unpacking bags every night, no repacking rinsed-out knickers before they were even dry, and no checking that you'd not left anything behind – worrying constantly that the tickets and the passports were no longer there.

They didn't normally travel in a group, and only twice before had they signed up as "Nature-seekers". But this was different. And very appealing. And it even had an appealing extension. At the end of the Brahmaputra cruise, they, along with just eight others from the current group, would be going on to the Sundarbans for four nights. This was the area at the mouth of the Ganges to the south of Kolkata. Here there were mangrove forests, more animals, more birds – and again, no tourists. Just a handful of Nature-nutters like themselves. Bliss indeed.

Well, so far it was shaping up fine. If, that is, one ignored the current case of the squitts, the local traffic and those bloody awful life-jackets. Other than those little wrinkles, everything had been as smooth as the lining on Brian's gut. The flights out to India had all worked, the hotel in Kolkata where they'd spent their first night had been terrific – and the MV Sukapha was all they could have wished for.

To look at, their current floating accommodation wasn't quite as sleek as the sort of stuff Mr Abramovich goes in for. But there again it wasn't built for the same purpose. It wasn't constructed to impress air-heads, but instead it was put together to carry a small number of passengers in cosseted comfort down the broad and shallow waters of the Brahmaputra. To this end, it needed to be more a floating brick shape than anything more traditionally ship-shape and it hardly needed a pointy bit at the front end at all. The Sukapha, you see, didn't cut its way through the water, it eased its way through – in the way a punt does – and with the same sort of draft as a punt. Only a very little of the Sukapha's hull was hiding beneath the water-line.

This submerged bit did, however, house a remarkable amount of activity. Small portholes just below the lower deck (the boat's ground floor) were reminders to the cosseted passengers that below them were twenty or more crew, cooking, washing, ironing, oiling, tending – and living – and generally doing everything that was needed to keep the cosseting at the highest level possible. And they were all so smart and friendly…

Above this working level was the lower deck of the Sukapha, which housed the passengers' dining room – and a spa. Not like Cheltenham of course, but like one of those places where they rub things on you and rub things off you, and sometimes they do things with your feet. Brian even thought of using it (for about two minutes). But then the thought went away and it never came back.

Then there was the upper deck, which housed all the cabins – and at its front end, the lounge. This was a lovely room. It had a bar in one corner and on the wall by the door there was a small library. This had nothing Russian in it and there were no football annuals. So not really ideal for Mr Abramovich. But it was full of books on flora and fauna and all things natural, the sort of reading material Nature-seekers have been known to digest in their sleep. The lounge also contained some fine cane armchairs and settees, a little clutch of low, glass-topped cane tables, and at its very front, there was a pair of sliding doors opening out onto a forward-facing balcony. Here one could act out that famous scene from the film "*Titanic*" where two people, whose names Brian had never committed to memory, pose dramatically on the prow of the doomed ship. Only, on the Sukapha it was even better than in the film. The balcony was just above the lower deck, and any falling-over mishap would therefore result in only a broken limb and not in the loss of an entire life through drowning or instant hypothermia.

Furthermore, there was very little possibility that any other passenger would be attempting to recreate the drama of that scene from "*Titanic*", as most of them had far more sense. So you would have the stage to yourself, so to speak, and you could give it your all. And finally, unlike the Titanic, the Sukapha was not a doomed ship. So you could come back into the lounge whenever you liked and have a welcome drink from the bar, safe in the knowledge that the vessel you were currently on was not going to hit an iceberg.

All these thoughts had passed through Brian's head as he rested on the next deck up – which has already been described. This didn't mean he was delirious, but it did mean he needed some interaction with other humans and he possibly needed some food. It was therefore very fortuitous that the Nature-seekers were now returning to the boat and that very soon lunch would be served.

It was curry. Indeed, lunch was always curry. Just like dinner was always curry. This, after all, was India, and in India, people eat curry all the time. Here, it was not regarded as a treat or as an option or as a post-boozer fill-up, but simply as a diet, as a natural way to eat, and virtually the only way to eat. For Brian, this wasn't a problem. He delighted in eating all sorts of curries, and the one on offer this lunch-time, laid out on the buffet table in the Sukapha's dining room, looked particularly inviting. All the more galling then that he had to decline the invitation. Sandra and his own reluctant common sense told him to do so. And instead to have a… well, why not a banana?

In the event, he had two. India's bananas were a little on the small side. Just like its elephants.

He also had the company of Pamela and Julian, and of Sujan, one of their two principal guides. Communal eating was part of the Nature-seekers' ethos, and here in the dining room there were just two long tables, so you always had enough table companions to field a football team. Although, of course, only a small proportion of them were within chatting distance. And on this occasion, for Brian and Sandra, it was Pamela and Julian, and sitting at the head of the table, next to Brian, the ever-smiling Sujan. They made an odd combination.

Pamela was a GP. In fact, Brian had noticed that she'd introduced herself as a GP and not as a doctor. In the same way, he thought, as a forger wouldn't necessarily introduce himself as a criminal. He'd want to be specific, wouldn't he? After all, "doctor" and "criminal" both cover so many different roles. Or was that being just a little unfair? Maybe she was merely making it clear that, thanks to the remarkable negotiation skills of the Department of Health, she was now a very high earner – and still couldn't believe her luck. But no. That was being more unfair than ever. And it entirely ignored the fact that Pam was a very nice lady.

In appearance terms she was indisputably very nice indeed. She was young looking and probably younger looking than her actual age, and she had a pleasing face. It was glowing with health (and why wouldn't it be?) and it even had a fine bone structure. It also had, as its natural expression, a faint smile and an air of rare serenity. This, Brian thought, might be a product of the caring nature of her work – or of her six-figure salary. Ultimately though, he decided it was just because she was a nice person. And not just in appearance terms. But in the way she spoke, the way she listened and the way she acted.

Julian was similar. He wasn't as attractive as Pam, and with Brian's height, a rather gaunt face and an indecisive sort of grey beard, he was never going to be. But he was clearly cast in that same caring mould as his wife. He wasn't a GP or even just a doctor. He was an academic – in some aspect of agriculture. Which must have been a source of endless hours of fun at academic gatherings... along the lines of: 'What field are you in?' 'Oh, I'm in cereals.' 'Mmm, well watch out for the combine!'

There again, academia might be a little more sophisticated these days, and Brian was sure there were just as many opportunities to show your caring qualities as a teacher and researcher as there were as a doctor. And no doubt about it; Julian was thoughtful, responsible – and nice. Just like his wife.

This did cause Brian a bit of a problem. When he'd first seen them, back in Kolkata, he had pictured them as the man and wife proprietors of a health-food shop. In his mind, he could see them very clearly, standing behind a counter full of mung-beans and lentils, relishing the prospect of another of their grateful customers stocking up on some of their nourishing foodstuffs. But now that this image had been swept away by reality, another more alarming one had taken its place. It was one based on their pervasive air of thoughtfulness, their very obvious middle-class sort of decency, their commendable listening ability – and their recently admitted interest in "culture". (Yes, they had admitted to being in that small minority of the party who put "culture" ahead of "nature" as their primary interest on this cruise.) It was, of course, the image of a pair of willing participants at a Gordon Brown inspired focus group, a gathering of the deluded and the demented who are prepared to take such a nonsense seriously, and who are even prepared for the possibility of having to confront our national embarrassment in person, of having to shake his hand and share the same air with him. The thought made Brian shudder, and it certainly didn't help the small talk. The longer the lunch went on, the more Brian expected the arrival of a dishevelled Prime Minister and a questionnaire on something like: 'What makes Britain British – other than its looming insolvency?'.

However, relief was available in the form of Sujan. This was Sujan Chatterjee, one of India's greatest ornithologists, joint leader of the tour, sole leader of the extension to the Sundarbans, and a man who both physically and temperamentally was the antithesis of Pamela and Julian.

Admittedly he did, just like Pam, always have a smile on his face. But his smile was not a benign smile; it was a wicked smile. And it spread across a face that was large, expressive, brown, and "full-cheeked". That is to say his cheeks echoed the rest of his body, which wasn't so much fat as expansively generous, and designed to match his character. Indeed he couldn't have been any other shape. It simply wouldn't have fitted his nature. A lean Sujan would have been an oxymoron, an affront to the way things should be, and destined only to make him fodder for a focus group or a fate even worse.

Like Pam and Julian, he also cared. But what he cared about was different. He cared about wildlife. He cared about birds in particular. And he cared about the planet in general. How else could one interpret his contentment with his one-child family, his one-female-child family, when so many others sharing his "culture" thought so very differently? He also cared about his stomach – as was always evident from a study of his dinner plate. (And his lunch plate, come to that.) And he cared about his charges, Brian and his fellow Nature-seekers. Although he probably had his own thoughts about them as well, his own wicked thoughts on occasions...

And how did Brian see Sujan? What role had suggested itself for this all too clearly "rounded individual"? Well, it was obvious. If Bollywood ever got round to making an Indian version of "*The Three Musketeers*", here was Portos, ready and waiting for a starring role as the overweight hero who is never seen without a smile on his face or a pile of food on his plate. And who knows? He might even have been a dab hand with a rapier as well.

This lunchtime, though, it was just a fork and then a spoon. And the spoon was needed for his helping of a creamy sweet, something that looked a little like an Indian version of Angel Delight. Albeit not so fluorescent.

It had been a useful lunch, in that Brian now knew a great deal more about two of his fellow travellers and one of his guides. But if challenged about what they had discussed, just two hours later, he would have found it difficult to recollect. Sizing people up, learning how to deal with them, knowing what to say and what not to say was, for Brian, such an all-consuming effort that it tended to obliterate the actual content of the exercise. And in any event, he suspected that whatever contributions he himself had made to the discourse, these were equally lost for all time in the minds of his lunchtime companions and almost certainly in the mind of his wife. She'd heard all his contributions so many times before that they were extinguished from her consciousness almost immediately. It was the way she kept sane.

She also made a lot of allowances for Brian. Not least when he was ill, whether it was one of his interminable migraines or one of his man-magnified afflictions, such as his currently hardly-discernible gut-ache. It was now mid-afternoon. Brian and Sandra were sitting on the sundeck of the Sukapha admiring the endlessly flat landscape of the Brahmaputra as it drifted on by, and Brian was sipping a glass of water. He didn't look happy.

'How are you feeling?' she asked.

'Oh, not too bad. I do feel a bit weak.'

'You need more than bananas.'

This was true. And not just in a Confucius saying sort of way, but in a practical way as well. Brian may have starved his stomach bug into submission, but he was also starving himself. Those Indian bananas were really very small.

'You haven't been to the loo.'

'I know. But I'm still a bit concerned.'

'Well, that's better than being a bit caught short all the time, isn't it? And anyway, you're a much better colour. You're obviously on the mend.'

Brian looked at his wife. He knew what this meant. It meant: 'For God's sake, you're not going to die and you're not even going to test the soundproofing in the en-suite loo any more. To all intents and purposes you're as fit as anybody else on this boat, and you should just get on with your holiday and stop being a pain.'

Conjugal shorthand like this must exist in many marriages, but for Sandra and Brian it had been refined into almost an art-form. And in common with other art-forms in the world, it could have an immediate and dramatic impact. It did so now. Brian put down his glass of water, took a theatrically large intake of breath, and announced that it was time to see Pauline again. With that he rose from his seat, picked up his new Canon Powershot, and started to walk towards the back of the sundeck where Pauline was standing looking over the stern of the boat.

'Hi,' he announced as he joined her. And as she turned to face him she gave him a disarming smile and a full frontal view of her two very large cameras. Both of them were hanging from straps around her neck.

'Blimey, they're big,' he observed bluntly. 'I mean, talk about whoppers.'

Pauline either didn't notice his gaucheness or she politely ignored it.

'This one's a long-shot and this one's a wide-angle,' she responded. 'I find I need them both. And well, it's just not possible to keep switching lenses, as you can well imagine.'

Brian could well imagine. Although he could barely imagine at all how anybody could deal with two great humping pieces of kit like that. And in this heat and with a pair of binocs as well. There was just no way.

'Of course, the lenses.'

This made it sound as though he had only just realised that it was the lenses that were very large and not the cameras themselves. Which was so alarmingly close to the truth that he began to blush.

Fortunately Pauline came to his aid.

'That's a Powershot, isn't it? May I have a look at it?'

'Of course.' And he handed her his camera.

As he did this, Yvonne appeared at his shoulder. Yvonne was the wife of Derek, and they were the other half of the Pauline and Dennis combo. All four of them were travelling together, as they had done on other similar holidays. And all four of them were into photography in a serious way. Indeed, Yvonne had a pair of cameras which if anything were larger than Pauline's. They now adorned her chest like a brace of serious artillery pieces – and they looked primed for action. Brian could hardly take his eyes off them. And only when Yvonne asked him about his Powershot did he properly acknowledge her presence.

'It's a Powershot, isn't it?' she asked.

'Errh... yes.' He nodded as a greeting. 'Errh... it's the first time I've used it. A digital, I mean. I've tended to avoid them. But…'

He paused to think. Why the hell was he telling these two technophiles that he was a raving technophobe who had to be dragged into the digital age kicking and screaming? But he had no choice. He had to plough on.

'Errh, well you see, it's got a twenty-times zoom. And that goes to eighty with the digital… thing. And well, I'm still trying to learn it.'

Pauline was now operating the zoom and observing the Powershot's display.

'This is really good. Take a look at this.'

She was now handing the camera to her artillery-festooned friend. Yvonne took it from her, repeated Pauline's inspection routine and concurred that it really was very good indeed and added that she'd been considering buying one herself. Although Brian could not conceive where she might have parked it on her person had she not laid down at least one of her existing weapons.

This was all going very well. Brian had two new and admiring Nature-seekers in his company, he was getting to know them, and they seemed very nice people. Not nice like Pam and Julian, but normal nice without all that depth of thought and concern. But then it started to get awkward. First, Yvonne asked him about what settings he used – which he assumed meant those other settings on that wheel thing on the top of his camera that he always had locked on "auto". And then, worse than this, Pauline asked him a direct question about something called ISO numbers. He flannelled. But he flannelled very badly, and he was soon into admitting that it was a fair cop. He would, he promised them, attempt to do better in the future, and as regards the ISO query, he could do no more than refer them to his wife.

This seemed to satisfy them and may even have won him some brownie points. Honesty, ignorance and incompetence in a male can often be very attractive to the opposite sex, and can lay firm foundations for a rewarding relationship, especially a temporary one where companionship rather than intimacy is the order of the day. He had made a good start with these two ladies and he looked forward to more of their company. And not just on the Brahmaputra. Pauline and Yvonne and their respective spouses were on the Sundarbans extension as well.

So too were Bill and Tina. With them, his start wasn't quite so good.

It was dinner time. In front of Brian was a curry. (He'd decided he could now risk more than a banana. And anyway he was desperately hungry.) And across the table from Brian were Bill and Tina. Bill was a man in his sixties who had an air of latent pugnacity about him, and Tina was of a similar age, much smaller and entirely pacific. More to the point, Bill was a chief examiner in biology for one of the exam boards and seemed to know all there was to know about birds everywhere. As did Tina – presumably through a process of osmosis or through her own observations as they'd journeyed round the world.

This was too much for Brian. He had to lay down a challenge.

'OK, Bill,' he started. 'Unique birds. How many birds can you think of that are in some way genuinely unique?'

'Sorry?'

'Well, I'll give you a prime example. How about a wrybill? You know, the only bird in the world with an asymmetric bill.'

'Oh, I see…'

Bill was hooked. Like Brian, he had visited New Zealand, and was well aware of a little wader that was found there, which had a bill that was curved to the left at its end. Or was it to the right? Well, that didn't matter. But what did matter was that this bird was the only known example in the world of an avian species that didn't have the normal symmetry arrangements for its beak-bit. What also mattered was that Bill was going to rise to the challenge.

'Right,' he said. 'Kiwis. They're the only species with nostrils at the end of their bill. And the only birds with two ovaries.'

'Mmmm… sorry, Bill, but I did say unique. And as you know, there are five different species of kiwis. So strictly speaking…'

'The vernal hanging parrot,' pronounced Tina. 'It's the only bird that sleeps hanging upside down.'

'Errh, I think you'll find that the Ceylon hanging parrot does the same…'

Bill was now looking more pugnacious than ever, and even Tina looked a little "aroused".

'Ah,' began Bill, his face now beaming in triumph, 'the turacos. They're the only birds in the world that have other than melanin and carotenoids pigments in their feathers. There's a red pigment called turacin and a green one called… errh… turacoverdin… yes, turacoverdin…'

'Errh… yes. But like the kiwis, Bill… well, you've just said it, haven't you? Turacos – in the plural. There's more than one species. So I'm afraid…'

Bill muttered something under his breath. Then he put his hands to his mouth and started to drum on his upper lip with his fingers. He was in intense thinking mode. Because what

Brian had said had implied that there were any number of other birds that were unique in different ways. And he clearly wanted to identify them himself rather than being told them by this lay-person across the table who probably didn't even know the difference between a scapular and a primary. Tina was clearly equally eager.

They were now sitting across the table from Brian, scowling in unison and occasionally making as if to announce the next member of this exclusive band of birds. But each time their announcement was frustrated by their own knowledge as they discovered in their memories another bird or another fact that scuppered the uniqueness. And now they were getting frustrated in their own right. Bill, in particular, looked potentially belligerent.

So now Brian began to question the wisdom of his challenge. Why, he asked himself, had he been so stupid as to set a puzzle to which he knew only one answer: the wrybill? As far as he knew there were no other birds that were unique as an individual species, and if there were he hadn't yet found them. So how was he now going to admit this fact and in doing so reveal to Bill and Tina that he had set them a misleading if not impossible task?

Ah, he had it! He'd thought of a way out. He would draw the contest to a conclusion on a highly humorous note. That always worked. The charade could be brought to an amusing conclusion. And no doubt another promising relationship would be set on its way.

'OK,' he began. 'Not easy, is it? And of course the reason it's not easy is that, as far as I know, the wrybill is the only truly unique bird on the planet...'

'What!'

Bill now looked like something that was about to burst. Tina looked simply perplexed. Brian saw these reactions and immediately began to doubt the wisdom of his end-game. But he had to go on. There was no other way.

'Well,' he started, 'there is one more, of course. But it's not what you'd call a biological uniqueness. It's more… well, more a cryptic uniqueness…'

Bill now looked wild. Brian felt himself reddening.

'Well…' he began to laugh nervously, 'you see, as well as the wryneck there is also the snipe.'

'The snipe?' challenged Tina.

'Yes,' responded Brian, wishing desperately that he hadn't started all this nonsense in the first place, and wishing also that it had been Bill who had posed this final challenge and not Tina. Because that way he wouldn't now be facing the imminent prospect of having to inform a woman in her sixties and whom he barely knew, that the snipe was a unique bird because it was the only bird in the world whose name was an anagram of "penis".

This time Brian felt not mildly ridiculous; he felt profoundly ridiculous. Bill and Tina, he suspected, felt something else.

3.

This morning, Brian was required to abandon his bed early, but not desperately early. There was to be a "cultural visit" to a fishing village – with, of course, bird-spotting opportunities. But the village was close to where they were moored, and therefore the day could commence without the need for a small-hours reveille. He and his fellow passengers were not required to rise until a relaxed 5.30.

This allowed him to bring his illness-ravaged body back into action at a manageable pace and even allowed him to cope with the demands of his life-jacket...

The village that the Nature-seekers were scheduled to visit was only fifteen minutes away. But fifteen minutes by the country boat away. And that meant that before they set out they all needed to don their bright orange life-jackets.

This might not sound like too arduous a task. But for Brian, and as soon became apparent, for all the Nature-seekers, it was a task that was more than arduous and a task that was deeply resented.

These life-jackets were not of the inflatable variety. They were of the "permanent buoyancy" variety. That is to say, they operated on the principle of buoyancy through the use of outsized bricks of some unknown buoyant material sewn into their fabric at their front and their back. Brian had last seen such life-jackets when he had idled away a wet afternoon back in England watching the umpteenth showing of "*The Cruel Sea*". Julian, however, thought they were rather more reminiscent of those they'd used on the Lusitania. And Dennis went even further back in time. He was convinced that they were just like those in use during the Boxer rebellion, a hypothesis which, at least, went some way to explain their "Made in China" origination.

But it wasn't their antiquity that was the real problem; it was their bulk and their failure to embrace the concepts underlying the science of ergonomics.

Nature-seekers, when they are about their business, bristle with all manner of equipment. Their tackle will include binoculars, cameras (often with humungous lenses), camcorders, water-bottles, bags, pouches, and sometimes even telescopes and tripods. It is therefore bordering on madness to then ask them to wear on top of all this gear, a massive, rigid, cumbersome, intensely awkward and ludicrous nautical bodice – which, to be held in place with a cord which passes under the arms and around the body and is tied at the front, needs the skills and manual dexterity normally only found in the ranks of the Venture-Scouts. And then there was the question of their safety…

The country boat was a little like an old-fashioned lifeboat, but significantly longer and with a roof. The roof was low. Brian and even the smaller Nature-seekers were all obliged to crouch as they found their way to their seats beneath this roof, seats which were simple benches running along the sides of the vessel. (Nobody had thought to arrange the seating in rows which would have enabled their occupants to look out of the boat rather than at the boots of the Nature-seekers sitting opposite.) When seated, the jacket-bound passengers were therefore enclosed within a space, shut off at one end by a small engine room and above them, by the low roof. The only exit was the open end at the front through which they'd entered, or through the more easily accessible gaps between the vessel's side and its much discussed and really very low roof. But because the roof was really very low indeed, these gaps were tiny. An unencumbered passenger would have had to struggle to squeeze himself through them. An unencumbered female passenger might have had to struggle even more. But for a passenger, of whichever gender, tied into one of those damned life-jackets, the struggle would not have been worth it. He or she would not have got through.

So here was an ultimate stupidity: sensible, responsible adults being required to submit themselves to a piece of equipment that was not only clumsy, unmanageable and plainly preposterous, but also a piece of equipment that, if called into use, would do the opposite of what it was designed to do. It would not save your life; it would ensnare you in the boat and it would lose your life. It wasn't so much a life-jacket; it was more a bloody death trap.

Brian had a loathing for "Health and Safety" as practised in Britain. The whole concept of a broad-brush, nanny-ish, don't-for-heaven's-sake-take-responsibility-for-your-own-actions approach to the population's wellbeing was not just a misdirection of resources and an unwarranted interference in people's lives, it was also counterproductive. The more people depended on others and on a system to protect them, the less care they'd take themselves. But surely this nonsense hadn't got to India? Hell, from what he'd seen on the roads here and from what he'd observed on their way out of Kolkata (like all that rickety bamboo scaffolding), he couldn't believe that Safety could get a foothold. And as for Health…

So this set him thinking. And what he did was to think from an Indian perspective, and not from his own, western-smart, find-fault-with-anything, rather supercilious perspective. From this viewpoint he could very easily see that the management of the Sukapha were clearly not attempting to put their passengers in the way of danger, but what they were doing was their level best to provide them with the very best protection they could assemble, and protection that very likely went far beyond any safety rules that applied in the country. They were doing more than they needed to. OK, the kit was not ideal, but it was probably all they could reasonably afford. Or maybe they really thought it the better option. 'If an inflatable fails to inflate, will our middle-aged punters have enough power in their lungs to do the job themselves? Wouldn't they be better off with something that doesn't depend on inflation?'

Brian also realised that this Indian perspective also explained the face-to-face seating in the boat. 'Why force our passengers to look at the back of other passengers' heads as though they were on one of those terrible Kolkata buses, when we could let them face each other and have a chat – like they do on those smart London tube things?' And well, thought Brian, why did they all look at each other's boots when they could just as easily have talked to each other instead?

This perspective switch was useful. Even if it didn't remove his despair at the sight of his life-jacket entirely, it did help Brian come to terms with it. A similar switch of perspective would now be needed for the fishing village.

They had just shed their life-jackets and disembarked from

the boat. Brian and his khaki band were walking along a path towards the village and taking in the first manifestations of its "culture". The very first of these was a gentleman pushing his bike along this path with a goat suspended from one of the handlebars in a comfortable looking sling contraption. The man smiled and some of the Nature-seekers smiled at the goat. Then the man indicated with a broader smile, a simulated cutting action to his throat, and the English word "offering", that the goat was on the last bike-ride of his life. Brian was taken aback. And how, he thought, do Hindus reconcile their commendable vegetarianism with animal sacrifice?

The second bit of culture was a guy on the bank with stacks of cracked clay pots, which he appeared to be mending with wax. It was his job. He was an itinerant cracked clay pot mender. Brian wondered whether by using such a questionable repair methodology his itinerary ever took him to a particular village more than once. Or was it, repair it, sell it and scarper? He could not, for example, believe that the bloke further up the path, ploughing a tiny field with an ancient wooden plough and two small bullocks, would ever give any of his hard-earned resources to someone who had previously sold him a cracked clay pot with the cracks covered over with "concealing wax".

They were now in the village proper. Here, around the base of a huge tree, was a shrine. It was essentially four concrete pillars painted blue, supporting a corrugated iron roof with a hole in its middle for the tree trunk, with, below the roof, a frieze of pictures of various Hindu deities, none of which Brian knew by name. Many photographs were taken here.

Then things got progressively browner. The homes in this village were thatched affairs built on bamboo stilts from more bamboo and some sort of cane. There were others, similarly thatched, but not on stilts and finished off in a mix of mud and cow dung – which is surprisingly workable and really very attractive. However, thatching, bamboo, cane, mud and cow dung are all brown, as was the beaten earth throughout the village. Therefore a sense of pervading brownness was unavoidable. For Brian at least. It was just as well that the inhabitants of the village were rather more colourful.

The women were very colourful. They were dressed in colourful saris. The children made patches of colour too. But in a different way. They all wore a mixture of shorts and shirts and skirts of every colour imaginable – none of which could ever be accused of "matching". They also smiled a lot and wanted their pictures taking – so that they could see themselves on those digital displays. Gratifyingly, that was all they wanted. Enough "strange people" had so far visited this place to allow these kids to learn about the features of digital cameras but not enough to allow them to learn about the techniques of soliciting for handouts.

Indeed the whole place was used to being visited. Brian could see this. But only used to very infrequent visits. There was no resentment yet. No questioning of the impertinence of foreigners tramping by their houses and staring at them. Not even a reluctance on the part of the grown-ups to be photographed – whether they were mending a roof or weaving on their doorstep, or cycling by on their ancient bicycles, tinkling out a warning as they approached.

How long these attitudes would remain was impossible to tell. But it probably wouldn't be for as long as these obviously very poor people had to continue to cope with their grinding poverty and their struggle to get from day to day. Nobody was starving here. But nobody was fat – or rich. Brian began to feel pity.

That's when he changed his perspective again – to their perspective.

What must they think – if they know anything about our lives in the West? Do they pity us? After all, he thought, they don't live in houses that force them to borrow four times their income (or even more). Other than the occasional passing bike, they don't have to cope with traffic, and traffic congestion would be beyond their understanding. They also miss out on work-stress, the threat of redundancy, being burgled, being mugged, being micromanaged by the state, and they don't even have to avoid "*Britain's Got Talent*". Then there's no social isolation, no lack of community spirit, no threat to their indigenous culture and no threat from Brussels. There's also no threat that if you take an innocent photo of a child, as virtually all the Nature-seekers had done repeatedly as they'd walked through the village, you'll end up in court and with an entry on the sex-offenders' register for the rest of your life. So, on balance, Brian thought they didn't have a bad life after all, and they certainly didn't warrant his pity. Indeed, in one respect he honestly envied them. For they had, in and around their village, a wonderful selection of birds. There were Indian pond-herons, Indian rollers, pied kingfishers, green bee-eaters, black redstarts, both blue-throated and coppersmith barbets – and even grey-headed canary-flycatchers... Although, if you're trudging around a field with a wooden plough and two bullocks, maybe you don't tend to notice...

A boat ride and a tussle with an orange life-jacket later, Brian had forgotten his Indian perspective and was focused instead on his lunch. He was also focused on his two immediate lunch companions: Dennis and Derek. These gentlemen, it will be recalled, were the husbands of the photographically intimidating Pauline and Yvonne. They were also, it transpired, even more intimidating. Because their interest was not in mere static photos, but in pictures which moved. It appeared that both of them, as they always did, were committing their holiday to film, and film of a professional standard – with slots in them for their respective wives' best photos. They were both serious cinematographers. This was commendable but another problem for Brian. He was pretty ignorant about "normal" cameras, but he knew as much about video cameras as he did about knitting, which was next to nothing. And there was no likelihood that he'd ever tangle with either. Still, he had to make an effort.

'So how do you choose what to keep, Derek?'

Derek was a retired pilot. He used to fly Concordes. One at a time, of course. And now, even as he sat there in his Nature-seeking gear, one could easily picture him sitting instead in the crowded cockpit of that wonderful machine, going through some checklist or other, or doing whatever it is that pilots do before they switch on the ignition. He had the right sort of decisive looking face and even the right sort of penetrating eyes. He did not, however, have the ability to make himself understood to Brian on the subject he was now expounding. There was something about the number of images per second, and some software and inevitably a computer. But Brian was lost after the first sentence.

He did venture a few nods when he thought this was appropriate, but he bottled out on making any comments or asking any further questions, as he was well aware that this could lead him into all sorts of untold trouble. Instead, he let Derek finish, treated him to some more vigorous head-nodding and combined this with his very best "I'm really impressed" expression. It seemed to do the trick, and it allowed him to turn to Dennis and try all over again, this time with an even more anodyne question than before. Dennis was older than Derek. Also, he used to run the production in a bottling plant, not fly supersonic aircraft, so he was bound to be less technical and more down to earth. Brian might even be able to understand something.

'And Dennis, how about yours?'

Well, as it turned out, there was a mini arms race going on between Dennis and Derek, and currently Dennis had the upper hand. His device was state of the art digital (and very expensive) and had features and functions and interconnectivity and God knows what else that made Derek's machine sound like a Box-Brownie. Inevitably, his explanation of how it worked and what he did with it was even more impenetrable than was Derek's, and Brian simply had to switch off. He still nodded and still made the right expressions with his face, but he was out of his depth and he knew it. Just as well then that the conversation eventually switched from the camera technical to the (UK) domestic political, where Brian could make a sensible contribution and, at the same time, establish that Dennis and Derek were as amiable as their wives and had a similar perspective to his own − when, that is, he wasn't taking an Indian perspective on life-jackets or a villager's perspective on the West.

The afternoon was a glide down the river. This allowed all those on board to take in the nature of the waterway on which they were floating and to take in its size. For the Brahmaputra is not just a river; it is a broad ribbon of water flowing as it pleases over an even broader flood plain, and it is vast. It is truly enormous. Its scale dwarfs even the largest rivers in Europe, and with its empty, endlessly flat sand banks to either side, its seemingly boundless width must challenge even that of the Amazon. Often, one shore of this mightiest of streams was barely in view, whilst at other times it was simply not possible to tell whether a sand bank in the distance was the shore or one of the countless islands of sand which shift constantly within the river's bounds. Brian found it awe-inspiring and more than a little threatening. Not in a personal sense but in the sense of what it could do when it was in flood, when it carried across this flood plain more water than he could ever imagine. Then, he could imagine, it would be terrible, and potentially deadly for all those people who fished and farmed within its reach – or mended clay pots.

This vista of the infinite lasted for more than two hours until they reached a stretch of the river which was the northern boundary of the Kaziranga National Park. Now, on the left hand side, was forest, the wooded eastern range of the park which they would be visiting tomorrow. And within this forest there were birds, visible from the boat, and Indian one-horned rhinos which were also visible. They saw two, although Brian thought it was just one seen from two different perspectives as the vessel floated by. But so what? It was an encouraging sign of what was to come.

Finally, it was time to stop and to moor for the night. Not on the south bank of the river, but in keeping with tradition, on the far bank, opposite the park they planned to visit the next day – and on a bank of sand. The Sukapha had sidled up slowly to a great flat expanse of the stuff and was now resting just feet away from where it met the water as a low crumbling cliff. Immediately two of the crew, dressed in their smart black Sukapha kit, leapt from the boat and began the mooring task.

This was not conventional. It couldn't be. This was not a

dockside and there were none of those big metal mushrooms one finds on a dock. That is, there was nothing at all onto which to tie the boat's mooring ropes. Step forward crewman number one, who, with a mattock, was now busy excavating a large hole in the sand about twenty metres from the bank. While he was doing this, crewman number two was dragging a mooring rope to the hole and then he returned to collect a large baulk of wood, two huge bamboo stakes and a Shrek-size mallet. The baulk of wood was passed through a loop at the end of the rope, and when the hole was complete the baulk with the rope attached was cast into it. Crewman number two then demonstrated his skills with the oversized mallet and drove the bamboo stakes into the bottom of the hole thereby pinning the wood and securing the rope. The end of this exercise entailed crewman number one backfilling the hole until the stakes were nearly buried – and then the two of them repeated the whole exercise for a second mooring rope. Brian was impressed. He was also impressed with the vigour and the size of the two young crewmen. They were in no way fat, but they were both about twice the size of any of the local villagers he had seen. It said a great deal about the diet available aboard the Sukapha and the diet available in the local villages. If Assam ever wanted to field a world-class rugby team, it would need to house them all on this vessel.

Currently, however, the Sukapha housed a party of Nature-seekers who were now all gathered in the boat's lounge to participate in the most important ritual of their day, and a ritual Brian had so far missed out on, first because of his indisposition and then because of his failure to join in the following day's expedition. But now, having visited the village and having observed the wildlife from the boat's sundeck during the afternoon, both he and Sandra could take their place in the "listing" session.

To the uninitiated, this might sound all rather nerdy. Anything up to an hour spent going through a pre-printed list of birds and animals and agreeing which of the species on the list had been spotted during the day. However, it was very useful and always good fun. Making comprehensive notes as one is walking around or riding around is not very easy. Better to make partial notes and mental notes and then be reminded in the evening of precisely what has been observed – and what you as an individual have observed. And the fun bit comes from the challenges, the misunderstandings, and on this trip, from the co-tour-leader and "list master". This was Tika, or to give him his full name, Tika Ram Giri.

Tika was a renowned ornithologist from Nepal. With Sujan, he was the guy who found the birds and the other wildlife for the party and identified them. But he also ran the listing sessions. This was good news. If Sujan was Portos, Tika was Athos; a thoughtful, "fatherly" man with a dry sense of humour and a grin to rival Sujan's own. He had been born on the edge of the Royal Chitwan National Park in Nepal, and despite receiving no formal education, he had ultimately become the park's senior naturalist and one of the very best naturalists on the Indian sub-continent. Remarkably, his knowledge of birds and mammals was all self-taught, as was his English. And so fluent was his English, that Brian had made a note to write to the Schools Minister on his return to Britain to suggest that the self-teaching of English should become the method of first choice for all those word- and grammar-challenged children currently drifting through our increasingly politicised and therefore terminally damaged "World Class" education system.

But now, as Tika was just getting down to the lapwings and plovers, Brian was getting down to a more immediate task, namely the feeding of his face. For not only were there alcoholic beverages available during the listing sessions, but there were also savoury snacks on offer. Therefore, as Sandra applied herself to their personal list-making, Brian applied himself to the nibbles. They were very tasty but very small scale, and far too small to simply pick from the bowls in which they were served. One therefore had to spoon a heap of them into the cupped palm of one hand, with the fingers of the other hand then coax them into its centre – and then lick them off – as meticulously and as discreetly as possible. Brian could not possibly have dealt with a pen and a list at the same time. And anyway, Sandra was a past master at that sort of thing. Just as Tika was the present master of the sessions themselves, combining authority with humour and knowledge with humility. He shouldn't have been running just these gatherings in the evening; he should have been running the whole of Nepal.

This was a view put forward by Brian to John over dinner. John was a scientist who specialised in the transmission of something or other through cell walls. He had a Scottish accent, and Brian hadn't quite caught what he'd said – or whether he'd admitted to being a chemist or a biologist. But it was really of no importance. He was a very pleasant fellow who always appeared jovial. Just as his equally pleasant wife, Vivien, always appeared rather timid – even though she was herself an accomplished marine biologist. Brian was also not sure whether they were still working or whether they were retired. They were distinctly middle-aged, but who knew how long people went on working these days? Especially if they enjoyed it.

John clearly did enjoy his science, and had, over his life, become a specialist in his field, someone who had channelled his obvious considerable intellect into a very narrow aspect of human knowledge. So when Brian made the tactless admission that he had abandoned chemistry immediately after university, precisely because he hadn't wanted to become a specialist like John, and end up being trapped in some tiny inconsequential pocket of science that nobody else knew about, John gave him a rather odd look. But no lasting damage was done. And although Brian had at first felt mildly ridiculous (again), by the time the meal was over he just felt rather tired.

This was partly due to the hour, but also due to his other table companion of this evening, the singleton traveller in the party by the name of Jim.

Little can be said about this gentleman other than that he had clearly not been made aware of the full potential of modern dentistry – and that it was as yet impossible to determine what his principal interests were on this current expedition. Furthermore, it was all too apparent that if ever a world championship were organised to find the world's worst conversationalist, Jim would be in there with a chance. His speciality was the simple non-response to an observation or even to a direct question. But he was also incredibly strong in the areas of out-of-the-blue announcements unconnected with anything said previously, mind-numbingly boring observations on the cost of chips (of the electronic variety), and comments which, if not rude, were distinctly crass.

Jim, it should be noted, was the only representative of the British civil service in the party. So, although Brian was very tired this evening, he was also very pleased that one of his deeply held beliefs had once again been confirmed...

He thought he'd seen it yesterday. But now he was sure. There were a number of the party who had adopted a banana diet. At the six o'clock breakfast there were at least three other Nature-seekers who had eschewed fried eggs or omelettes in favour of this stomach-friendly fruit. Whilst Brian's bowels were now quiescent, those of others in the group were clearly not and were in active revolt. It remained to be seen, therefore, whether all of them would join the expedition to Kaziranga.

They did. Either through a resolve which put Brian's in the shade, or through the ingestion of a generous dose of Imodium, they all made it into the country boat, and thereby committed themselves to a whole morning in the park. There was, it has to be said, a longer than normal mass-relief session as they arrived at the gate to the park. Although, in truth, this could have been more to do with the fact that males as well as females were allowed into the facilities here – and with the state of these facilities. Doing anything in them that required the loosening or losing of any of one's garments was necessarily a very delicate and consequently a very slow procedure. And if squatting wasn't in your cultural make-up it could be a very slow procedure indeed.

Eventually, however, all the Nature-seekers were empty and

were ready to go. And waiting for them were six jeeps.

Now, Brian and Sandra had, on similar safari rides in Namibia and Botswana, become used to jeeps that were constructed out of girders and plate metal and went by the name of "Land Rovers". They were apparently very well known. They were also very powerful, large, comfortable, and could cope with just about any sort of terrain. It wasn't just a marketing claim; these Land Rover things really could manage anything. Furthermore, if they were being used for game-viewing, they were always equipped with forward facing seats, all of them raised above the chassis, and with each row of seats set marginally higher than the row in front. In this way all the passengers were afforded a clear and uninterrupted view of whatever there was that required viewing.

Kaziranga's jeeps were not, unfortunately, Land Rovers. They were "Maruti Suzukis". Brian imagined that this meant they were Japanese designed jeeps manufactured in India. But wherever they were made, it was not where there was any tradition in the use of girders and plate metal, and it was not where there were any European-sized humans. They were insubstantial and they were tiny, tiny in the extreme. In that pecking order on the roads referred to earlier, Brian imagined they would rank somewhere just above rickshaws, but only those rickshaws with fainthearted drivers. Those with a more determined soul at their helm would probably take precedence. And when they left the roads... well Brian could not imagine them being left in a garage, but instead in a cellophane-fronted cardboard box, just like the sort his Dinky toys had arrived in. Then there was the seating...

This was in the style of the country boat. Behind the jeep's cab, two padded benches faced each other across its miniature rear. But unlike in the boat, for those who used these seats, there was no clear space and a view of the boots of those opposite. But instead, there was just a cluttered space, full of their own legs, knees and feet, intertwined with those of the other three unfortunates crammed tightly into the same vehicle. And needless to say, a clear and uninterrupted view only of the faces of their fellow facing passengers. Brian was not too encouraged.

He was encouraged even less when he saw who one of these passengers would be. He and Sandra had crawled onto one of the jeeps and were now sitting facing each other directly behind its cab. And now, following them onto the vehicle was Jim! As he scrambled aboard, Brian looked at Sandra and Sandra looked at Brian. But there was nothing they could do.

Fortunately Rajan then joined them as well. He was a little bigger than ideal for the last place available, but he was a great deal less daunting than the odd civil servant. In fact, he was not daunting at all; he was very pleasant and easy to get on with. He was the guy who had put the whole tour together. He was Indian, but he now lived in England where he worked for the Nature-seekers set up, and was out on this particular tour acting as the tour manager. While Sujan and Tika, as the two tour leaders, did all the nature stuff, he did all the other stuff – like worrying. He was officially responsible for worrying about schedules, transport, connections, logistics – and now, the growing number of upset stomachs. However, this morning he had a break from this responsibility. For the next four hours he could virtually stop worrying at all and instead simply ensure that his legs, knees and feet were kept within bounds – along with Jim's verbal aberrations…

They were about to move off. Their jeep and two others were going to take a clockwise route around this part of the park; the other three would take an anti-clockwise route. And each trio of jeeps would have two guides. Sujan and Tika had been joined by two local guides, Imran and Babajan. Imran and Tika were responsible for Brian's trio, and the way they were going to discharge this responsibility was by switching between jeeps as they drove round the park. At any one time, one jeep would be without a guide but the other two would have a resident naturalist-guide who'd be pointing out the wildlife. And as all the jeeps were to stay close together, even the guideless jeep would receive instructions as to where to look.

They were now moving. Brian's vehicle was sandwiched between the other two jeeps in his group, and it was the one that was presently guideless. It was also presently without conversation. Everybody on board was too intent on absorbing their surroundings. This area of the park was wooded, but between the trees there were stretches of open grassland and patches of swamp. It was a little, thought Brian, like a soggy savannah. It was also good for seeing things, things that liked this combination of trees and grass and wetness – and that didn't mind being seen. So very soon, even in the cramped and imperfect-viewing conditions of the jeep, Brian had seen any number of adjutant storks (both lesser and greater), loads of little cormorants, piles of pond-herons and swathes of swamphens. There were also wild boar, hog deer and water buffalo on show. And back with the birds, there were fish-eagles, and here and there, a novice bird-spotter's nightmare: changeable hawk-eagles, earning this name from their habit of having a changeable plumage. As if identifying birds wasn't difficult enough already...

This silent safari went on for some time, until Jim started telling Rajan about the cost of microchips and what a great deal he'd secured on the ones he'd just bought...

Fortunately this tiresome discourse coincided with the arrival of a muddy puddle. The first jeep had managed it. But a certain lack of momentum and an additional lack of tread on the tyres meant that Brian's jeep didn't cope quite so well. In fact, it became stuck. Immediately. Brian was incredulous. A Land Rover wouldn't even have noticed the puddle. Hell, even a rickshaw would have made it. But this poor old jeep... Well, it had done brilliantly; it had brought Jim's explanation of his artfulness in the art of chip-procurement to a premature and permanent stop.

Rajan pushed the vehicle out with the help of Imran. Imran then used this unscheduled stop to switch jeeps. When he'd assured himself that the following jeep wasn't going to fall foul of the minor water hazard, he climbed aboard Brian's jeep to commence some onboard observing.

Now, much has been made of the less than generous proportions of these jeeps and how their passenger accommodation in the rear was no more than stingy. Three standard-sized whities and an oversized Indian consumed it entirely. Imran, therefore, was obliged to station himself not in the jeep but "behind" the jeep. That is to say, he was now onboard, but only onboard the jeep's back bumper, standing up and holding onto a U-frame, a U-frame the official purpose of which was to hold a tarpaulin in place – and not a naturalist with a rather large stomach. But it seemed to work. It still being sunny, the tarpaulin was folded over the roof of the cab and not, itself, in need of the U-frame. Furthermore, this stand-and-hold-on technique gave Brian an idea. There were two other U-frames, one midway between the back of the vehicle and its cab and one immediately behind the cab. By holding onto this front one, Brian might be able to stand up himself. This would give him a much-enhanced view of his surroundings and it would also allow his wife to see more. He wouldn't be facing her and blocking her view with his head.

He did it. He stood up and he grabbed the forward U-frame. He did need to hold on quite tightly to allow for the bumpiness of the track, but it worked. So well that the same "stand and spectate" system was now being adopted in the other jeeps, with as many as three of their occupants on their feet and hanging on. And it was fun as well. The jeeps had now become chariots. And Brian was now Charlton Heston!

But there was still the serious stuff as well. There were birds everywhere, and Imran was finding them all the time. Unfortunately though, Imran needed to convey to his charges where these birds were, especially if they were skulking around in the trees. This was never easy, even when the jeep had come to rest. But as Imran had learnt his English from an ex-patriot, hyper-active auctioneer, it was not easy at all. His spoken English may have been the best of all the guides, but he delivered it so rapidly that Brian could never decide. Neither could he ever decipher it. He was reduced to following Imran's hand movements instead, or to just training his binoculars in the direction of Imran's own.

This was not what Jim was doing. He was just sitting in the back of the jeep and barely using his binoculars at all. Indeed the only sightings that seemed to stir him into action were the sightings of buffalo, rhino or elephants. None of these were around in great numbers. But whenever one was spotted his interest was aroused – and he would reach for his camera. Eventually, Brian worked out what was going on. Jim was on this tour to capture photographs of large animals. Nothing much else seemed to matter. No matter how rare or how colourful any other representative of the local fauna might be, if it wasn't large and it wasn't readily available as a fairly straightforward photographic subject, he just wasn't bothered.

Brian considered this hypothesis. It did seem to fit his observations of his companion's behaviour, and it was also supported by all that tedious stuff about the cost of the chips in his camera. Furthermore, it was in perfect harmony with what he knew about this chap's nature. Jim, remember, was a civil servant. And what do civil servants do? Answer: they undertake tasks that are really only of interest to themselves; they choose simple tasks and avoid those that are more demanding; the tasks that are chosen are not only simple but they are also discharged sporadically, and the activity then created is almost inevitably sandwiched between much longer periods of complete inactivity... Oh, and civil servants very rarely have an insight into the wider picture either... Yes, there was no doubt about it; Jim was on a shoot-the-obvious-and-effortless photo-shoot, and he was more or less blind to all else.

'But so what?' thought Brian. 'He's not harming anybody. And if that's what he wants...'

So Brian ignored him and got back to his game-viewing and bird-watching – with the help of Imran's arms, and then, as their journey progressed, with the help of Tika's instructions.

Tika had now replaced Imran, and as his English was more moderately paced than Imran's, Brian had no problem in understanding his every word. He was also shit hot at spotting anything and everything. So much so that the bird count and animal count (including five-striped palm-squirrels) proceeded to mount rapidly. It was proving to be a very interesting and very rewarding morning.

Eventually, Brian's trio of jeeps, on their clockwise circuit, met the second trio coming the other way. They all stopped and notes were compared and advice exchanged – about the whereabouts of particular sightings by each party. And then a jeep was exchanged. The clockwise route had apparently brought Brian's jeep over the more manageable half of the circuit, and it now faced a more demanding half where the terrain was more uneven and the puddles more muddy. And as it had the handicap of a cracked suspension, it was thought prudent to allow it to return whence it had come (with a new set of passengers from the second party), and to re-house Brian and his buddies in the jeep these passengers had relinquished. Their jeep was just as small and just as insubstantial, but it possessed a currently un-cracked suspension and was therefore considered a rather better bet for the remaining, more challenging part of the journey.

The swap was completed and Brian re-established himself in the standing position. The new jeep had the same U-frame arrangement as the first. He was therefore able to continue his enhanced viewing of his surroundings, albeit that he now had to hold on more tightly than ever. The track was just as promised: far worse than before. Indeed at one point it was almost impassably far worse.

Brian's vehicle was in the lead and had just stopped to allow its occupants to observe a red junglefowl. When it started off again it almost immediately came into a long stretch of track that was no more than a series of muddy holes joined together by a series of muddy ruts. It got through this hazard, but only because its driver exhibited a criminal disregard for its engine, pushing its rev-level into Formula One territory. It screamed as though it was about to die, smelt as though it had died, and sounded none too well even when the rev-level subsided. But it was through. It was the same for the second jeep – although this one nearly came to a stop, and just possibly the mud-menace was getting worse. The little traction there had been was now degrading under the wheels of each vehicle as it passed.

No surprise then that jeep number three did stop. Right in the middle of the mud-bath. The initial reaction to this was to attempt to push a piston rod through the engine block as quickly as possible. The jeep's engine wasn't so much screaming now as shrieking in pain. If Brian had been carrying a gun, he would have wanted to shoot it. Put it out of its pain and let it lie where it had died – in the middle of a mud pool. But then the revs died instead, and the other drivers and Imran advanced towards the stricken vehicle with sticks and branches, which they then proceeded to place under its wheels. This was a tried and tested means of providing more traction. However… when the revs were applied again the jeep didn't move an inch – other than downwards and even deeper into the mud. Only when more branches were pushed under the wheels and the two assisting drivers mounted the sides of the jeep to give it greater weight, did it move forwards. And even then it was slowly, and not without further shrieking. It also entailed a lot of mud-splattering. Pamela and Julian had been sitting in the back of this jeep and they were now sitting there in mud-splattered shirts. As the jeep's wheels had spun, so had the mud flown up and onto their clothes. They looked like a couple of human Jackson Pollocks. But they didn't seem to mind. Maybe they were Pollock fans.

After this there were more buffalo, more junglefowl, and a tree full of vultures. This caused a bit of a stir, in that it could have been a sign of a recent kill – by a tiger. Tigers were, after all, resident in Kaziranga. But no. They were not here today, and Brian and his companions would have to console themselves with a well-earned lunch, back on the Sukapha. Their first jeep safari was now at an end, and it was time to don their life-jackets again and return to the boat.

Lunch was a curry of local Brahmaputra fish with the usual accompaniments. Brian made do with just the accompaniments. He'd seen how many bones there were in the fish – and how little flesh they had, an observation not apparently made by Ron. Ron was the husband of Irene and an ex-employee of Jaguar. When he'd worked for this company he'd worked as a technician. He'd been involved in some of their special vehicles and occasionally in the launch of their new models. He had worked with his hands. This was just as well, as he now needed all the manual dexterity he possessed to extract a mass of needles from his mouth, his hopes that the fish-bones would merely melt in his mouth having clearly been dashed with his very first mouthful. And Irene was trying to ignore him.

These were the pair who had already won the "most down to earth" award in Brian's assessment of the whole party. They were always willing to chat and Ron, in particular, always had something to say. Irene was less verbose, but she was rather more confiding. She even confessed to Brian her opinions on certain sensitive issues back home, opinions that wouldn't have earned her too many plaudits from the liberal establishment in that country, but opinions that didn't upset Brian in the least. Oh, and Irene was afflicted with the stomach bug. She was sitting at the lunch table with a banana and a slice of bread on her plate

So was Tim. Tim was an accountant from West Yorkshire. Now, many people regard accountants as dull and unworthy of any real respect. Brian, however, did not. This was primarily because he had been one himself, and like Tim, had worked as a partner in one of the "Big Four" firms of accountants, the quartet of "professional services" firms whose activities span the world. He therefore knew how demanding an accountant's job could be, how difficult it was to meet all these demands for a whole lifetime – and also how many accountants, despite all the rumours to the contrary, were almost normal. They were also, he knew (when they had remained in the profession), not bankers, not "no win, no fee" lawyers, not estate agents, not politicians, and most importantly, not civil servants. And these credentials alone, he thought, should have earned them rather more respect than they received.

Tim was a prime example of this breed of professional heroes. He had done his time with one of Brian's firm's competitors, and was now semi-retired and doing just some specialist work for this same firm on a salaried basis. He was also seeing the value of his retirement pot shrinking rapidly (through the efforts of bankers, politicians and civil servants). But that is another story and has no place in an account of an expedition to India. Just let it be said that he and Brian shared some very similar views, and although they had formerly been in competition with each other, they were now in complete harmony on many issues concerning both the creation of wealth and its rampant consumption.

Tim also had a charming wife: Karen. She was slim, beautifully turned out (even when occupying the rear of a tiny jeep in near-tropical temperatures), and she had a delightful vice. According to informants she was a bit of a boy-racer. Tim had retained his dependable mid-range Mercedes Benz when he had semi-retired. Karen, on the contrary, had retained her interest in burning rubber, and now raced around the environs of Leeds in her convertible Porsche. Brian just hoped she knew where all the speed cameras were.

This last thought was drifting through Brian's mind as the Sukapha now drifted down the river. They were now moving a small way down the Brahmaputra to enable a mooring to be established closer to the next entrance to Kaziranga, the entrance they would be using the following day. So it was time to relax again and time to absorb more of the surroundings. Yes, one could take in more of the grandeur of the river itself, and if one was feeling very active, one could look out for dolphins.

Brian found it difficult to believe, but this river was so immense it really could sustain its own species of this higher mammal – in the shape of the "Gangetic dolphin". He had seen one on his very first day on the boat. Just a glimpse, but it had been the very obvious shape of a curved dolphin back as this wonderful creature emerged silently from the water and disappeared immediately beneath it. It was difficult to see more. The water was full of silt and impossible to peer through. Gangetic dolphins do not jump out of the water; they only ever just break its surface. So it is almost pot luck. Be looking in the right direction at the right time and you might see one emerge. And if you're very lucky it might be really close and it might emerge towards you, and then you can see its face and its head as well as its back and its tail. That was what Brian was doing now, having some time ago forgotten about speed cameras around Leeds. He was still doing it as they arrived at their mooring.

This was the previous mooring's twin brother. It had the same expanse of unstable-at-the-edges sand and it required the same dig-and-bury mooring technique. However there was a difference here. The boat had arrived early enough to allow time for a game of beach-volleyball!

Yes, as soon as the mooring ropes had been secured, the moorers turned their attention to creating a volleyball court. Two long bamboo poles were driven into the sand and between them was hung a volleyball net. As this was going on, one of the crew, who had been blessed with a sense of accuracy found in few men and a sense of spatial awareness found in no women at all, drew out the boundaries of the court with his foot. He simply drew it through the sand in one uninterrupted movement, taking it through the right angles at the corners as though he had a GPS fitted in him. Then the court was ready for use.

Regrettably, in neither team were there any ladies kitted out in miniscule Lycra bikinis with large expanses of tanned, bare flesh on show. There weren't even any lady Nature-seekers on show. There were just the fit and athletic crew members. But almost all of them, it seemed. Brian even picked out the ship's master from his gallery vantage point on the ship's sundeck. And he was pretty good too. Although not quite as captivating as a nubile young woman in Lycra. Brian quitted his seat in the gallery and went off to prepare himself for the evening.

This began in its conventional manner with a listing session in the lounge. But then there was something different. The evening meal was to be an Indian barbecue on the "beach".

And there it was. As Brian followed Sandra down the narrow gangplank to the sandy shore, before him was a pole with a light at its top and a car battery at its bottom, and around this pole in a large circle were two dozen plastic chairs straight out of "*You've Been Framed*" and the raw material for hundreds of those Harry Hill quips. This was a little disconcerting. A wind was now getting up, and unless Brian and Sandra were joined by their fellow Nature-seekers and they all sat themselves on those chairs pretty damn soon, there was a very good chance that they would all be blown away and end up in Bangladesh in a couple of weeks' time. They really did look as though they were about to be whisked off.

Fortunately, the other Nature-seekers were very soon assembled, and Brian's concerns evaporated as twenty-three middle-aged bums were brought into action as chair-weights. The danger had passed. Now all he needed to do was secure a drink for himself and his wife and wait to see what happened. He had never attended an Indian barbecue before and he didn't know how it might work. He did suspect it wouldn't entail too many burgers or too many beer guts, and he doubted there'd be any serious accidents with lighter fuel. But other than this he just didn't know what to expect.

Well, in the event, it was delightful, and a great deal more genteel than many of the barbecues he had attended in England. In the first place the portions were manageable. They were little more than bite-size. But they kept on coming. All sorts of wonderful ingredients and tastes. Like curried prawns and curried fish and differently curried lamb and a dozen other delicacies. And all delivered on silver platters by the ship's two waitresses – and all delicious. This seemed to go on forever, and it gave Brian and Sandra an opportunity to meet the final instalment of their Sunderbans team, the last couple making up the ten Nature-seekers who would be going on to that further destination when Assam was behind them. This was the spouse and spouse duo of Alan and Lynn.

Alan was a revelation. Like Brian, he had studied chemistry at university, and like Brian, he had abandoned it immediately. But unlike Brian, he had not then sought sanctuary in the bosom of a profession, but had hurled himself into commercialism in the shape of a management career with the Royal Mail. He had done well and he'd ended up as one of its directors. But then there was never going to be any other outcome. Alan was not just very intelligent, he was also an addict. Yes, he was addicted to challenges. He simply could not resist them, and this had taken him far. It had not only taken him into a Royal Mail directorship, but it had also taken him into the higher echelons of Deutsche Post and then into running the Post Office in Ireland. And that addiction was still there. He had eventually retired. But now, in his mid-sixties, he was back in again, this time taking on the challenge of a start-up business. Brian wasn't quite sure what it did. But it was something to do with a mail service. And it was all about satisfying his addiction. Or satisfying it nearly…

Work challenges were not enough. Alan was a heavy user, and before he'd retired officially he had supplemented his fixes through work with some fixes through sport. He'd been an orienteer, a competitive orienteer. But now his body had decided that this tramping around the countryside was no longer on and he needed a new competitive challenge, something that, like orienteering at the highest levels, would take him around the world, something indeed like "competitive" bird-spotting – where the competition was all about the number of birds he could spot. How many of the world's nearly ten thousand species he could observe and record.

This makes Alan sound a little like a nerd. Like a train-spotter in a badly fitting anorak, scribbling numbers in a notepad. But Alan was anything but a nerd. He was bright, engaging, always ready to laugh, and he was just enjoying himself with the sort of challenge that allowed him to take himself and his wife to some of the most remarkable places on Earth. He was, therefore, just like Brian, only just a little bit keener on his bird-count. And on top of all this he looked like a cross between Michael Bentine and Clint Eastwood, and he had a jacket. Sitting here, at this Indian barbecue, he was wearing a smart tropical jacket – and it was uncreased! But how had he done that? How had he managed to get all the way to the Brahmaputra with an item of apparel that was so free of creases? Brian never found out.

His wife was uncreased as well. This was Lynn, smooth-skinned and young-looking, not least because she was an awful lot younger than her husband and indeed may have been no more than forty. But this was of no consequence. She still shared his enthusiasm, his intelligence and his interest in wildlife. Albeit she wasn't quite so addicted to a challenge. Brian discovered that she had other interests: cooking, swimming and reading, and these served her just as well as Alan's more focused attention on birds.

She also liked food. This was apparent when a more substantial part of the piecemeal barbecue arrived. She managed a full plate. Brian and Sandra did not. They had already had too many of the countless nibble-size bits of the feast and could face no more. They were also aware of the time. It was almost ten o'clock and they were very conscious that tomorrow's planned escapade would require them to rise from their bed at four in the morning!

They therefore made their excuses and retired for the night, comfortable in the knowledge that they had met another pair of people on this cruise who might prove to be the most amiable and interesting pair in the party. And who didn't seem too interested in photography...

5.

The generator burst into life. This was the boat's alarm clock. It was so noisy that it was impossible to sleep through. And although a minute or so after it had been switched on, one of the boat's crew would knock discreetly on everyone's door to ensure they were awake, there was no way they'd not be. It was now rumbling away, and Brian was trying to drag himself into consciousness. Four in the morning was really pushing it, and he still had to shave...

He managed, and by 4.45 he, with all the other Nature-seekers, was sitting on the country boat, encased in a life-jacket and coming to terms with the day. He was also counting his companions. They were all here, a further testament to the efficacy of Imodium and, he suspected, the growing realisation within the group that as long as you didn't fart, even if your stomach was at the peak of its upset, you'd probably be OK.

The boat trip took just minutes, barely longer than it took to put on and take off a life-jacket. And now they had disembarked and were walking towards two minibuses. They were the same two buses that had ferried them to the gibbon sanctuary on their first day. They must have followed them down the river, shadowing the progress of the Sukapha and stationing themselves for their next use by its passengers. Brian was impressed. Rajan was obviously good.

Brian chose a back seat. He thought that a clear view of the road ahead might not be a very good idea this early in the morning, and a shunt in the back didn't hold quite the same degree of terror as a head-on collision. He needn't have been so concerned. The road trip was short, uneventful (at least for those at the back), and it was now over. They had arrived at an entrance to the Kaziranga National Park that gave them access to its extensive grasslands – and to its elephant rides!

Brian was quite excited. He might have ridden a donkey when he was very small, but he had never ridden a horse and neither had he ever been on a "holiday" camel. But here he was, about to mount a bloody great pachyderm, the riding equivalent of jumping in at the deep end. And probably with minimal Health and Safety. It was worth getting up for.

The buses came to a stop, and there they were, a dozen or so saddled elephants, waiting in a neat line like a row of bulbous, grey taxis. And the first thing that struck Brian was that they weren't bloody great pachyderms at all, but that they were quite small pachyderms. Compared to African elephants he had seen, they were lightweights, just like those Indian bananas… Brian thought that if Hannibal had made it over the Alps with the African variety, then maybe these chaps might just about manage the Mendips. But then he thought that possibly it was Indian elephants that Hannibal had got his hands on, which rather undermined his first thought, but did remind him again of how little he knew about anything and the wonder he found in ignorance.

They were bigger when one came to mount them. This boarding process took place in a concrete edifice that looked a little like an unfinished water-tower. One climbed up some concrete steps, an elephant squeezed its way through the tower's concrete pillars, and when it had come to rest adjacent to the top of the steps, one pulled oneself on. Without being allowed to give it any considered thought, one was then on its saddle, a broad, three-seater saddle with each of the seats facing forward. Now, just to make this clear, this means that one was now sitting on an elephant in the same way that one would sit on a horse, with one's legs hanging down either side. Only, of course, they don't hang at all; they splay. The back of even a modest-sized elephant is a great deal wider than that of any horse, and riding one of these creatures involves doing the splits for as long as one is on it. And testing splits. Brian soon decided that elephant riding of this sort would plainly be inadvisable for many, and especially for the arthritic, for the obese, for the infirm and for the intact. And maybe it wasn't going to be too good an idea for him.

He was on an elephant with Pamela and Julian and their new change of shirts. Sandra had become separated in the mounting tower and was now on another elephant with Bill and Tina. They both seemed to have forgotten Brian's injudicious reference to the uniqueness of snipe at the dinner table and had made Sandra welcome. She'd even been given the front seat – just behind the mahout. And what a strange word that is, thought Brian. It sounds more Scottish than Indian. As in: 'Duncan had a fine wee mahout, which he kept tucked away in his sporran'. Or maybe it might be a Scottish term of abuse…

It must have been all that getting up early. Brian reminded himself that he wasn't here to have irrelevant, inconsequential thoughts; he was here to observe wildlife from the back of an elephant. And it was around him already. Their squad of eight mounted elephants was now in elephant-size grass, and standing there, in a small clearing in the grass, but just a few feet away, was a substantial wild boar. Beyond him there were hog deer, more than ten of them. And beyond them there was something grey. It was a rhino, one of the hundreds of Indian one-horned rhinos for whom this park is a crucial sanctuary.

Brian had been told that these rhinos didn't much bother about elephants, even elephants decorated with a topping of humans, and he had been told correctly. The phalanx of organic people-carriers advanced in the direction of the sighting until the something grey had become the very clear and very close view of a rhinoceros. And it wasn't in the least concerned. Nor were the elephants. And nor were the Nature-seekers aboard them. They were obviously all fascinated with such a close encounter, and Brian himself was simply thrilled. Here was one of the most unbelievable creatures in the world, just like its African cousins, a masterpiece of natural engineering, with a hide that defies description and a face which belies the animal's awesome power. For when one studied those delicate lips and when one looked into those remarkable eyes, one could see only sensitivity, a gentleness which would take a great deal to budge, and certainly a great deal more than a contingent of nosey tourists.

This creature proved to be just the first. During their sixty-minute ride through the grass, they encountered another four, all, like the first one, models of serenity and indifference – with possibly some nonchalance thrown in there as well. But then the ride was over and it was time to dismount.

This, it transpired, was to be more of a challenge than the original mounting. Legs no longer responded to commands and newly discovered muscles had to be pacified to avoid pain. But eventually Brian was off and had now only to coax his legs into walking. They managed the distance to the minibus and he got on board to sit next to Sandra.

'They only do two a day, apparently,' she announced.

'Two what?'

'Two rides. And we were the second. So they're off for the day now. They've done all they need.'

'You mean the elephants?'

'No. I mean the bus drivers. We've been abandoned for the day… Oh come on, Brian, of course I mean the elephants.'

'Oh, splendid!'

And he meant it. As enjoyable as the experience had been, riding tamed elephants was a bit "circus". But, there again, if they had such a short working day, and for most of the day, the rhinos and the other animals were just allowed to get on with it, then fine. Or even splendid. And it even made him wonder how you became a mahout. Far shorter working hours than those of an accountant.

He tried to advance this thinking with Tim at the breakfast table. But Tim wasn't really prepared to engage. He doubted anyway that there were many openings for mahouts in West Yorkshire, and in any event, riding an elephant wouldn't be quite the same on the Leeds ring-road. Brian was forced to agree, and immediately deserted his thoughts on mahouts in favour of a mouthful of toast.

They had come to a simple lodge just outside the park where, after refreshing themselves, they had sat down to an alfresco breakfast. Brian and Sandra were seated at a table with Tim and Karen, Ron and Irene, and a couple who answered to the names of Jerry and Edith. Now, earlier Brian had made some remarks about how difficult it must have been for those with bowel problems to splay their legs for a whole hour, and how surprised he'd been that there hadn't been any accidents, or at least none that he'd been aware of. This observation didn't appear to go down very well with Irene, and even Ron looked a little concerned. And whatever they thought, they then just talked between themselves. Which is why Brian had initiated a discussion about mahouts with Tim. But this was now at an end, and Tim had re-activated Irene and Ron, and Sandra had engaged Karen. Which left only Jerry and Edith.

This was a problem. And it was a problem because Jerry and Edith, in "social sophistication" terms, had a good deal in common with Jim. They could certainly never be described as riveting company, and in many ways they were rather two-dimensional. Indeed, in terms of their appearance and their dress, they could have been created by Donald McGill. Jerry, in particular, was a seaside postcard come to life. It was the combination of his bouffant hair (on his ancient head), his British Home Store trousers and his sensible sandals – aided and abetted by the fact that these two aforementioned items of gentlemen's apparel were permanently estranged from each other. (His trousers finished halfway down his calves and may never have met an ankle in their life.)

So, suffice it to say that Brian had not gone out of his way to bond with Jerry and his wife. Whenever he had overheard them talking or observed their rather bewildered reaction to what was going on around them, he had, in fact, gone out of his way not to bond with them. How could he? He now believed that they were only on this trip by mistake, that they had gone to the wrong check-in at Heathrow or had got on the wrong baggage-belt. But now they were here with him at the table and the only people to talk to. So he had no choice. He had to take them on. And he did. He started talking to them about the state of the economy. After all, everybody has a view on the state of the economy. And maybe even Jerry did.

Brian was correct. And more. Not only did Jerry have a view of the economy back in Britain, but he also had a view about Britain in general, how it had been reduced to its present state, and even a suitable remedy for those responsible for its downfall. Yes, he was of the firm opinion that Blair and Brown between them had completely ruined the country, and that for doing this, they should be hanged or emasculated or both.

So Jerry wasn't so bad after all. He was still an odd-looking wally, but at least he was a wally who could cut through that web of conflicting evidence and arrive at that nugget of truth: that the two aforementioned gentlemen had really screwed things up.

This revelation was as refreshing as it was unexpected. It kicked out the remnants of Brian's early-morning weariness and he now felt up and ready for the next part of the day. This was just as well, as what was now on the agenda was another long jeep safari in what was becoming the hottest day so far.

They had returned to the Kaziranga Park through the "elephant gate" and they had once again disembarked from their minibuses to re-board their jeeps. These were the same jeeps they had used the previous day – and came with the same companions. That is to say that Sujan instructed his charges to pair up with the same jeep-buddies they'd driven around with before. Which for Brian and Sandra meant… Jim. This rather detracted from Brian's recently revitalized state, and his revival was further impaired by the realisation that this would be Jim without Rajan. Their tour manager had not joined them today because of an overload of official worries, and this meant that he and Sandra had no one to shield them from Jim's "conversations". They might be assailed with a discourse on microchips without any warning whatsoever.

As it turned out, Jim was no problem at all. He sat for most of the time quietly and unobtrusively, again taking only the occasional photo and not much interest in anything else that was smaller than a buffalo. He did get very agitated once. But understandably so. Imran had indicated (silently) that he'd possibly seen a tiger.

The jeeps had split into two groups and were taking clockwise and counter-clockwise routes around this grassland area of the park – just as they had in its more forested area the previous day. Brian's trio had Imran and Tika in attendance, and whilst Tika was majoring on birds, it became apparent that Imran was using his local knowledge to locate a big cat. This part of the park with its eight-foot high grass was where they were most often found.

His possible sighting brought all three jeeps to an immediate halt, and while all their occupants waited in expectant silence, Imran started to conduct a more thorough search. This didn't involve him in an excursion through the hidden depths of the grass (for obvious reasons). But it did involve a lot of moving around and crouching while he peered through the gaps in a line of trees that bordered the track.

Jim was clearly getting impatient. Brian, however, was simply getting resigned, resigned to the fact that he was not going to see a tiger. Even if there was one around he knew they wouldn't see it – even if the tiger was seeing them. That's what tigers are like, masters of concealment and as careful as they come. That's why there are still any tigers left in the world at all. And maybe those that now survive have a race memory imprinted on their minds that makes them even more careful than their forbears, a race memory concerning a band of tossers whose blinkered view of the natural world required them to blast any tiger they saw.

So, if Brian wasn't going to see a tiger as such, maybe he could still spot some tiger poo. That would be something. And he started to scour the sides of the track for a pile of anything that might be further investigated and then identified by the experts. He did this first with his eyes and then with his binoculars. This was when Sandra asked him what he was doing.

'I'm looking for tiger poo.'

'Why?'

'It's supposed to keep cats away.'

Jim was listening to this exchange – whilst still intent on Imran's inspection of the grassland. So was Tika. He had just walked up to the back of their jeep in readiness to join it. He looked slightly puzzled.

Sandra continued.

'So you're looking for some tiger poo in Assam to keep cats away in Worcestershire?'

'Well, yes. You can't find it in Worcestershire…'

Tika joined in.

'Did you say you wanted tiger poo… to keep cats away?'

'Yes,' replied Brian. 'We get loads of them at home, and they're a real bloody menace. And apparently tiger poo works a treat. I suppose it must be like us finding some human poo, but… you know, in six-foot lengths. That'd certainly put the wind up me…'

'Brian!'

'Well, Tika asked. So I was just explaining.'

'Cats and glass,' pronounced Jim suddenly.

Brian, just for a second, thought that Jim had once again made one of his peculiar unrelated utterances. But then he realised what he meant and he thought he ought to expand on Jim's observation, if for no other reason than putting Tika out of his misery. He was clearly entirely perplexed.

'Yes, cats and glass – as in glass windows. The two biggest killers of birds in the world...'

'Followed closely by the Maltese,' observed Sandra.

Brian looked at his wife in disbelief. He knew that she had a very poor view of how the Maltese shot everything in sight (during the migration seasons). But it was very unusual for her to express such a forthright view in the company of others, and especially when she wasn't sure of her ground. But he needn't have worried.

'Oh yes,' agreed Tika. 'I've read about it many times. The RSPB tries very hard, but they can't seem to stop them. They're now worse than Cyprus. '

'We should kick them out of the EU,' added Jim. 'They're breaching their terms of entry.'

'Blimey,' thought Brian. 'He *has* got an interest other than in big animals. Or maybe the Maltese have upset his bureaucratic cool. Breaching the terms of entry 'n all. That certainly won't do. But hey, whatever his reasons, he seems to be on our side. So well done, Jim. Hope you get some good snaps...'

This unexpected charitable train of thought was brought to an abrupt end by Imran announcing that he hadn't found a tiger and that the jeeps should move on. And Brian had drawn a blank on the tiger poo as well. But he didn't think anybody would be too interested in that and he didn't announce it. Instead, he just steadied himself against the forward U-frame. The jeep was now in motion. And even if they'd drawn a blank on tigers for the present, there was still plenty more to see.

The first sight was of a pied harrier. It was flying slow and low (as all harriers do) over a stretch of marshy ground within the grass. It had the grace of its marsh and hen-harrier cousins, but it also had its own unique plumage: the black and white of a truly pied bird. And this combination of finesse in flight and elegance in appearance was quite breathtaking. It was not only one of the most splendid wildlife sights that Brian had ever witnessed, but it was also one of the most splendid sights of anything at all that he had ever witnessed. It was quite incredible, and for Brian, just as exciting as seeing a tiger or any big cat. Albeit this probably wasn't how Jim would have seen it.

The second sight was of another black and white bird, a little ringed plover, not quite so remarkable as the harrier, but still very welcome. Then there were a whole host of other birds including crested serpent-eagles, shikras, swamp francolins, Alexandrine parakeets – and lesser whistling-ducks, who appropriately were doing a lot less whistling than Brian would have liked. In fact they were doing none. They were as silent as a troupe of terrapins who were spotted on a log in a pond. They were lined up along its length staring heavenwards, and looking for all the world as though they were awaiting the arrival of some terrapin supreme being, some hard-shelled redeemer who would lead them to the promised lake and to a future free of raptors. And wouldn't that put the Pope in a spin?

Brian was at it again, letting his leaps of tortured imagination get in the way of his enjoying the now, of observing properly what was around him.

'Come on,' he said to himself, 'get a grip. And anyway, terrapins are hardly going to get swept away by that sort of nonsense…'

His renewed focus on the real paid dividends. There were buttonquails, there were rufous treepies, there were striated babblers, and in the bigger league, there were dozens of deer and dozens of rhinos. Indeed there was one rhino "at ease" in a flower-decked mud-pool, which was so close and so unconcerned and such a perfect photo opportunity, that Brian became almost as excited as Jim. And Brian's resulting photo was superb, his subject looking directly into the lens – and clearly pitying the photographer. 'What a stupid thing to be doing when you could just be lying here in this pool…'

They'd now been out on the jeeps for over three hours. They'd met the other trio of jeeps and exchanged news (although, on this occasion, not jeeps, as the suspension crack seemed to have gone into remission), and they were now approaching the end of their safari. And as a finale to it, there appeared before them a whole herd of elephants. And not of the tame, rideable variety, but of the wild, would-stamp-on-you-if-you-tried variety. Brian was impressed. Even though Indian elephants were noticeably smaller than their African counterparts they still had that same incredible air of dignity about them that no other animal possessed. They also made Brian want to cry. But that was probably more to do with Brian than it was to do with the elephants.

Lunch was at another lodge a few miles from the park gate. It had only recently been opened and, with its square of bamboo and concrete huts arranged around a large rice field, it looked more like a set for a remake of "*Apocalypse Now*" than it did an Assamese lodge. No matter. It was owned by the same people who operated the Sukapha. Accordingly the food on offer for lunch could only be described as excellent. This was good news for Brian and all those others in the party who had either recovered from their stomach ailments or who had not yet been struck down. But for those who were in the all too active stage of the malady, it was not such good news. More bananas than ever were consumed by the group.

Some of these banana-eaters were among those who returned to the boat directly after this lunch, along with the wimps in the party, including Brian and Sandra. They had now been up for over ten hours, the day was hotter than ever, and there was no way they wanted to indulge in a further safari. However, some others in the party did. Brian suspected they were on drugs. How else could they do it? God, most of them were older than he was!

He thought about this some more while he was relaxing on the boat's sundeck and imbibing his own drug of choice: alcohol. It came wrapped up in a nice lager-type beer called Kingfisher, which, of course, is also the name of an airline in India – owned by the same proprietor. He then thought of the likelihood of ever flying on an airline in Britain called Boddingtons, and decided that this was highly unlikely.

Dinner was with Derek and Yvonne and Dennis and Pauline, the quartet of fellow travellers who excelled in the arts of photography. This was a little awkward for Brian to begin with as Pauline began to ask him about the settings he was using, and Brian couldn't even remember their names, let alone provide her with anything like a proper answer. He therefore had to use all his skills of deflection to take him past this hazard and into the far more rewarding sphere of: "Where have you been?". Virtually all of the Nature-seekers on this trip were very well travelled indeed, and names such as Costa Rica, Belize, Madagascar and Botswana could be heard being bandied about all the time. But the quartet members were particularly well travelled. Indeed they had met on one such travel, on an expedition to Antarctica, where presumably their shared interest in the still and moving image had drawn them together. So it was only natural that Brian took this route, hoping if nothing else that he could trump their Antarctica with his and Sandra's Papua New Guinea. But then another country emerged, one to which all six of them had ventured – and one which was hardly a usual destination for anyone.

They had all visited, it turned out, Guyana. This not only meant that they were all in that minority of Britons who knew that Guyana was in South America and not in Africa, but it also meant that they were all members of that much tinier group of Britons who had actually been there. About six hundred visit it each year. And here, around this table, in the dining room of a boat on the Brahmaputra, were six of them, a full one percent of Guyana's annual visitor total from Britain. What's more, they had all visited the same places within Guyana – which isn't quite so incredible. Because if you are there on a wildlife trip (which is really the only reason you would be there), you very soon discover that there are only a handful of possible destinations. Guyana makes rural Assam look like a heaving metropolis. Its minute population clings stubbornly to its coast, and its interior remains delightfully empty (for now) with only one dirt track making its way through the forest and all the way to Brazil.

Brian had to compare notes. What had they thought of Karanambu? Well, as he soon found out, not quite as much as he had. Which was a bit of a disappointment. After all, Karanambu was (and hopefully still is) a little slice of heaven. It is a very basic lodge deep inside Guyana, where the forest melts into more open savannah. It is a working cattle ranch, but a cattle ranch that is so vast that as a visitor one never encounters a single cow; they are all miles away on some distant pastures. Instead one encounters just a beautiful, untouched sliver of

South America, simply stuffed with a whole host of the most wonderful birds and animals imaginable. One also encounters the lodge's matriarch, Dianne, a lady whose life has been devoted to the care and rehabilitation of injured or abandoned giant river-otters. She is often observed swimming with them in the nearby river.

She is also seen, every evening, doing her duty with the bat droppings.

Meals at the lodge are taken around a table that is just large enough to take the six guests who can be accommodated in the lodge cabins, together with Dianne and her nephew and niece. This table sits in an open-sided dining room under an enormous thatched roof – in which there are bats. Early in the meal these bats are not a problem. But as the evening wears on, and the bats wake, they tend to do what many others do when they wake – but without the benefit of a flushable lavatory. The inevitable result is the arrival on the table of one or two, or nine or ten bat spraints.

Now Dianne is very old school. She was born in Guyana, but she was the daughter of the local District Commissioner (when Guyana was British Guiana), and she would not be out of place in Liberty's – where, in fact, she worked for a while in her youth. She is now over eighty, but still has the cut-crystal voice of a well-brought-up English lady of the early Fifties, and she still has the manners of a well-brought-up English lady of the early Fifties. So much so that she is able to charm you with her engaging conversation at the dinner table, and without pausing for a second in her discourse, brush away the offending poo with an accomplished but discreet sweep of her used napkin and virtually convince you that the poo was never there in the first place. That it was just your imagination and the effect of the heat. How could this elegant woman, chatting to you in her refined tones about her days as a "young gal" in Guyana, also be wiping bat excrement from the dining table? For Brian, this display of old English etiquette in the oddest of surroundings was one of the highlights of his trip to Guyana.

Apparently though, not for the photographic four – who came away from Karanambu with insect bites and, although laden with a haul of photos and film from the surrounding area, not with the cherished memories of an eccentric but wonderful heroine living out her life with rescued animals.

But hey… that was Guyana. And, as Brian eventually reminded himself, this was India. This was Assam. And it was late. Time to retire again and get a few hours' sleep in a bat-proof cabin, in order to be ready for another early morning. Because tomorrow, it was boats. Not boats on the Brahmaputra, but boats on a far away river. And boats full of air.

As full of air as Brian was full of apprehension.

6.

*B*rian had considered asking for half a fried egg. But when he was faced by the chef behind his hot-plate he bottled out of it and asked for a whole one, a single, fried-on-both-sides one. So here he was at the breakfast table, chomping his way through two rashers of bacon and two fried-on-both-sides fried eggs. Not that he minded much. It was going to be another long day and lunch was hours away. He probably needed the additional sustenance. Furthermore, he'd become distracted as he ate, and he hardly noticed the over-abundance of egg matter. And what had distracted him was the word "rasher". He was quite interested in words, and especially words that had limited use. Words like "clench". For although "clench" could replace "grip" on occasions, it was generally limited in its use to the act of clenching one's teeth, clenching one's fist or clenching one's buttocks. And that was about it. One could never clench one's nose or even one's legs. But with "rasher" it was even more limited. It only ever meant a thin slice of bacon or ham cooked by frying or grilling. And how did a word like that arise? Who, one day, sat down to his breakfast of cooked slices of bacon and said: 'Mmm... I think I'll call these slices "rashers"?' And why "rashers"? Why not "lashers" or "tashers"? Or "sliggers" or "giggers" for that matter? Was it just pot luck, or was there some more rasher-nal explanation?

This was when he emerged from his distraction. Even Brian couldn't manage such an appalling play on words this early in the morning. So now he was back in the world around him and intent only on clearing his plate and finishing his coffee. After that it was a quick trip back to his cabin and getting Sandra to check that he had all about him that he needed for the day – including the advised change of clothes…

They were setting off today for the Nameri National Park and a white-water river ride. Brian could not quite believe that this was a suitable diversion for a group of middle-aged naturalists. But the tour organisers apparently believed otherwise, and Sujan had been very reassuring the previous evening. But then there had been this instruction to bring along a change of clothing, and that seemed to undermine the reassurance completely. Nevertheless, nobody had backed out of the trip, and that meant that neither could Brian and Sandra. So it was out of the cabin with a bag-full of spare shorts, shirts and socks, onto their appointed minibus, waiting for them at the foot of the gang-plank, and off to Nameri.

This park was north of the river and a long way away. So the minibus and its following twin were now embarking on a two-hour journey along the south bank of the river, over the only bridge that spans the river for miles in either direction, and on and up to where the province of Assam borders that of Arunachal Pradesh. And Arunachal Pradesh is the bit of India that sits by Tibet, and which, at its western end, abuts Bhutan, a country which interestingly contains all the letters required to spell the word "abut". That, however, was just another glancing thought that went through Brian's mind as their journey began, and very soon he was more absorbed in the journey itself.

The roads to start with were not completely manic. There

were only a few vehicles around, and the only real challenge that the bus-driver had was to avoid a reduction in India's goat, dog and bicycle population. As regards the goats and dogs, this was no challenge at all. They all have traffic-avoidance built into their DNA, and there was therefore very little avoidance left to the driver. He just drove and the animals did virtually all the avoiding on their own, even if, on certain occasions, they did seem to be tempting fate. Generally by only a few inches. The bicycles, however, were not quite so evolved, and only through a series of improbable miracles did their riders not discover what the underside of a bus looks like as it was rolling over them. Fortunately miracles around here were not in short supply.

Ultimately, however, the minibuses emerged from a tangle of country roads onto what was clearly the main thoroughfare leading to the bridge. Here there was more of a real challenge – made even more challenging at the outset for Brian's minibus by the loss of an atmosphere in one of its tyres. Both buses stopped, their occupants decamped with their binoculars, and the two bus drivers set about replacing the flat tyre. This gave everybody an opportunity to conduct some impromptu bird-watching and an opportunity for the locals to observe at close quarters what white people look like. For it had now become apparent that Assam was essentially white-people-free and that Brian and his companions were as rare in this part of the world as green people were in England. There were simply none, and therefore the Nature-seekers represented no less than a double-fifty-pointer in "The Assamese Eye-Spy Book of Non-Assamese". 'Goodness gracious,' you could imagine an onlooker saying as he watched them with their binoculars. 'These fellows aren't from West Bengal or Bangladesh; they're from somewhere where there isn't any sun. I mean, look at them; they're so pale. And look, they all have such poor eyesight as well. See how they have to carry around those monster pairs of specs and how they need them to see even a tree. Amazing. And how do they ride a bicycle with those things?'

The tyre was mended and the rarest of rare species rejoined their transport. As it pulled away to become part of the traffic again, the clutch of locals who had gathered to gaze and to ponder looked on in wonder. Would any of their friends ever believe them? Would they even believe it themselves after a few days? It could, after all, have been a dream.

Brian had this very same thought – about it being a dream – when his minibus failed to make contact with the front of an oncoming lorry. Because it was not possible that it hadn't met it head on. It was therefore more than possible that the avoidance of the collision was just that: a dream. And that the reality was that Brian was now lying in a crumpled wreck of a bus, so seriously injured that he was hallucinating and imagining that he was still OK – and not about to breathe his last.

He pinched himself and he felt the pinch. Maybe it wasn't a dream. Maybe they had missed that lorry. And then Sandra spoke to him, and he knew they really had.

'Did you see that road-sign back there? I can't believe it.'

Brian thought for a moment. 'How can you notice road-signs,' he thought, 'when you don't notice lorries, lorries bearing down on you and intent on ending your life?' But he didn't say this. He just said: 'Errh… no dear. What road-sign was that?'

'Well, it was a proper one. You know, an official one. And it said: "Don't gossip, let him drive." I mean, let *him* drive. Can you believe it?'

Well, Brian not only could believe it, but he also thought

that the message was commendably pragmatic and admirably free of political correctness. Heck, women drivers here were almost as rare as white people were, and it was never men that gossiped anywhere. But he didn't say this either. Instead, he just shook his head in mock disbelief and emphasised this with the observation that it was: 'Incredible. Quite incredible'.

This seemed to satisfy Sandra, and Brian was able to get back to worrying about the oncoming lorries and trying to calculate whether there was any realistic chance that they'd even get as far as the bridge.

They did. Brian was in the middle of the minibus with far too good a view of the road ahead, and stretching out before them now were the two miles of the enormous bridge that spanned the Brahmaputra at one of its narrowest points. It was only two lanes wide but it was very impressive. It was also, apparently, quite wide enough to take the largest Chinese tanks – when their armies surged in from Tibet to overrun India. Brian wasn't sure that this piece of information, which had been provided by Sujan, was meant as a joke or as a rueful comment on what might really happen in the future. He decided it was a joke. But he also decided that the joke might eventually be on India.

Intriguingly, there was a military presence on the bridge even now. There were armed soldiers and military trucks. However, this was not in anticipation of a Chinese onslaught, but as a deterrent to civil unrest. India's general election would be taking place in just a couple of weeks and it couldn't be guaranteed that it would be entirely free of incident, especially up here, in this remote and some might say neglected corner of the country. And so the soldiers and trucks. Brian had a good look at them as the minibus drove past. The soldiers looked "well turned out" and the trucks looked new, and nothing at all like all the other ancient "public carriers" that lumbered around the roads threatening the lives of people in buses. It said a great deal to Brian about how the country was run and how it set its priorities. So did another road-sign a few miles from the bridge. It said "Assamese Rifles Urinals". Hell, nothing less than a military versus non-military apartheid!

They were now in a built-up area that could have been a town or just an agglomeration of dwellings and shops around the nucleus of a military camp, a garrison of the Assamese Rifles. But whatever it was, it came with more than its fair share of goats, dogs, cyclists, rickshaws, lorries, and fortunately more than enough of that other dimension, that new dimension in space that Brian had first observed five days previously on their way to the gibbon sanctuary. It was needed. Maybe it was the build up of election fever. Or maybe there were rumours of an invasion. But in any event the locals this side of the river used the road as though there was nobody else on it. Vehicles turned in front of other vehicles without warning (and clearly without enough space). Cyclists went about ignoring everything including other cyclists. And pedestrians just strolled – often in the middle of the road and often in defiance of either sanity or common sense.

Brian was now becoming tired. All this lunatic behaviour was proving wearing, as was the bus-ride itself. They had now been travelling for over two hours, the tyre change having put back their schedule by at least twenty minutes. So he was very pleased indeed to see that they were now turning off the main road and onto a much smaller road that led to the park. Sujan then confirmed that they were no more than a quarter of an hour away, a time that was then devoted to spotting "their river", the body of water that would soon be carrying their bodies – in inflatables. They did see quite a few streams, but nothing that looked quite the right job for a squadron of dinghies. Then the spotting stopped. They were at their destination. This, of course, wasn't the river. It was a toilet. Or more precisely, two toilets – at the rear of two tents within a tented eco-lodge. Males had one and females had the other. And relief was enjoyed by all.

Sufficiently drained, the Nature-seekers then re-boarded their buses and set off once again, this time for the real destination, the river itself. On the way, the game of "spot my river" was resumed with the sort of gusto only ever observed as a manifestation of nervousness. The white-water river experience was now very close, and clearly for most of the Nature-seekers, the prospect of the experience was all rather alarming. It certainly was for Brian. So why not join in and take some reassurance from all that gusto? Why not indeed? After all, it did seem to help. But then the buses pulled off the road, which had now become a track, and before them was the river. It was called the Jia Bhoreli River and it was enormous. The inflatable dinghies, which were lined up on its bank, were, in contrast, miniscule. Brian relapsed into nervousness which almost immediately translated itself into a sort of whimpering panic.

Matters were not improved when he then noticed that not all the Nature-seekers were here. He soon established by talking to Sujan that six of their number had decided to stay at the eco-lodge to conduct some leisurely and, more particularly, some safer bird-spotting. This was not good. Neither were the life-jackets. They were not of the permanently buoyant variety, but more of the too-tight-for-comfort variety – and of questionable worth. That river was not only enormous, but it was also flowing down its course like a horizontal waterfall. Life-jackets would serve no purpose whatsoever. Brian really could not believe that they were all going to be launched onto what was nothing less than a raging flood – with or without these useless life-jackets.

But they were. He and Sandra, now bound into their chest-hugging life-savers, were summoned to the shore and encouraged to step over some slippery stones and into their vessel. "Into", however, is not really the appropriate word. Their vessel was a very tiny inflatable dinghy, across which had been laid two short planks. These planks were simply resting on the dinghy's inflated sides. And Brian quickly realised that they were supposed to be interpreted as the dinghy's seats. His panic rose further. But before he really knew what was going on he was sitting on one of these "seats" with Sandra sitting on the other in front of him. He was immediately aware of the hardness of its unpadded wooden surface, but more disconcertingly, of the wobbliness of the dinghy's un-inflated bottom beneath his feet. He and his wife were separated from the water of the river by a millimetre or so of plasticised rubber. Or who knows? It might have been a millimetre or so of reconstituted plastic shopping bags. But whatever it was, it didn't feel too reassuring; it just felt immensely unsettling.

Brian then turned his mind to the matter of dinghy propulsion and navigation. How the hell were they supposed to get this thing down this raging torrent without drowning within yards? The answer was a pair of paddlers, the two local lads who had helped them into… no, onto the dinghy, and who had now joined them on their miniature craft, and were sitting, paddles in hand, on the inflated bit at the back. They were even less in the dinghy than were their passengers.

Brian was about to ask for a recount, to demand a further debate on the wisdom of the entire project. But too late. The paddlers had now pushed the vessel away from the shelter of the bank and their little rubber toy was already in the maelstrom. They were off down the river whether they liked it or not, and at a pace that made Brian wonder what he'd done to deserve it.

The river was very broad. There was an awful lot of water in it, and this water was in a terrible hurry. It swept down the river like a true torrent, and, of course, it swept down with it any small vessel that was foolish enough to join it. Brian and Sandra's dinghy was now racing down the flow in the company of eight other dinghies, and, as Brian quickly established in his mind, all of these vessels were now completely at its mercy.

The paddlers, as he noticed on the other dinghies, were not paddling at all. They didn't need to. And indeed any attempt to paddle in this flood would have been as difficult as it would have been futile. No, instead they were acting as rudders. Essentially, each dinghy was equipped with a human-held double rudder, the so called "paddles" being used to do no more than to keep the dinghies facing forward and then, increasingly, to prevent their being swept into the wilder parts of the water. For it soon became apparent that this river was not only broad, but it was also "braided". It had within its course huge banks of pebbles, some above the waterline and some below it – creating in its flow enormous stretches of not quite white water, but viciously undulating, constantly agitated, worryingly swirling, grey water. Just the sort of water that could provide an experience that would not only be immediately deflating but pretty soon after that, decidedly lethal.

Brian gathered himself. The rudder system was working.

They were avoiding the vortices. They were still inflated. Maybe the "paddlers" actually knew what they were doing. And Sandra didn't seem unduly concerned. If, that is, she hadn't fallen into a state of catatonic shock. And no, she hadn't. She turned her head slightly and uttered the word 'pratincoles'. And yes, there they were, a flock of small pratincoles, fabulous pale-coloured little birds sweeping this way and that over the river like a host of ghostly swallows. They were superb, and they were a bird that Brian had been hoping to see for some time. They were also his salvation. This river trip might be a little alarming, but it really wasn't that bad. As long as these two chaps behind continued to do their job, all would be well, and Brian might as well just get on and enjoy it. He might never do it again. Even if he survived it.

His change of attitude worked. Within a very short time he was relishing the experience, not just of what he was seeing, but also of the mad dash down the river itself, with its constant threat of mishap or worse. Indeed in retrospect he would compare it with a visit he had made to Disney World in Florida (for the benefit of continued good relations with some family members who possessed young children). There he had exposed himself to the delights of such things as "*The Duelling Dragons*" and "*The Hulk*", terrifying roller-coaster devices which were designed to make you scream, and the design of which had worked. But there, one felt in danger even though one knew one was entirely safe. The potential size of American lawsuits made sure of that. Here on the river, however, it was the opposite. After the initial shock had been dissipated by all those pratincoles, one felt safe even though one knew one was not far from danger. If the guys at the back got it wrong just once, the dinghy would soon be in shreds, and even if you weren't too, through the action of vigorous pebble-pummelling, you would probably be drowning. The life-jackets would be useless and so too would all your colleagues in those other dinghies. Quite simply, they could not have manoeuvred themselves against the flow to come to your aid, and the nearest professional rescue services were certainly miles away, if not days away, and would arrive at just about the time your body was entering the Bay of Bengal.

Fortunately, it wasn't retrospect time yet, and Brian was still in full relishing mode. He relished the further birds he saw: river terns, river lapwings, wreathed hornbills, green sandpipers – and nearly a great thick-knee. He also relished the scenery: luscious open forest in the foreground and in the distance, to the north of the river, the densely forested ridges of Arunchal Pradesh, the "Land of Dawn-lit Mountains". They were spectacular, and on their own well worth putting one's life on the line for an hour or so at least.

Indeed this dinghy experience risked becoming absolutely outstanding. But that would have been to ignore the contribution of Brian and Sandra's paddlers. They were young and fit, but they were also stupid and irresponsible. They had clearly become bored with their role within minutes of setting off, and to relieve this boredom, had taken to talking, whistling and singing badly. This was not only distracting, but it was pretty irritating as well. Although not so irritating as when they then started to steer into other dinghies. They obviously thought it was the height of good fun to knock into their companions as though they were on the dodgems at a fairground, completely ignoring that this was not only puerile but also life-threatening – in what was already a perilous predicament. Brian wanted to make his irritation known. But with his life-jacket on, he could not turn to talk to them, and even if he could, he doubted they spoke any English. He therefore calmed his irritation by again trying to look at their behaviour not from his perspective but from theirs.

Here they were, giving up probably a whole day of their lives. And for what? Maybe for no more than twenty rupees. Nothing. And for that they had to sit in discomfort on the back of a tiny inflatable, struggling against the currents of a huge river, and without even the novelty of the scenery or an interest in birds to relieve their exertions. On top of that, they were probably under instructions to dive into the river if either of their passengers abandoned ship without prior notice. They would no doubt be expected to put their own lives at risk to save the lives of people they neither knew nor cared for. And these people were so old! Were their lives worth saving anyway? So why not chatter and whisper? And why not spice things up a bit with a spot of dinghy-ramming? 'Heck, these people are just sitting there staring around. Surely better for them that there's a bit of excitement, something they'll remember, something they'll bore all their friends with when they get back home.' And Brian had to concede; he wouldn't be forgetting this trip in a hurry, and neither would he be forgetting the added frisson, courtesy of a couple of mischievous mariners.

The headlong rush down the river took just over an hour. When they'd arrived at their destination, a muddy bank above which were their two mini-buses, Sujan informed them that their "cruise" should have taken twice this time. However, because the river was so swollen, it was running at about twice its normal pace, and hence the rapidity of their journey and its earlier than expected conclusion.

'And now he tells us,' thought Brian. 'It *was* bloody

dangerous. And far more dangerous than those Duelling Dragons or that incredible Hulk. Wait till I tell Sandra's brother...'

But he wasn't really angry. How could he be? After the initial panic he'd enjoyed it. And look, here was the bearer of this quite shocking news, and he hadn't even got a life-jacket on. Sujan was just too portly. There hadn't been a life-jacket big enough to fit him. So he had embarked on this river adventure without one – in his own personal dinghy (there was only room for him and his two paddlers) – and in the honest belief that no matter how much water there was and how fast it was flowing, he and all his charges would be well. And, of course, he had been right. Result: Health and Safety nil, Sujan three. No, make that a four to one defeat. After all, they hadn't even got wet, and they didn't need to change their clothes. And that was worth another goal at least. And unsurprisingly it wasn't just Brian who wasn't angry; nobody was angry. All of them, quite obviously, had been exhilarated by the experience and felt just elated and alive – and now very hungry.

So back to the eco-lodge to rejoin the bird-spotting landlubbers and then to set about some alcoholic refreshment in preparation for a delicious lunch. It was curry and it was consumed in an open-sided dining room at the lodge. Brian and Sandra were joined at their table by Pam and Julian, and by Judy and Rosamunde. Now these last two ladies were as yet an unknown to Brian. He and Sandra had never found themselves in chatting distance of them before now, and his only communication had been a short one with Judy on the very first day. He had introduced himself to her and she had introduced herself to him – by announcing immediately that she was married and that her husband had not wished to join her, which is why she was on this trip with Rosamunde – who was a friend through work. Brian had heard similar announcements before, made by ladies who were travelling together on holiday. They were always made as soon as possible and they were always designed to send the very clear message that the two ladies in question were not lesbians.

Brian entirely understood this. There were, after all, ladies travelling together who *were* lesbians, and this way it prevented all that "are they, aren't they?" nonsense. Notwithstanding that most of the ladies he'd met on holiday who were lesbians were generally far better company than their heterosexual counterparts. After a few minutes at the lunch table, Brian began to suspect that this might be true in this instance as well. All that he could extract from Rosamunde was that she was a physiotherapist, and from Judy that her husband wasn't with her because he preferred real tennis to real wildlife. Brian was therefore soon obliged to discuss the subject of over-population with Pamela and boats with Julian. This most unseaworthy-looking chap had apparently ordered a new one from a boat-builder, and it would be ready for him when he returned to England. Brian just hoped that Julian would be ready for it.

After lunch there was an unscheduled treat. This was a walk to a small protected compound behind the eco-lodge which was a breeding centre for pygmy hogs!

Pygmy hogs are the world's smallest pigs. They are native to Assam, but for reasons that are far too obvious to explain, they are now threatened with extinction. Just a single tiny population is thought to exist in the wild. Cue Durrell Wildlife Conservation, which has stepped forward to set up a captive breeding programme in Assam, in the hope that eventually there will be enough mini-porkers to allow their release into the wild, and through this, to secure their survival in the future.

The place the Nature-seekers were visiting now wasn't the principal breeding centre, but it did have half a dozen or so of these rare animals and was well worth a visit. Brian certainly thought so, but only initially. When they arrived at the compound they discovered that within the compound, and behind electrified security designed to keep predators at bay, there were some small enclosures, not full of hogs but full of closely packed grasses and other vegetation in which the hogs like to live. That is to say that the hogs were not going to make themselves visible.

It was quite a sight. More than twenty grown men and women, peering over the low walls of these enclosures at a hog-free plant landscape – for more than twenty minutes. And it was getting very hot and there was no shade. The twenty grown men and women were now beginning to glow.

Brian was all for giving up. This was just silly. But then Vivien thought that she'd seen a hog in a hole. And indeed she had. As everyone gathered around her, they could see for themselves that in a small hole under a bush, there was a patch of hog-hide. One could even see that the hide was stretched over a hog leg, or maybe it was a hog haunch or even a hog shoulder. But it was definitely hog. No doubt about it. Just not much of it. And as it was a pygmy hog to start with, that wasn't very much at all.

Brian soon felt like giving up again. It was as hot as hell and he didn't have a hog-hole to hide in. Then others were clearly losing their enthusiasm as well, and the party began to drift towards the compound gate. That was when the first hog strolled into full view in the first enclosure, to be followed by another in the adjoining enclosure just a minute later. There was delight all round, cameras were called into action en masse, and Brian was overcome. He immediately regretted those rashers on his breakfast plate back on the Sukapha. And how could he have amused himself on the etymology of rashers – when there were these little darlings here, who were so small and so sweet and so enchanting? Yes, Brian could be a bit soppy when he put his mind to it.

He could also be quite mean-minded. Having had their fill of lunch and of pygmy hogs, the Nature-seekers were now boarding their minibuses in readiness for the return journey to the Sukapha. As they were doing this a police jeep and a white Hindustan Ambassador pulled into the eco-lodge's car park. Ambassadors are cars still produced in India for use as taxis and government vehicles, but they are based on a very old model: the Series III Morris Oxford that was built in Britain in the Fifties. This Ambassador, being a white one, was carrying a government official. He was clearly someone "important", and a flourish of rifles and rather too much shouting was required to announce his arrival. Brian was entirely underwhelmed and just pleased that they were leaving. He would not have enjoyed sharing the eco-lodge with anyone who turned up in such a pretentious manner. However there was worse to come. For as they were driving away down the track towards the main road, three more white Ambassadors appeared up ahead, racing towards them with their horns sounding and with the clear expectation that these two lowly minibuses would simply get out of their way. More "important people" were on the way to the eco-lodge.

Brian hated this. He had seen so much poverty in this country, that the idea of some fat, spoiled officials (for that's what they undoubtedly were) acting like tin-pot potentates, bulldozing their way through the masses, when all they were really doing was heading for a relaxing afternoon at an eco-lodge, made him extremely angry. He wanted to tell them what he thought of them. Tell them how fat they were, how spoiled they were, and how ridiculous they were. Didn't they know? Morris Oxfords were not cool any more. In fact, they had never been cool. They were old, stuffy and distinctly uncool even when they were first introduced. And that was in the depths of the last century. So wouldn't it be great if he could take this convoy of white museum pieces – complete with their occupants – and drop it down in the middle of Birmingham say. Or anywhere in Britain where the hoots of laughter that would greet its arrival would soon leave those same occupants with a very clear understanding of not only how unimportant they were, but also of how very silly they were. And maybe even of how truly naff white Hindustan Ambassadors really were.

But that wouldn't happen, would it? Things like that never do. And probably just as well. It might lead to unintended consequences, and that would never do. Brian was always happier when he knew exactly what was going to happen as a result of his own actions. Just as he was very unhappy when he had no idea of what would happen as a result of the actions of the driver of the minibus. And anything could. The traffic on the way back seemed heavier than ever and more intimidating than ever. It was just as well that he'd swapped his aisle seat on the bus, with a good view through the front window, for Sandra's window seat, where he could just stare out of the side and pretend there was no oncoming traffic. Regrettably, however, this didn't deal with the menace of being overtaken. As often as not this manoeuvre was embarked upon by lorries and buses which had all the overtaking power of a milk-float with its brakes on. Accordingly, they often seemed to be just outside Brian's side window for what seemed like minutes. And all the time Brian was only too aware that they were in the wrong lane on a two lane road. He just hoped that that all-important "other" dimension hadn't packed up for the day.

It appeared that it hadn't. Brian and all his companions made it back to the boat entirely unscathed. Although a wind had now blown up.

This was a pity. For after the bird-listing session in the bar in the early evening, all the Nature-seekers were then invited to gather on the shore beneath the boat to witness a local dance troupe in action. This would have been fine, had not those same plastic chairs that had been employed at the barbecue been brought into use. As before, they were secure when they were being sat upon by the Nature-seeker audience, but as the wind became more severe and as more and more of the Nature-seekers were plucked from their seats by the dancers to join in the show, they were anything but secure. The wind had them leaping about all over the place, often with more verve and more style than the dancers themselves. There was also sand blowing all over the place, and one couldn't help coming to the conclusion that local dancing on a windblown sandbank wasn't going to establish itself as the highlight of the day. Although if some of those chairs actually made it to the water's edge, and from there into the Brahmaputra, it might just stand a chance.

It was good to be out of the wind and eating. Tonight Brian and Sandra had Bill and Tina again. Brian avoided birds in general and snipe in particular. Instead he got back onto his old hobby-horse of overpopulation. Maybe it was all those people out there, crammed together in houses and buses, but whatever it was, the theme just kept suggesting itself. Bill seemed to warm to the topic immediately. And then Brian warmed to Bill when he pronounced that from his perspective as a biologist, he was now convinced that the human species had just another twenty years to go. And then that was it. Brian had thought the same thing for years. But here was somebody knowledgeable thinking the same thought. In a very, very perverse sort of way, it really made his day.

7.

rian awoke before the generator came on. It rumbled into life at 5.30, but Brian had been awake since five. It reminded him of how old he was. Because now, at the age of sixty, he could easily adapt to mandatory early mornings, and so much so that he was waking up even before he needed to. And this was all so different from how it had been in his youth. Then he'd had problems with rising early all the time, and quite a few problems with rising later as well. At university he had never been known to make a nine o'clock lecture, and had soon learnt to copy other people's lecture notes as a matter of course. There was even one day when he'd managed to extend his sleep and his rising to seven – in the evening. He had then retired again at nine. A mere two hour day! It had been a real achievement. But here he was now, a full forty years later, stripped of virtually all his skills in the art of slumber, and all set up to spend a similar two hour period just waiting for the real day to start. It was such a downer and it made him feel really morose.

So did the sight of those rashers of bacon in the hot-dish. He couldn't face them, not after that pygmy encounter of the previous day. Instead he restricted himself to just a fried egg, assembled as usual from the contents of two eggshells. And he filled up on toast and jam, something he normally avoided at the breakfast table as his youthful dexterity had abandoned him as well (and dealing with a china butter dish and a china jam pot, sitting together with other pots and other dishes and all laid around with knives on a huge china plate, was more than he could countenance). However, on this occasion, the plate of conserves was close at hand and he risked it. He did have a bit of a hiccough with the butter, which was still a little hard, but he did manage it. And his success cheered him immensely. So much so that when he came to embark on the day's first activity, he was morose no more and instead chirpy and breezy and more than ready for his next bite of India.

This was a walk. The party of Nature-seekers was splitting up into two groups. One group would visit a tea plantation and a temple; the other would go for a leg-powered trek in the Kaziranga Park – near to which they were still moored. For Brian and Sandra there was no choice. They would be in the walking group.

So off they set. Eleven of them in just one minibus, while the others set off down the river. It was an interesting schism involving the breach of partnerships. Sandra and Irene, its only female members, were accompanied by their husbands, but they were also accompanied by three further husbands: Derek, Bill and Alan – who were all on their own. There were also three guides: Sujan, Tika and Imran. And then there was Jim…

It was only a short ride to the start of the park trail, and Brian had decided he would keep himself fresh by really concentrating on what was around them as they drove along, rather than on the oncoming traffic. And it was fascinating; little snippets of India that said as much about the country as a million words would ever say.

Here was the site of a recently disassembled travelling fair, a huge expanse of open ground now blanketed with litter. Litter, for which as far as Brian could see, there was no means of clearance. It would probably stay there forever. Compare that to a small children's playground further up the road. It was pristine. It was full of slides and climbing frames and there were shrubs and small trees, and it was surrounded by a neat, brightly painted fence. It was also quite clearly unused. The fence looked as though it was there to keep the children out, less they damage its slides or injure any of its shrubs.

What would Ghandi have made of that? He was further along the road, a small bronze statue looking a little out of place within a confusion of small huts and rickety shelters. He also looked a little irrelevant. Then there was a man with a bicycle. He wasn't riding it, but he was using it to transport six very long lengths of bamboo. It was as much as he could do to push the bike along. How he'd got the thing upright and moving in the first place was something Brian could not imagine. He also had a little difficulty getting his head around the Indian approach to dental hygiene. It wasn't that it was novel or peculiar; they used toothbrushes here just as Brian did back home. But Brian would never have considered using his brush at the gate to his house or on the pavement, a practice which seemed to be almost obligatory around these parts. It was as though one not only had to practise good dental hygiene, but one also had to be seen to be practising it. And there was no ignoring it. At this time in the morning, public teeth-brushing was at its height.

And so it went on: garishly decorated but empty election booths for the forthcoming elections, tumbling down shops with adverts for mobile phone networks, very small cows trying to eat plastic at the side of the road, road-signs extolling the virtues of good driving, people with threadbare clothes, people with colourful clothes, women with especially colourful clothes, people with mobile phones to their ear, people in a hurry, many more people not in a hurry – and now people with guns. Yes, Brian's minibus had just pulled into the park rangers' office to collect their entrance permit – and their armed guards. Walking in Kaziranga means walking through tiger territory. And one does not do this without weapons to hand. Even if, as Brian suspected, the weapons had no ammunition…

It was just as well they met no tigers. All they encountered were birds, flowers, trees and the exquisite delights that are awarded to all those who stroll slowly through an unspoiled landscape.

There were birds of the forest: warblers, flycatchers, babblers, and a wonderful example of painted extravagance: a golden-fronted leafbird. Then there were hornbills and vultures and a pair of red-wattled lapwings. They were nesting in an open stretch of marshy meadow between the trees and didn't take kindly to the presence of some nosey strangers. They shouted at them. A rapid, high-pitched 'did he do it, did he do it?' and for as long as the strangers lingered. Brian and his companions weren't wanted here. So they pressed on – to discover dragonflies, butterflies, strange indigo stains below holes in earth banks, fungi that looked as though they'd been carved out of turnips by talented chefs, fungi growing out of cow pats (or were they buffalo pats?) – and ants.

Actually it was Brian who discovered the ants, directly after he'd discovered a single ant on his leg. (He had discovered it through the medium of pain.) Brian was dismayed. Since he had arrived in India he had been pleasantly surprised not to have encountered biting insects. Indeed, he had encountered few insects at all, whether of the biting variety or otherwise. On the first night on the Sukapha there had been a very well-attended convention of big beetles on the sundeck, but these had been harmless. They had clearly possessed no teeth or no desire to nibble on humans. All they did was forget to leave after the convention's conclusion and end up getting swept off the sundeck's flooring the following morning. Then there had been a few moths around the ship's lights, and these had posed no threat whatsoever. But now he had been bitten. His dread of biting insects, which for the past few days had been pleasingly quiescent, had now been aroused. It was a dread that was well justified.

Brian was normally bitten by anything that could bite, by any insect that had the facility to inflict a wound on his person that would either be immediately painful or interminably itchy. At home he was frequently bitten by horseflies and clegs, and not that infrequently by gnats, midges and mosquitoes, and on holiday he was bitten by everything that knew he was coming. He was still convinced that on one occasion, as he drove off the ferry at Calais, word of his presence in France and of his intention to travel its length into the Camargue, was passed to the mosquito population of that terrible place within hours. Only by knowing that he was on his way so expeditiously could they have assembled themselves in so great a number and then inflicted so much pain through so many bites. He would never return there again.

Nor would he ever again fly to Perth in Western Australia, proceed immediately to the veranda of a friend from the past to share a few tubes of Fosters, only to allow the local mosquitoes to make a meal of him as he drank. The next day he had so many bites around his ankles in such a disgusting state of suppuration that he could hardly walk. Then there was his first ever meal in Belize (in the civilised surroundings of a Belize City restaurant, but again on a veranda). Here he had sat down, picked up his napkin, and before he'd even delivered the napkin to his lap, the biggest mosquito in Central America had landed in the exact centre of his forehead, directly above his nose, and had bitten him as though it had a personal grudge against him.

Mosquitoes were his principal tormentors, but there were plenty of others. Sand flies, which left him looking like a new species: a bare-skinned, red-spotted primate previously unknown to science. Ticks, which in Brazil, he had been obliged to coax off his person with a cognac-soaked cork, and which always threatened to depart without their mouthparts which then became septic. Or tsetse flies in Botswana, which could bite through armour if they chose to. And let's not forget the stings as well. Like that time in a montane forest in Costa Rica where, when he had carefully brushed off his hand an apparently harmless variety of montane bee, it had flown away, only to gain height, take aim, and fly down in a literal bee-line to sting him on the top of his head.

There was no doubt about it. Brian was irresistible to all biting insects and even pretty attractive to the stinging variety as well. And now word might be out. The ant grapevine was probably already in action, spreading the message throughout the length and breadth of Assam, to every insect with nipping and stinging tendencies, that the Big One was here. That the most delectable of feasts was within their midst. And currently he was in Kaziranga and without any Deet. It was true. He wasn't at the moment wearing any insect repellent. It was so awful, and, of course, he'd been lulled into this false sense of security. Only now he knew he wasn't secure. There could be a swarm of mosquitoes gathering even now, ready to pounce on him in the next few minutes. Or later on, back on the Sukapha, when he'd lowered his guard. And what about the ants? There were loads here on the ground. This was all very unsettling. It rather took the shine off the rest of the walk. And for once Brian was relieved to be back on the minibus and facing whatever hazards lay in wait on the road. At least if he lost a leg in some horrible accident, his leg wouldn't itch.

As it transpired, the journey home involved no horrible accidents and Brian and his companions were soon back to their floating haven. They were not, however, back on board their floating haven. The other group of Nature-seekers had not yet returned. This meant that the country boat had not returned. This presented a problem in that the depth of the water at the mooring spot had prevented the Sukapha from edging close enough to the shore to allow the use of the gangplank in the normal manner. Instead the country boat had been drawn up between its bigger brother and the shore to act as floating gangplank and a platform for the real gangplank to the shore itself. Without the country boat there, the real gangplank was not long enough, and it now sat uselessly on the sand, where Brian and his colleagues stood uselessly, marooned from their final destination and with not even a grappling hook between them.

The problem was soon resolved. Four of those fit crewmen appeared, first with some bamboo poles, then with some twine, and then with an additional length of gangplank. Within minutes this resourceful quartet had constructed a super-length gangplank, supported by the bamboo poles at its centre, and with a bamboo handrail – supported by themselves as they stood in the water. This boat was quite a vessel and its crew were quite a revelation. Brian was delighted and impressed.

He was also delighted that for the rest of the day he simply had to eat lunch, then stare at the Brahmaputra and its banks as the Sukapha made its way down to its next mooring, and then attend the bird-listing session and finally eat dinner. Nothing much more was required of him and that was just fine. Riding in jeeps was tiring. But walking all morning (in the heat of the near-tropics) was simply exhausting.

Lunch was served as soon as the culture vultures had returned to the boat, and the boat set off down the river as soon as lunch was consumed. Virtually everybody then gathered on the sundeck to take in the sights, or if you were Tim or Dennis, to take a few nods. They were asleep within minutes. The others remained awake and they all had their own way of observing what was around them. Some like Julian kept a vigil at the deck's railings. Others like Pauline preferred to observe as much as possible through the lens of a camera. And then there were those like Brian who found that they could easily combine drinking, biscuit-eating, chatting and lounging with viewing and spotting whenever they chose.

Brian also squeezed in some thinking. He thought about his companions and where they all lived. Because, quite remarkably, if one made Norfolk an honorary county of the Midlands, eighteen of the twenty-three members of the party hailed from this middle of England. Only the heterosexual pair of Judy and Rosamunde hailed from the south (Hampshire and West Sussex), and Tim and Karen, together with Jim, were the only representatives from the north. Tim and his wife came from West Yorkshire; Jim came from somewhere near Blackpool. So the overwhelming majority of these Nature-seekers were Midlanders, drawn from just Warwickshire, Worcestershire,

Gloucestershire, Northamptonshire and Derbyshire.

What did this mean? Why were there so many mid-England provincials on this trip and so few from elsewhere? And why no "metropolitans" at all? No one from London and no one from any major city. (Everybody in the group, no matter where they were from, had their houses in the countryside or in a modest-sized town.)

Perhaps it was a UK version of the American phenomenon. Because Brian had discovered that to whichever odd and out of the way place he had ventured, so too had some Americans. But that these Americans would always be from either the West Coast or from the northern part of the East Coast, from California, Oregon or Washington state, or from any of the New England states. Those Americans in the centre of America or in its south never seemed to make an appearance. And maybe they never made an appearance anywhere outside America – or even got as far as its coast. But most definitely they'd not have made it here to Assam. The reason, Brian believed, was not just their lack of opportunity, but also their lack of interest. If the good lord had meant them to go to Botswana, he'd have issued them with a ticket. And he hadn't. So they'd stay where they were.

Yes, America was two countries, not one. There was the almost secular, almost sophisticated, almost normal coastal America, and there was the completely non-secular, completely unsophisticated and anything but normal middle. This second America did not send its sons and its daughters to anywhere where their blinkered and rather warped view of the world might ever be challenged. Only coastal America did this. And in this way they could continue the war. The Civil War. For that's what it was. That war was not over. The forces of reason and advancement were still locked in mortal combat with the forces of superstition and ignorance. And if not quite *mortal* combat, then at least a pretty entrenched combat, and one that would only ever be resolved if some light was let into the centre. Maybe by exposing its citizens to real foreign travel.

But how could you argue for a similar two states in Britain? You couldn't, could you? The Midlands were rather more sophisticated than they were given credit for and they were hardly a hot-bed of fundamentalism. But it was very difficult to argue that the other parts of Britain were unenlightened and full of God-fearing people either. There was really no case at all to support a view of two Britains at each other's throats and reconciled only to non-reconciliation. So that couldn't be it. It had to be something else.

Then Brian had it. It was more to do with city versus country, cosmopolitan values versus the values of middle England, a middle England in sociological terms that was now at its strongest in the physical middle of England. The Midlands might have more than its fair share of urban centres, but in some way it had retained an outlook that was still based on good old-fashioned rural rumination, a rumination that required a constant supply of new facts and new experiences that could be chewed over indefinitely. It was not an outlook that was based on contrived sophistication, nor was it an outlook that owed anything at all to that arrogant, metro-centric refinement that is generally no more than a shallow, follow-the-leader desire to conform and that leaves no room for real choice or for real self-improvement.

So whilst Midlands Nature-seekers might not be the most polished individuals in the realm, and they might even be regarded as a bit nerdy, or even very nerdy, they did see things and they did experience things that few other people did. They saw wonders that many other people were simply unaware of, and they experienced places and people that gave them a more informed and more intense view of the world than was enjoyed by most of this world's population. They were not just interested in birds; they were interested in everything. So interested that they sought out the obscure and the odd and the ignored – and the new. Whenever they could and whenever they could afford to.

The metro-thinkers did not. Their interest took them only as far as the Sunday colour supplements when they were choosing where to go. So this year it might be that place with that fabulous infinity pool, and next year it might be that charming, out of the way place in Portugal, which was so off the beaten track that there was only one golf course there. Even though Ryanair got you within twelve miles of it. Or how about that newly built spa resort in Malaysia, where not only could you get a pile of hot stones laid on your back, but you could also enjoy "The Real Malaysia" – safe in the knowledge that back in your room there was a wi-fi connection, a flat-screen TV and a phone by the side of the loo.

'What,' thought Brian, 'do people do in these places? What do the Sunday supplements suggest they do in these places? Or maybe they don't suggest anything. Maybe there's the assumption that it's not activities and experiences their patrons want, it's just the opportunity to conform and, before the heat rash sets in, the opportunity for some hot-weather sex.' Then he checked himself. It wasn't that he thought that everybody should buy a pair of binoculars and go off and frighten birds. No, he believed there was just as much legitimacy in a horse-riding holiday or in a wine tour or in looking at cathedrals or fine buildings. That wasn't Sunday supplement conformism and neither was it a denial of curiosity. Indeed these sorts of holidays were just the sorts of things other Midlanders might choose…

Then Brian checked himself again. He was becoming as bigoted and as ridiculous as some of those American fundamentalists. He knew there was a kernel of truth in his thinking, but he always took it too far. Then he tended to throw out balance and detachment and end up where he was now: in the realms of pure fantasy. That wasn't good. He should never forget that despite his own frequent travels around the world he still knew very little about anything, and clearly not enough to explain why this current contingent of Nature-seekers included nobody from the nation's cities and certainly nobody from its capital.

It must be time to stop thinking quite so much and get back to some more biscuits and some more watching.

This change of occupation was timely. The Sukapha was now well west of "the bridge". Some time ago, it had sailed under the same bridge that they had travelled over by minibus the day before. They were therefore now into a stretch of entirely bridgeless river which would retain this status until they reached their final destination in two days' time, the at-least-one-bridge-equipped city of Guhawati. But it wasn't an empty stretch. There were boats here and there, and occasionally there were people on the shore. Brian studied them.

The boats were fishing boats, tiny skiffs with an elegant shape but with little else. They were hardly more than floating platforms for the fishermen, and would easily be overwhelmed by the smallest wave. Fortunately, here on the silky-smooth Brahmaputra, there were no waves, and therefore no threat to the boats' occupants. All they had to worry about was catching some fish. That was clearly not easy. Brian had yet to see a fish removed from the water.

It was the same with the people on the shore. Most of these were fishing as well. They were using either large, anchored bamboo and net constructions or smaller hand-held bamboo and net devices (which looked to Brian like food umbrellas with the netting stretched across the bottom rather than over the top). Both worked on the same principle: the dip into the water, wait, hope and lift principle. Or rather they didn't work. Brian still hadn't seen a fish removed from the water.

It was a tough life. Tough for the fishermen – and tough for the men on the rafts. There were three of these, three bamboo rafts measuring in Brian's estimation about thirty metres by maybe fifteen metres. Each had a little shelter at its centre and each had a crew of six men. At any one time three or four of these men would be at an edge of the raft rowing with long oars and their colleagues would be punting with long bamboo poles. It looked desperately hard work, and Brian's initial thoughts were why on Earth hadn't these guys built themselves something rather more manageable, something smaller for example, and something a little more Cutty Sark and a little less Kon Tiki. Then it occurred to him; these rafts weren't the crews' vessels, they were their stock. They were their stock of bamboo, and they were taking it to market. Sujan confirmed Brian's conclusion. These chaps had assembled a huge quantity of bamboo, had then bundled it together to make these colossal rafts, and they were now guiding these rafts down to Guhawati where they would be sold and then turned into houses or scaffold.

It was awesome. Sujan explained that the rafts were like icebergs; most of the bamboo was below the surface. What one was seeing was just the top slice. This meant that the rafts could easily get caught on underwater sandbanks, of which the

Brahmaputra had an unending supply. So not only were the rafts' crews faced with an enormous physical effort, but they were also confronted with the threat of running aground. They had to know the river and where the sandbanks were (and where they had moved to), to stand any chance at all of completing their voyage without mishap. And it wasn't as though they had any respite from these challenges. The river flows constantly. Anything floating on its surface flows with it – constantly. So their physical effort, their rowing and punting to keep the bamboo rafts exactly where they needed to be, was unremitting. Brian even wondered how they ate and did all the other things that took his companions so much time.

It was extraordinary. And it was humbling. Brian wished there were some Londoners here to witness it.

The Sukapha was now approaching its new mooring and Brian was feeling a little subdued. The combination of all those fishless fishermen and those wretched rafters had really got to him. He was in need of a lift. It was therefore fortunate that he and Sandra had stationed themselves at the front of the sundeck, just next to the wheelhouse, when a Gangetic dolphin decided to rise from the water and expose himself in the nicest way possible just yards from the boat. He had risen from the muddy waters face-on to their vessel, and Brian and Sandra were therefore treated to a superb view of his snout, his head, his back and his tail in that traditional order. The view was only a brief one but it was as good as they get, and it provided Brian not only with a lift, but also with a memory that would stay with him forever. It also provided him with a marital dispute. He was sure the dolphin was a "he". Hadn't he just been described so? But Sandra was equally sure that "he" was a "she". Nothing male, she argued, could be that beautiful. Brian, however, decided not to stoop to a full-blown argument over the matter. He had no wish to spoil the moment. Neither, in truth, did Sandra. So a truce was established quickly – through the use of facial gestures. And Brian and Sandra stayed at their post in silence, scanning the waters for another glimpse of the sublime (which never came) and then watching the shore approach as they came in to moor.

Soon, ropes had been buried into pits, the Sukapha was securely anchored, and it was time to prepare for the evening.

This kicked off with the normal bird-listing session which, on this occasion, proved more challenging than normal. After all, there had been two excursions today undertaken by two groups. So there were birds (and animals) seen by one group but not by the other. There was therefore a whiff of competition in the air. And this is possibly what stirred Alan into a lively debate with Tika on the distinction between Indian crows and thick-billed crows and whether there should be any distinction at all. It did drift a little close to the nerdy, but Tika's professional handling of the matter made the exchange interesting in itself, and moved Brian's opinion of him up at least two more notches. He thought Alan was good value as well.

What he then thought about dinner was that it was unique. It was the first time in his life that he had sat next to a woman who was married to a real tennis nut. This, it may be recalled, was the gay-only-in-the-sense-of-her-expression Judy, companion of the not-even-gay-in-the-sense-of-her-disposition Rosamunde, and whilst she herself was not a real tennis nut or even a real tennis player, she had very little else to talk about. So Brian got it all: her husband's involvement, the history of the game, where it is played now, and a host of other truly trivial facts.

Brian was not in the least bit upset. For him it was just another insight into another subject he knew virtually nothing about. And even at the end of the meal, he could see that he had still learnt very little and he knew that what he had learnt he would probably soon forget. That was one of the delights of not knowing things. You could even add to your store of the unknown by discarding in your mind what you'd known in the past. And with Brian this top-up process had always worked a treat, and in his advancing years was now working better than ever.

There were inevitably certain facts concerning real tennis that would stick in his mind for some time. Facts such as the employment in the game of a handicap system, a feature of real tennis that allowed Judy's husband, who was apparently eighty-four, still to play people half his age and still to win. Then there were its roots: French and Italian monks in the Eleventh Century, who presumably had not got round to installing cold showers. And where it's played now: England, America, Australia and France. And with our twenty-six courts to America's ten, Australia's six, and a paltry three in France, why, thought Brian, haven't we got this game into the 2012 Olympics? Hell, we could even get the silver behind Australia!

The only other fact that would stick was a half-fact. It was something to do with the French only being able to count up to sixty, because that was the top score in real tennis. (Or so Brian half remembered.) This was why after sixty, the French resort to *soixante-dix* and then *quatre-vingt* and *quatre-vingt-dix*. That is to say they have no proper words for seventy, eighty and ninety. Brian wasn't convinced about this half-fact. He thought he remembered that there was a word *nonante* that had meant ninety in the past, but probably not past the Eleventh Century.

For all he knew there might be equivalent words for seventy and eighty as well. Such words might undermine the not-above-*soixante* theory. Or as Judy had presented it, the not-above-*soixante* fact. However Brian didn't challenge her. He wasn't sure of his ground and he didn't want to offend her. Furthermore Judy's dissertation on real tennis wasn't so much important for what it included, whether this was right or whether it was wrong. No, it was important (and welcome) for what it was: another expedition into the unknown, a new experience, an event which may only be encountered by travelling to the wilds of Assam, and which you're much less likely to be faced with in Marbella or Cancun. 'Those Londoners just don't know what they're missing,' thought Brian.

8.

*B*rian had bacon with his eggs. His conscience lacked fortitude.

He wasn't on his own. The rasher and ova diet came under sustained attack on this morning as the banana option was entirely abandoned. Everybody, it seemed, was back in control of their bowels. This was just as well, as the next expedition involved another excursion in those tiny jeeps, vehicles which offered nothing in the way of emergency facilities. Yes, they were all off to the Orang National Park, about which Brian knew very little other than that "Orang" was an anagram of "groan". He was sure it meant nothing.

The park was on the north bank of the Bramaputra. So was the mooring of the Sukapha. It was no more than a few hundred yards from the park entrance. But despite this apparent convenient proximity, access was not possible along the shore itself, and once again the country boat was brought into service. So after the extravagance of the breakfast it was the stringency of the life-jackets. Brian donned his own and boarded the boat. Within minutes he was out of it again and onto dry land.

Just yards away were the jeeps. It appeared that they had made it from Kaziranga and were now expected to make it around this new national park. Furthermore it was expected that they would carry the same combination of Nature-seekers that they had previously. Sujan announced that everybody should deploy themselves around the jeeps with the same jeep companions they'd had in Kaziranga. This was good news. Jim hadn't come. He had a sore neck or a guilty conscience or something, and this meant that Brian and Sandra had a jeep to themselves. They would therefore have all the room they might need, and Brian wouldn't have to worry about offending anybody through a careless remark or a cutting observation. Normally he had to make a conscious effort not to do this, but if there was nobody else there, all he ran the risk of was upsetting Sandra. And he had done that so many times in the past he now hardly noticed it. Even if Sandra still did. So the outlook was good.

They set off and within minutes the outlook was more than good; it was gob-smacking. The jeeps were going to split into two groups, and as before one group would take a clockwise route through the park whilst the over drove anticlockwise. But it was so close to their departure point that they had not yet split up. This meant that everybody enjoyed the gob-smacking outlook – and the sight of something that was truly remarkable.

Now most people would dispute with some vigour that what the Nature-seekers saw here was remarkable in any way, and they would be vehement in their challenge to the use of the term "gob-smacking". Instead they might just concede that what had come into view was mildly interesting. Or they might grudgingly accept that if you were inclined to the nerdy and you still hadn't found a life, then maybe, but just maybe, the sighting of a Bengal florican could constitute a noteworthy event. But they would be wrong.

Imran had seen it first, and he'd reacted as though he'd seen a tiger. For a Bengal florican is rarer than a tiger, a bird only very infrequently encountered, and even when encountered, more often glimpsed than seen properly. But this chap was right out in the open, strutting along slowly, and, whilst hardly within touching distance, not that far away. Everybody had a fantastic view of it, and all those with cameras were able to take all the photos of it they could ever want. Even Brian managed a couple.

But what is a Bengal florican and why was it such a coup? Well, a Bengal florican is a species of bustard. Bustards are big birds that spend most of their time on the ground, and that have therefore, in many parts of the world, largely been "cleansed" by an ape species that claims most of this ground for itself. Great bustards, it might be recalled, have recently been re-introduced into England after the ape species there cleansed it completely. So, to start with, the sight of any bustard should bring warmth to the heart. Especially to the heart of any representative of that ape species who is now only too aware of what his kind has "achieved" – of what his kind has been culpable of. But, on top of this, not only is a Bengal florican a rare bird, it is a very rare bird, and it is also a fascinating bird. For it doesn't just strut, but it "bombs" as well.

Like another bustard, the black korhaan of Southern Africa, a Bengal florican rises into the air and then curls up its body into nothing less than a large football. And as large footballs depend for their aerodynamic credentials on a Wayne Rooney type kick, and as no Wayne Rooney type is normally available, the Bengal florican then falls to the ground – like a football-shaped brick. Now, most people would regard this as remarkable, and it really is. Brian had seen it for himself in Africa. He was not, however, to see it here. Floricans only adopt this bizarre behaviour to attract female floricans, and clearly not only was there no Wayne Rooney type in the vicinity, neither was there a lady florican. Or possibly it was the wrong season, or the guy they were all looking at now had a headache, and all he could contemplate was a slow strut and then maybe a peck of something before he had a kip. But no matter. Although Brian and his companions had not witnessed a "bombing", they had, nevertheless, just been given an audience by one of the rarest and most extraordinary birds on the subcontinent, and a real audience. This hadn't been just a fleeting encounter; it had been a protracted reception, and in more prosaic terms, the best view that either Sujan or Imran had ever enjoyed. Apparently if one does see one of these birds, it is not just only a glimpse, but it is normally only a glimpse of their head or maybe their long thick neck as they creep through the grass. But this one was strutting. In full view! So it was gob-smacking and it was truly remarkable. Brian knew this and so did the whole party. And that was all that mattered.

This incident was going to be difficult to top. But that's not to say that there wasn't still plenty to see. The jeeps had now split into their two groups and Tika had joined Brian and Sandra in theirs. Brian thought that Tika appeared even more cheerful than his normal cheery self, and immediately ascribed this to the absence of Jim. It wasn't that Tika was in any way more or less exasperated by Jim than anyone else was, but Tika shared a room with him... There was restricted accommodation aboard the Sukapha; its twenty-three guests were occupying all of its twelve cabins. But Jim was a solo traveller with a cabin to himself, and had obviously come to some arrangement with the tour company to share his room – with Tika. This must have been a trial (for Tika). Brian knew he would never have wanted to change places with him, even on those very rare occasions on this voyage when Sandra had been less than her angelic self, and he could well understand Tika's reaction to being without his roommate for a while.

His mood even seemed to stimulate his spotting abilities and in no time at all he had started to discover new delights. Many of these were little jobs in trees, difficult to find and difficult to see even when you've found them. But Tika made sure that everyone did see them. He would satisfy himself that all the Nature-seekers on each of his three jeeps had clocked that white-rumped shama or that white-tailed stonechat or that hair-crested drongo, or whatever else had been skulking around in the foliage, before he allowed the jeeps to move on. And they just kept on coming, more and more birds – and more and more animals. For Orang had its own share of buffalos, rhinos and elephants as well.

It also had an ominous meteorological outlook.

The morning had started off "sticky" and it was now positively adhesive – as was Brian's shirt. The humidity of the atmosphere seemed to be approaching the saturated. But now there were sounds as well, the unmistakeable sounds of thunder. Then the sky began to darken, and in the not too distant distance the sky was now black. They were in for a downpour.

The jeeps were not without protection against such events; they had those U-frames and a tarpaulin that could be pulled across them to make the rear of the vehicle rainproof. But even if this transformation from an open-back to a closed-back machine could be achieved in time, which Brian considered unlikely, their safari would become a nonsense. The tarpaulins provided side and back cover from the elements as well as a roof, and that would make any kind of viewing from the vehicle completely impossible. The only birds and animals they would see would be those that were daring enough to seek shelter onboard, and they were unlikely to be many.

The sky was now darker than ever and a deluge was imminent. The tarpaulin had not been deployed, and Brian was now convinced that not only would he soon be sitting in the gloom of a covered vehicle when the tarpaulin *was* deployed, but that he would also be sitting there in dripping clothes, because the deployment would not have been made soon enough. However he had forgotten something entirely, something called serendipity.

There, in front of them, was a rest house. This was a house in the park where one could obviously stop for a rest, or stop to secure some shelter. It was perfect, and it was perfect timing. Brian and his travelling companions had just exchanged their jeeps for the sanctuary of the rest house, their drivers had just made their vehicles waterproof with their tarpaulins, the other trio of jeeps had just pulled in – with their occupants and their waterproofing dealt with in a similar manner – when the rain arrived. And it didn't arrive as it arrives in Britain, in drips and drops with occasionally a small gust of wind, but it arrived as it usually arrives in the near-tropics: instantaneously and dramatically.

A wind had blown up from nowhere, the day had become night, and there now appeared to be more water in the atmosphere than there was air. The rain was bucketing down. Indeed, it wasn't so much rain as an airborne torrent. It was difficult to believe that any cloud, no matter how black and how threatening, could unleash the amount of liquid that the one above them was now doing. It beat down on the roof of their shelter without mercy and with the help of the wind it lashed against its sides. Around the shelter, puddles began to form, then shallow ponds and then streams. The jeeps were now standing in water. It swirled under them and around them. And while all this discharge of water was underway, the Nature-seekers could do nothing but wait – and marvel – and thank whoever it was who had thought to build this shelter in the park. It was just so convenient. And thankfully, so rain-proof...

The downpour lasted almost half an hour. Then it stopped, just as suddenly as it had first arrived, and the sun came out. This was the signal to move on again. And when the tarpaulins had been rolled back from the U-frames and when all the Nature-seekers had been prized away from a wonderful view of a purple heron that had just emerged out of nowhere, the jeeps started off.

The rain had turned the tracks into mud. Progress was therefore slow, and the rest house seemed a distant memory by the time they'd arrived at "The Office of the Park Officer". As they had originally entered the park through an unmanned entrance, they still had to obtain their park pass and pay for this pass. Hence this visit to the Park Officer's office. This was a scruffy building embellished with a veranda on which there were the skulls of an elephant, a rhino and a buffalo and the bodies of three of the officer's park rangers. The bodies were still alive, although not very animated. Their duties may have been no more than guarding the three animal skulls. Or maybe they brought them out each morning and took them back into the officer's office each evening, in the same way that Arkwright moved his tin baths and his brooms out of and then back into his shop in "*Open All Hours*". But Brian doubted that the skulls were for sale.

Securing the necessary pass and paying for it was a protracted process. For all Brian knew, it required a phone call to Delhi and the approval of a minister. But it certainly wasn't straightforward. No matter. It simply gave everybody an opportunity to stretch their legs and to have a look round. All six jeeps were still together, so there were now Nature-seekers all over the place either peering into trees or just being nosey. For the Office of the Park Officer was flanked by a number of houses, which Brian assumed must be the homes of the guardians of the skulls and some other park rangers who were currently on more active duties. They weren't very salubrious, and indeed it was difficult to tell which were occupied and which were "resting between tenants" – and might well be resting until they collapsed into total dereliction. Brian was upset. On whatever the modern state of India was spending its resources, it wasn't spending much of them on the Orang National Park. Then he almost got angry. This was a country with a space programme.

Fortunately nature rescued him from his simmering fury. A large cuckoo-shrike had just been spotted, and it was now sitting on a branch in full view. It was engrossing. Then somebody found a blind snake. That isn't to say that somebody had poked its eyes out; it was born that way. It was a Diard's blind snake and it was sightless because it spent most of its time under the ground or under leaf litter. But here it was on the surface and quite happy to have its photo taken. Bill was especially interested in it. So much so that he became temporarily visually impaired himself. His glasses fell into the leaf litter as he leaned over the snake to get that last prize-winning snap and they immediately disappeared. Needless to say, keener eyes were soon there to help and it wasn't too long before Bill was returned to his normal eagle-eyed vision. He was then able to join in the fun centred on Ron and Irene's jeep.

The postcard models, Jerry and Edith, had not come to the park. Brian thought that they had finally realised they were in India and they needed time to come to terms with this. When he'd communicated this to Sandra, Sandra had informed him that he merited the word "despicable" and that she sometimes wondered why she had married him and had not yet remembered. This is by the way, but Jerry and Edith's absence did explain why there was one jeep that was the sole property of Ron and Irene. On the previous safaris they had formed a quartet with the missing duo and, just like Brian and Sandra, they therefore now had a jeep to themselves. Unfortunately, however, it was not a well jeep. While driving around this morning it had already stalled on a number of occasions and would then not start again. Each time it had to be push-started by the drivers of the other jeeps travelling with it.

But now things were being sorted out. The jeep's engine cover was up and all the jeep drivers were gathered around its engine administering some mechanical aid. To be precise they were administering the contents of several water bottles. Part of the group's stock of drinking water was being poured over the engine block and presumably over anything else near the engine block that was looking anything like sickly. Brian's first thought was that this was a libation, the offering of a precious liquid to appease the god of jeeps. But no, this was a piece of genuine mechanical therapy designed to restore the engine to rude good health. Unfortunately it was not a piece of effective therapy, and the engine remained sick. Ron looked on in amazement. He thought he knew what the problem was (something to do with worn bushes, whatever they are). But he also knew that water pouring would not only not cure it, but it might also make matters worse. There were electrical things next to that engine, and even Brian knew that water and electricity are not the best of playmates and that they often squabble. So don't pour water over your engine!

After fifteen minutes of this treatment further damage had miraculously been avoided, but inevitably the jeep still wouldn't start. Muscle power once again had to replace the starter motor, and Brian watched as Ron and Irene disappeared along the track, their jeep sandwiched between two others, its driver over-revving its engine to avoid another stall. He later found out that this didn't work. Further stalling and further push-starting was to plague them to the end. (The water treatment was abandoned.)

Brian's trio of jeeps moved off in the opposite direction. More marvels were sighted, more photographs were taken and more challenges were overcome. The tracks were still very slippery from the downpour, and some enthusiastic driving was called for, not least when their route took them through a series of deep gullies. One of them in particular was almost too much of a challenge. But with each jeep summoning up about eight thousand revs and their drivers summoning up the assistance of that jeep god (who may well have existed after all), they all got through. And a brown crake and an elephant with calf later, they were back with the country boat. The jeeps, despite Brian's reservations and all his defamatory thoughts about them, had done their job. Sort of. And he now felt almost sad that he'd not be seeing them again. He just hoped they'd make it back to their cardboard boxes with those cellophane fronts.

But now it was time for his next encounter – with a life-jacket. Or should he just mutiny?

He didn't. He didn't want to delay lunch. And he didn't want to delay the departure of the Sukapha. As soon as the

Nature-seekers had seated themselves at the dining tables, the Sukapha was casting off its moorings and setting off down the river. The afternoon would be another session of relaxed observation from the sundeck, and that's where Brian and almost everybody else returned to when the meal was at an end. What would this stretch of the Brahmaputra reveal to them?

To begin with it revealed more of the same: immense expanses of water, endless flat landscapes and the biggest skies Brian had ever seen. Then there were more boats. Some of them were little bigger than the tiny fishing boats they had seen before. And some of them were ferries. They had aboard them cycles, motorbikes, other chattels and lots of people. They were all clearly licensed to carry a maximum number of people exactly equivalent to the maximum number of people they could carry without sinking. If these boats had been any lower in the water, they would no longer be on the water but in the water – with the water in them. But obviously they knew what they were doing. They didn't even bother with bright orange life-jackets.

This was Brian's initial view. But then he began to wonder whether they just didn't care. Whether they were just fatalistic, and if the boat sank then the boat sank, and that was that. What made him think this was the appearance along one bank of the river of increasingly large "cliffs".

The Brahmaputra runs through a colossal flood plain. Its waters are full of silt, washed away from its sides and deposited in any number of huge sand banks within and beside its flow – and eventually in the Bay of Bengal. There is a constant reshaping of its course. Nothing about this mighty river is permanent, and that includes its cliffs.

Theses cliffs are cliffs of sand, scaled-up versions of the sand banks which occur all along the length of the Brahmaputra. And whilst Brian had already seen some really high banks over the last few days, he had not before seen banks quite this high – up to thirty feet tall – nor banks that were quite so unstable. Because this was their outstanding feature: their collapsibility. If one stared along a stretch of these cliffs of sand, one had to wait no time at all to see a piece of cliff dropping off. With the help of the flow of water beneath them, small slivers or sometimes great wedges would simply detach themselves and then slide into the river. It was real-time erosion, a disintegration of land that was happening so quickly as to be unreal. But it was real. One minute land was there; the next minute it was gone. And in hours, days or months, it would be land somewhere else or just river bed or sea bed. The river would decide.

Now, this was endlessly fascinating to watch, but it was also the cause of Brian's reflection on fatalism. For the land that was disappearing was lived on. In many places, just beyond the cliff edge, there were houses. Brian had always thought it must be deeply unsettling to live on the slopes of a volcano. But volcanoes are normally quiet and unthreatening. They are just potentially dangerous. Whereas the Brahmaputra is anything but unthreatening and it is constantly dangerous – and constantly eating away the land on which people live. How many months would have to pass before one of those houses was in the river? And how long would it be before one of their occupants was in the river? For what was truly amazing was not the proximity of the dwellings to the cliffs, but the proximity of the people. They would be not just yards from their edge, but inches. Men, women and children would be lined up on their very brink, waving at the boat or even running along and waving, and never more than inches away from where the land disappeared – and where a slice more of it might disappear at any second. But they just didn't seem to notice or to care. Hence Brian's thoughts on fatalism and his increasing concern that the transit of the Sukapha might locate a weakness in this fatalism's armour, and deliver some poor hapless villager into the clutches of the Brahmaputra along with half a ton of sand. It was extremely unnerving, and especially so with the children. It was as though they weren't even aware that there was an edge there at all.

Inevitably nobody did fall in, and maybe these river folk knew a lot more about crumbling cliff edges than Brian gave them credit for. But he still found it deeply unnerving. Because there was one thing he was sure of: these people, and particularly the youngest of these people, were distracted. And when people are distracted they are inattentive and they are careless.

The cause of the distraction was the Sukapha itself. It was as clear as day that the Sukapha's passage was a big event. Indeed, the Sukapha was not just a big event for these riverside dwellers, it was also the biggest thing they ever saw or were ever likely to see. It dwarfed all the other boats on the river and it also dwarfed their buildings, even their temples and their meeting houses. It was also a manifestation of another world, a world that used metal and glass rather than reeds and mud, a world where energy sprang from an oil-powered machine and didn't have to be coaxed out of overworked bullocks or out of their own overworked limbs. Rural, riverside Assam was a place where machines of any sort were largely non-existent, a place where nothing was on more than a modest scale, and a place where modernity had barely made a mark. So to see some enormous, out-of-their-world palace floating past on the river must have been for them an enthralling experience and an almost incomprehensible experience – and a distracting experience. Even if they knew everything there was to know about crumbling cliff edges, as far as Brian was concerned, they were in real danger, the sort of danger that only fatalism can deal with. 'There again,' he thought, 'if their fatalism can cope with the prospect of their homes disappearing into the river in the foreseeable future then I suppose it can cope with just about anything'.

But he knew that he'd have stood well away from the edge.

He'd even stay well away from the edge of the sandbank where the Sukapha had now moored. It was no more than three feet high, but it was as crumbly as a child's sandcastle and not meant to bear the weight of an overfed Brit. He and Sandra were on the sandbank. The mooring pits had been dug, a beach volleyball game was in progress, and the Nature-seekers had been invited to stretch their legs on dry land for an hour. There was not much to see, but it was pleasant to be left to one's own devices for a time whilst not on the boat.

Brian and Sandra just walked – and just avoided the edge. And as they walked back to the boat they spent a little time watching the volleyball game and watching the local villagers who had turned up to watch too. They were all slender. They were all as lean and spare as Brian had been when he was in his school's cross-country team and had not yet started to shave. They were fishermen and farmers. One of them was carrying a wooden plough and a wooden rake over his shoulder. They were all hard workers and light eaters. They were not emaciated, but just the shape our species was designed to be, with no hamburger fat around their middle and no fat anywhere. Whatever problems they might face in their lives, obesity for sure wasn't one of them. And from what Brian had observed of the pace of change along the Brahmaputra, it never would be.

Brian was still thinking about these people when he sat down to dinner. He was thinking about what they might be eating this evening. He was also reflecting on all those disintegrating cliffs and what such a state of constant instability must mean for these people's lives and for their sense of permanency. Did they see "temporary" and "permanent" in the same way he did? How could you see it in a "western" way if your home might not be there in a little while or the ground you were actually standing on might not be there within the next few seconds? After all, aren't all our concepts of permanency rooted in the unmoveable? And what's more unmoveable than our homes and the ground we stand on? And if these aren't permanent, then how can we develop the concept of permanency or indeed the concept of the temporary? For these chaps, everything is temporary. Even the course of this humungous river beside which they live.

Brian thought that his musings were worthy of discussion with his table companions. He also thought that there might be an opportunity to broaden this discussion by using the life of a Brahmaputra local as a metaphor for all their lives, and in particular how permanence in the way that they understood it was possibly a construct. How it was much more realistic to see everything as temporary and our whole lives as just a fleeting ripple in the torrent of time.

But he couldn't get any takers. Instead Dennis kicked off a conversation about the worst people on TV and radio back home, and this soon drew contributions from the whole table.

To begin with there were the no-brainers: Jonathan Ross, Russell Brand and Graham Norton. And Sandra made a very astute observation about what it was that made these people so offensive – when somebody like Julian Clary, who could be equally outrageous, always managed to do this with a certain degree of charm and without causing offence. It was, she said, that Mr Clary, for all his rudeness, was genuinely funny, a vital qualification that allowed him to get away with just about anything. The aforementioned trio, on the contrary, were not funny and just grotesquely smutty, although all three of them were under the misapprehension that they were the funniest thing since an Alastair Darling budget. Brian could only agree with Sandra's observation.

The no-brainers out of the way, it was then the turn of the more esoteric turn-offs. First to get a mention was Sandy Toksvig, who all on her own has ruined forever "*The News Quiz*". Everybody agreed that she suffered from the same delusion as the initial trio: she thinks she is funny. It has clearly never occurred to her that she is not in the least bit funny, and that the combined effect of her inane giggling and her gross unfunniness in the company of so many others who are funny has destroyed the programme completely. Why don't the producers see this? And why don't they see that Griff Rhys Jones isn't quite the national treasure he's made out to be and that neither is Toyah Wilcox (who has now developed the very irritating habit of popping up on programmes about Seventies music and presenting her highly distorted views on its principal players – and her supposed significance within their number). And then how about Ann Robinson? How could anybody think she was a good idea?

Anyway, having exhausted who not to have on the telly or the radio, the conversation then turned to what to put in their place. This was easy. There was no shortage of contributions. More bird and wildlife programmes of course with, if possible, Sir David Attenborough narrating every one.

Just pottering about

The Sukapha's tender (and very caring)

'Have you tried the sat-nav?'

Heaven afloat

Bamboo-zling

Living on the edge

Many hands make something work

A kite in flight

The Sundarbans in style: the M B Sundari

'I dare you.'

Ample transport for sixteen people…

Spot the tiger

More Clive James talking common sense and exploiting more of that moral authority he's earned. Then there was more of "*Have I Got News for You*", but with the power given to the panel to subpoena people. With this, not only could they ridicule those of the great and the good who deserved it in their absence, but they could also do this in their presence – and cross examine them. It would be great. And how about a modern "throwing to the lions" type programme, where it was MEPs who got thrown and the public who were the lions? One MEP per programme. And he or she need turn up with just their expenses record and their attendance record. It would certainly be a way to engage the public with European politics.

This idea led to another on a political theme: the repeated showing on consecutive nights for the next ten years of every episode of "*Yes Minister*" and "*Yes Prime Minister*". That way the great British public might finally wake up to how they are ruled and who is doing the ruling. This proposal met with unanimous support. Although Alan suggested that it might be better to make it compulsory viewing in schools. Or even to have it as the entire syllabus for Politics A level – on the basis that everything one would ever need to know about British politics was contained within its five magnificent series. Brian thought this was a brilliant use of a brilliant piece of writing and acting, and wished he'd thought of the idea himself.

The conversation wound up in the area of excessive salaries paid to the BBC's management and to its creative director, and clearly made about as much sense to a puzzled-looking Tika as had the debate on media personalities. Brian thought that maybe he should have been more forceful with his initial idea about existential impermanence, which would have allowed Tika to join in more. But it was now too late. For dinner was finishing, and the Nature-seekers were rising from the table to make their way to the boat's lounge for a film.

It was a film about tigers in the Sundarbans, the mangrove forests in the mouth of the Ganges, to where Brian, Sandra and eight other Nature-seekers were heading after they'd done with Assam. It was also a very bad film. It was American and its theme was the man-eating proclivities of these tigers. It had no redeeming features in terms of real science or real enquiry into the tigers' habits, but just an unrelenting, sensational and impressively tacky focus on the danger that these animals posed. It was full of truly over-the-top dramatic statements, embarrassingly bad reconstructions of people disappearing – but no actual footage of tigers. And it had a commentary that would have made the sainted David Attenborough reach for a sick-bag. In short, it was as bad as "*Friday Night with Jonathan Ross*" even though Ross wasn't in it. Brian and Sandra left after just ten minutes.

Only in the morning did they discover that the expert brought in to solve the disappearances (that is, to ascribe them to man-eating tigers) was Sujan, their lead guide and the guy who was going to escort them to the Sundarbans. And he'd been in the lounge to watch them leave it after just ten minutes and before his starring role had even commenced. In retrospect, Brian had to admit to himself that this wasn't the best way to bond with someone who was going to be responsible for their safety in the tiger-full Sundarbans, or as the dreadful film had described it, in the "Killing Zone". But what could he do? And anyway Sujan didn't seem offended.

Furthermore, the early retirement from the lounge had given Brian a chance to catch up on some reading back in his cabin. And the reading proved a great deal more rewarding than some appalling film about a "Killing Zone". It had been provided by Kunal.

Kunal was the expedition's "cultural guide". He was the chap who led the visits to the villages and the temples. While Sujan and Tika would be on the lookout for new birds on these excursions, he would be on the lookout for new "cultural" experiences. He would point out how the houses were built, he would explain how the weaving looms worked, and he would generally ensure that the Nature-seekers got all the information they needed about how the Assamese lived.

He was a very jolly character and looked a little like a dark Benny Hill. He was Assamese himself, but his still discernible Assamese features were now softened by a rather round face that was mirrored in a rather round stomach. Like many other Indians who have access to large quantities of good food he was obviously making the most of it. That said, his appearance suited his character and his jolliness was infectious. Brian liked him a lot.

He also liked the way he had gone to so much trouble to entertain and to inform. For when one returned to one's room in the evening, there, on one's bed, was not only a typed-up copy of the next day's schedule (in case one had not absorbed the earlier verbal briefing), but there was also an "extract" from Kunal. He had combed through a variety of chronicles and books from the past that were either about Assam or contained references to Assam, and had made "extracts" from these writings, purely to add a little bit more to the Nature-seekers' experience – in bite-sized nightly helpings.

This night, Brian had a chance to catch up on these extracts. He had been less than diligent the two previous evenings on account of his falling to sleep too promptly. But now he was fully awake and he collected together the three unread extracts.

The first was an extract from "*A Tea Planter's Life in Assam c1890*". This contained an informative but depressing commentary on the Assamese jungle "in all its magnificent vastness". It also contained a reference to the reason that this "magnificent vastness" no longer existed: the practice of jungle-burning as practised by planters and natives whenever they wished to make a clearance for a plantation, jungle-burning being "the most expeditious method of removing the tangled vegetation". Brian found it difficult to argue with that.

The second extract was almost as dispiriting. It was an extract from Shihabuddin's description of Assam in 1662 during the Mohammadan wars, and it described the country then. For example, the extract starts with the observation that: 'Assam is a wild and dreadful country, abounding in danger'. It then goes on to state that: 'The trees of its hills and plains are exceedingly tall, thick and strong', and that, 'large, high-spirited and well-proportioned elephants abound in the hills and jungle'. Brian thought that should old Shihabuddin get himself reincarnated and make a second visit here, he might spot a few changes.

Then finally there was an extract from the 1910 edition of "*Encyclopaedia Britannica*". This was not in the least dispiriting. It was just hugely embarrassing. It contained the following passage:

'The Assam peasant, living in a half-populated province, and surrounded by surplus land, is indolent, good-natured and, on the whole, prosperous. He raises sufficient food for his wants with very little labour, and, with the exception of a few religious ceremonies, he has no demand made upon him for his money, saving the light rental of his fields. Under the peaceful influence of British rule (!) he has completely lost his ancient warlike instincts and forgotten his predatory habits. In complexion he is a shade or two fairer than the Bengali. His person is in general short and robust, but devoid of the grace and flexibility of the Hindu. A flat face, with high cheek bones, presents a physiognomy resembling the Chinese, and suggests no idea of beauty (!). The women form a striking contrast to the men; there is more of feminine beauty in them than is commonly seen in the women of Bengal, with a form and feature somewhat approaching the European (!!!)'.

Brian thought that Kunal must have found great amusement in making this extract, and it provided him with a whole new perspective on what must have been Kunal's perspective on them, this band of travellers who one hundred years ago, despite their enlightened views on TV scheduling and TV personalities, might well have written similar words themselves.

9.

obody had relapsed. Bananas were now very clearly "not wanted on voyage", and instead everybody at the breakfast table was tucking into fried comestibles. A couple of them were also coughing. Brian didn't really take this in. But he would remember it later.

Breakfast completed, a full contingent of Nature-seekers was soon on its way to another village for another cultural inspection. This involved another trip in the country boat and another confinement in one of those damned life-jackets. They weren't getting any easier. But soon the parole board had authorised their release and Brian and his companions were disembarking from their vessel to begin their tour of a place called Ganesh Pahar.

This was a fishing village. It was of linear design, with a row of simple houses along the length of an unmade path, on the other side of which there was a slope to the river. As with many of the settlements Brian had observed the previous day, this place was really living on the edge. Its only plus point in this respect was that the slope to the river didn't appear to be in a state of constant degradation and that it was protected from the worst of the Brahmaputra's power by a spit of land. There was a channel between this and the village itself, and this must have moderated the abrasive power of the river significantly. That said, one of the first things that Brian observed was a lady climbing up the slope with a basket of earth on her head. This she was about to add to a pile of earth at the top of the slope, clearly about to be used to repair a section of path that had simply crumbled away. He now not only worried for the future of the village but also for his own safety. From now on he would keep to the village side of the path as much as he could.

The village was quite pleasant. The houses were small, but all of them were well maintained and most were surrounded by a tidy courtyard. Many of them were also decorated. Around their doors was a border of white hands, each with a patch of red at its centre. These borders, Kunal said, were to keep something bad out of the house. Or something good in. Brian couldn't quite catch his commentary.

However, there was something they certainly weren't keeping out, and that was the god of fertility; there were countless children everywhere and most houses seemed to have at least half a dozen. 'Where,' thought Brian, 'will all these children go when they want children? And is there anywhere for them to go?'

He immediately chided himself. What about looking at it from their perspective? What did this abundance of children mean for the locals?

Well, whatever it might mean for the future, for now it meant a lot a little hands to get on with the re-plastering of the houses (with the much-used mud and dung concoction), more little hands to help out with the baby-minding (even the smallest of small girls was often holding a toddler within her arms), and more little hands to earn the families some money. This is where changing his perspective didn't work. There was a group of five children sitting on the flat bottom of an upturned boat, and all five of them were making tiny little pots out of clay. Brian heard Kunal explaining that they were oil pots to be used with the offerings made in temples. None of the children was more than five years old and none of them was enjoying it. They looked sullen and bored – and resigned to their task. So too did the two three-year olds who were collecting the raw material for this work and bringing it up a slope from a creek below. It was child labour. Not in the depths of some sweatshop in Mumbai, but out here in the open in a small village in rural Assam.

Brian felt uncomfortable. Maybe he hadn't really taken on the local perspective. And just look around. There was a woman winnowing grain in a way that hadn't changed in millennia; there was another crushing grain with a foot-powered see-saw device that must have been around for the same sort of time. And wherever you looked people were working and toiling, trying to carve out a life with the minimum of resources and with only ancient technology. Any wonder then that they tried to supply themselves with some help – even if the truth was that all this help just added to their burden?

Brian was getting out of his depth. It was just as well that Tika distracted him by pointing out a fly-past of Himalayan swiftlets and then brought his attention to some weaver nests in a palm tree, complete with some baya weavers hanging from their sides. But then Brian came to the village shop. It was more a booth than a shop and it contained some sweets and other delicacies, all of which could have been carried away in a single Sainsbury's shopping trolley. It made Brian think again – about the place he was in. And he felt troubled again. This village, he thought, might be neat and tidy – and peaceful and safe – but there was something being stored up here that was frightening.

There were just too many people and very soon there would be far too many people. And of course, it wasn't just this village. Or just Assam. Or just India. It was everywhere in the world. Brian knew all this already, but it wasn't too often that he was confronted with it so forcefully.

So he was glad when they left, relieved that he would soon be back in his cocoon and not quite so challenged by reality. Even if to start with he had to put that life-jacket on again and even if the cocoon wasn't quite so accessible as usual…

For what had happened while the group was walking around the village was that the Sukapha had gone walkabout herself. She had cast her moorings and was now sailing down the river with her crew on board but with no Nature-seekers. In doing this she had made the country boat's return trip a very short one (as she was now almost down to the fishing village), but she had presented its boatmen with something of a challenge. They would have to catch her and then transfer their passengers to her while both vessels were still on the move.

There were two boatmen; one was the captain and the other was his crew. They were a remarkable pair. They lived on the boat. While the Sukapha's crew would bed down in that boat's basement cabins each night, the country boat company would settle in the vessel's tiny engine room, ready, should the need arise for any reason, to untie it from its mother craft and take it to safety. But despite the complete absence of comfort aboard the country boat, and despite a similar absence of any apparent facilities, each morning they would be ready, smartly turned out in their black uniforms, to welcome aboard any Nature-seekers requiring their services.

Well, now it was the turn of the captain to demonstrate that his remarkable qualities didn't stop at just his appearance and his courtesy, but that they also extended to his boat craft. The country boat was approaching the stern of the Sukapha which, whilst not at "water-ski speed", was still going at a fair old lick. The country boat was obviously going faster but only marginally so, as would be expected. The captain was trying to dock with the Sukapha, not to ram it.

He was sitting on top of the engine room. He was out of sight of the Nature-seekers, but Brian had seen him in action from the sundeck of the Sukapha on previous occasions and knew how he "drove". For on top of the engine room he had access to the rudder, which he held in his left hand, and to a piece of string attached to the engine's throttle, which he held in his right hand, and with which he could control the speed of his craft. He was therefore now pushing on his rudder and pulling on his piece of string in the expert manner that he must have learnt over years, and bringing the country boat towards the side of the Sukapha with no apparent effort whatsoever. It glided into and then against the side of the bigger vessel with barely a nudge, and within seconds the crew of the Sukapha had secured it tightly with ropes and the Nature-seekers were being invited to change vessels. Brian wondered how much the captain of the country boat got paid – and whether his crew of one got paid at all. Maybe he just made do with food and accommodation. But no. That was just the village getting to him, a reaction to all that hardship he'd seen – and to all those children and the sort of hardship they'd face in the future. Soon he had returned to reason and was up on the sundeck with far different thoughts in his mind.

The Sukapha was now approaching Guhawati. In his "*Lonely Planet*" guide the introduction to this city reads: 'Sprawling almost 20km along the Brahmaputra's southern riverbank, the Northeast's gateway city is a major business centre servicing tea and oil industries. Although not that attractive overall, green hillocks rise curiously above Guhawati's noisy smog and the city's water tanks and riverbanks are patchily pleasant. Come here to arrange tours to other Northeast states, see a few of the fascinating temples and then move swiftly on.'

This was the 2007 edition of the guide and it gave the population of Guhawati as 964,000. Brian thought it was a fair assumption that the population was now in excess of a million, but he wanted to check out some of those other facts himself – about the patchy pleasantness of the riverbank and the curiousness of the green hillocks. And where better to do this than from the sundeck, right at its front, as they approached the conurbation. He might even get an insight into the advice to 'move swiftly on'. Not, he thought, the most enticing of comments to write about a city. But who could tell? He might have a pleasant surprise.

He didn't. The Sukapha had made its way down the river through especially murky water, which was so murky and so swirly and therefore so full of hidden sandbanks, that the boat's pilot had been deployed. He'd stood a few feet away from where Brian was sitting with Sandra, peering over the front rail of the sundeck and passing steering instructions to the boat's master inside his wheelhouse. Thanks to him, they were now past this watery murk, and instead into the murk of river-side Guhawati. It wasn't very nice. Suffice it to say that the inhabitants of this city did not appear to regard the river upon which it sat as an amenity to be exploited for pleasure but as a utility to be employed for rather less laudable purposes.

The Sukapha came to a stop. It had dropped anchor some way from the shore and just a little up-river from Peacock

Island. This was a tiny hillock-shaped island in the middle of the river, which no longer boasted any peacocks, but which, at its summit, did provide a site for one of those "fascinating temples" referred to earlier. And that was where the Nature-seekers were off to next. They were about to make their second cultural visit of the day, and it wasn't yet lunchtime...

The country boat took them there. It deposited them at a decrepit looking landing-stage, and with Sujan, Tika and Kunal, the assembled party then strode off in search of the temple. This wasn't too difficult. The island was no more than one hundred metres in diameter, and the only exit from the landing-stage was a stone stairway. This, it transpired, led to the top of the island and to the home of the holy place.

Brian started to climb the steps of the stairway. The first thing he noticed was an official sign at the side of the stairway which announced that: 'Beautification Cum – Development Works of Unananda Temple Hillock is going on under GMDA'. The sign looked old. So too did the generous drift of litter that carpeted the hillside above it. It looked as though it had been there for years. Brian wasn't so much shocked as bemused. He now knew that tidiness wasn't an innate quality of this country's population, but this wasn't just anywhere, this was a small, discrete island, only accessible by boat, and the location of a temple, a holy place visited principally by a procession of "worshippers". How could it get this filthy in the first place and how could it be allowed to stay this filthy (especially when the GMDA were on the case – whoever the GMDA were)? Perhaps it would be better at the temple itself.

It was. But only relatively so. And this represented something of a dilemma for Brian – in the sense that he didn't know how to react.

He was a self-confessed atheist. There was no question about it. He didn't believe in a responsive supreme being and he thought all religions were a product of the past and wished that education and enlightenment would one day sweep them all away. Only then, he thought, would either the world or the human species stand any chance at all. However, that was not going to happen in his lifetime, and meanwhile he couldn't find too much wrong with people following a religion, particularly if somehow it made them better people and it didn't turn them into people who only wanted to blow up other people. He had friends who were religious. Aspects of religion interested him. And here he was now experiencing a slice of a particular religion, and paying it its due respects – by being diffident in his manner and by being un-shoed in its place of worship. And he was finding all sorts of faults. And should he have been? As an atheist, wouldn't he have been finding faults with this temple anyway?

Well no. He didn't find many faults with his local parish church. It was a bit cold if you ended up there for a winter funeral, but it was really a very nice place. He even took his bad-atheist ass up there to help keep the grass mown in the churchyard. Not as an act of worship in any way, but just to recognise that the church was a piece of his cultural heritage, and a piece of it that needed maintaining – with a lawnmower. Just as it would in his longed-for post-religion nirvana.

But here, in this small temple… Well, it could have done with a clean. And the guys manning the shrine thing in the middle… Well… And there wasn't a lot of serenity here, just a lot of people who seemed to be… well, paying for favours, just like his relatives did in his youth, when they lit a candle in his local Catholic church and made an offering of money. 'Here

God, here's a little something. And now I've got your attention, you couldn't see your way to doing me a little favour, could you? You see, I want...'. And that's what was happening here. Brian was sure of it. He also thought he knew what they were asking for: fertility. Indeed there was an inner sanctum in the temple which was down some steps and so packed with worshippers that none of the Nature-seekers ventured down, and in which, Kunal admitted, was an enormous phallus and, in addition, another giant organ of some sort. And not, thought Brian, of the sort with pedals and stops that Mrs Grubbins plays at evensong every night. Yes, fertility was in high demand in this place, and he had to concede that the punters more often seemed to get what they wanted than not, as was only too clear in the village...

And so the dilemma. Were these atheist-inspired misgivings or vestigial-Christian reservations, or was he just being objective? He didn't know, but he hoped he was being objective. Indeed, he always hoped he was being objective. But in any event, whatever he thought and however misguided he was in his thoughts, it wasn't going to stop what was going on here. Or even get any of that litter cleared. It was time to leave Peacock Island and go and have some lunch – and to keep his thoughts to himself.

Lunch was as delightful as ever. Brian even treated himself to a chilli on a stick. Just to prove to himself that he had now fully acclimatised to the Indian way of eating – and to give warning to his stomach that he would countenance no further misbehaviour on its part, and that whatever he fed it, it would have to deal with without complaint. And anyway, a chilli might chase away this feeling he had in his throat. It felt almost sore...

After lunch there was another expedition – to see a flock

of greater adjutant storks. Brian and Sandra decided not to join it. They had seen many of these storks before and they were not desperate to seek out further of their number. Furthermore it was now stiflingly hot and the prospect of any expedition at this time of day was much less than appealing. But the real clincher was the location of this flock of storks; it was on Guhawati's principal rubbish dump.

Brian's sensibilities had already been tested on this holiday, and he now knew his limits more clearly than ever. He could not cope with a rubbish dump. Not a rubbish dump in India, complete apparently with dump-dwellers and no doubt lacking in any deodorisation measures. From all accounts it was a very smelly place. So as the other Nature-seekers were packed into minibuses to be ferried to hell in Guhawati, Brian and Sandra retired with a supply of brewed nutrition to the comfort of the sweet-smelling sundeck.

The Sukapha had now moved a very short way down the river and was moored off a section of the Guhawati riverside that definitely would not have qualified as one of the "*Lonely Planet*"s "pleasant patches". It also offered no views of any green hillocks rising curiously out of the smog. No, all it had going for it was a graveyard of long dead metal boats, an assembly of… well, there was no other term for them; an assembly of rusting hulks, not so much lined up on the shore as cast about it like pieces of oversized litter – which is precisely what they were. They were thrown-away boats, boats that had once plied their trade from maybe the Bay of Bengal, up through Bangladesh to this inland port. Or maybe they were the ancestors of the Sukapha, smaller versions of the craft from which Brian was now viewing them – and marvelling at them.

They were predominantly white, pale blue and pink. The

white was off-white and was what was left of the paint with which they'd once been coated. The pale blue was also a remnant from their painted past, when clearly blue was the non-white colour of choice around these parts. The pink was rust. It covered as much of the redundant vessels as the white and blue did together. No doubt in twenty years' time it would cover the vessels completely. And they would still be here then. Brian was convinced of it. Unless the price of scrap metal went into the stratosphere and somebody came here with the right kit and the right authority, these shells of past shipping would remain here until the second coming. In fact, they'd probably still be here after the second going as well. They were now just part of the land and a lot less moveable than much of the "real" land that borders the Brahmaputra along its length. Brian found them fascinating.

He was also interested in their inhabitants. Because this was India, and no matter how decrepit and how uninviting a location might be, if it has some shelter to offer, or a vantage point to peer from, or just a flat bit of space to sit on, it will be inhabited. Consequently each hulk had a human tenant. One was sleeping, one was smoking, another was playing cards with his mate, and yet another was fishing (albeit he wasn't actually "catching"). And there were other human passengers on these literal junks who were cooking, eating, phoning or reading, and that's only what was going on outside. Brian could only guess at their hidden pastimes. For all he knew, these guys weren't just using these ex-boats as a convenient daytime roost but also as their full-time homes. For them this might be a very pleasant patch of riverside despite all the visual evidence to the contrary.

Of course, it wasn't perfect for them. There was a riverside "re-sculpturing" going on just next to their haven. This took the form of a couple of ancient, heavy-duty "public carriers" that were repeatedly trundling onto the sandy riverbank, where a gang of labourers would quickly load them with as much of the riverbank as they could publicly carry away. These labourers would wield their spades and within minutes another few tons of sandy land had become a load of sand for sale presumably to builders. Not a bad business really: labour costs low, transport costs very low, and raw material costs, zero. You just dig the stuff out of the ground – and presumably ignore the fact that you don't own the ground, and that very soon the ground will have gone and the Brahmaputra will be just a little bit wider (and a little bit closer to the row of shanty dwellings at the top of the bank, and to that fleet of marooned rust buckets).

Brian occupied himself with this view all afternoon. Sandra had taken herself away with a book, but Brian became captivated. It wasn't like looking at birds and new animals; Brian appreciated that the cast of characters in this diorama were all of his own species, and that had he been born in Guhawati, he might have been amongst their number. But he hadn't been born here; he'd been born many hundreds of miles away in England in a place called Rugby, a town that has given the world a game that is now even catching on in such far-away places as New Zealand. And that made him an outsider in Guhawati, an observer, and an observer of a way of life he could barely get to grips with. Did the guys on the boats have families? Where did they find the money to eat? Where did they find the money to buy the playing cards? Would those lorries keep on coming here until they physically couldn't, until they'd carted away the whole riverside? Would anybody try to stop them? Was what they were doing illegal or just entrepreneurial? Did they abide by all the Health and Safety regulations – insofar as these extended to removing the sides of rivers? There were so many questions in his mind. And none of them with a satisfactory answer. Perhaps he should have gone to the rubbish dump instead.

But then the Nature-seekers returned from the rubbish dump, and many of them were of the opinion that perhaps they should have stayed on the boat. The dump had lived up to all its advance billing, and although there were the promised birds there, there was also the smell and, even worse, the people who lived with this smell and with the total degradation of a rubbish dump life indefinitely. In comparison, Brian thought, lazing around, playing cards on a derelict ship seemed like a fairly easy number.

Better though that none of those guys out there knew what life was like aboard the Sukapha. They wouldn't "understand". And especially on this night aboard the boat – which was the night of the Nature-seekers' "Final Brahmaputra Dinner". For tomorrow, they would be heading back to Kolkata, and from there either straight back to England or, like Brian and Sandra, down to the Sundarbans. So tonight was a bit special. This was immediately apparent in the lounge where all the Nature-seekers had gathered for the final on-board listing session. They had all dressed up. Not only in their uncreased party best, but also in their life-jackets. Tim had started it. He'd argued that these life-jackets had been such a low point of the Brahmaputra experience, that now, on this final night, they should be made a high point. Not for the whole evening but just for as long as it took to send a clear message to the boat's management and to the guides, that these useless pieces of kit were much despised but had been worn valiantly and without actual rebellion, and might even have found their way into people's affections.

It doesn't take much to keep Nature-seekers amused, and everyone, without exception, had joined in. So when Sujan and his colleagues arrived to join the party in the lounge, the party was all orange. The effect was even heightened by the Indian and Nepalese choice of dress. They had all donned their achkans, the long collarless shirts worn on the subcontinent to denote rank and status, and donned this night to add to the sense of celebration.

This sense of celebration was then maintained after the listing process – and after speeches of thanks to Tika, Sujan and the boat's crew. This was accomplished in no small part by the ship's management and through their use of the ship's wine stocks. "Riviera Red" and "Riviera White" flowed like the Brahmaputra itself – figuratively speaking. And although this product of Bangalore might not have made it in a competitive field, here on its own, on this night in Guhawati, it proved a champion of champions.

It also softened Brian's mood. Despite the earlier jocularity with life-jackets and a general overflowing of bonhomie, Brian had been feeling a little depressed. He had become very aware that he had spent a whole day which had been very anti-Indian. He had visited a village and had come away with dark thoughts about child labour and even darker thoughts about the number of children. Then he had visited a temple and had thought some very unreligious thoughts about the local religion – and its impact on that number of children again. And then he had sat and observed what could only be described as a mix of squalor and disfunctionality. And even for an aspiring misanthropic recluse, none of this was good. If only he could work that perspective trick a little better. See everything from their point of view. And then it wouldn't look anything like as bad. Or would it? And it was just that they weren't acknowledging what they saw… But no, that couldn't be right. That would defy human nature. 'And anyway,' he kept telling himself, 'if you were born here and didn't have all those hang-ups we have, you'd wouldn't see anything wrong at all. And if you went to England, you'd see a hell of a lot wrong there'.

Eventually this mantra had some effect. Assisted as it was by the Riviera White, the table conversation and a growing realisation on his part that this really was his last dinner on board this boat. And with Brian, there was nothing quite like sentimental melancholia to take his mind off his congenital sense of guilt – whether that guilt concerned his vindictiveness towards people like Jim, his near lecherous thoughts about women such as Joanna Lumley, or his having had an "everything's wrong with India" sort of day.

He also had something else to distract him: the beginnings of a painfully sore throat and a small cough. He kept washing it with Riviera, but to no avail. He was getting a cold. From the sound of the other coughs in the dining room, he wasn't on his own. Perhaps he and all those succumbing to this next epidemic should have been provided with Kunal's "extract" for that night a little earlier. It was taken from "*Sport in British Burmah, Assam & the Cassyah & Juntiah Hills*", by Lt. Col. Pollock, published 1879. Part of it read:

'It does not do for a man in Assam to drink, or be given to sedentary habits. He should wear flannel and be ordinarily careful, and I believe he can go anywhere without running any great risk of fever. The one thing he must remember is, if he encamps near the foot of a range of hills, to avoid sleeping within the influence of the wind which nightly rushes down from the elevated plateau to take the place of the exhausted air of the plains, through one of the numerous gorges which abut onto the plains and through which generally a river flows.'

So that was it. They'd got everything wrong, and Brian was convinced that he hadn't seen anybody wearing flannel anywhere. What's more, maybe all those negative thoughts about India were just a product of all that exhausted air. It had been especially stuffy today, and now he thought about it, he had no recollection of a wind blowing down from the plateau last night.

Lt. Col. Pollock clearly knew his Assam very well...

10.

*J*t was morning. Brian had eaten breakfast to the accompaniment of more coughing and was back in his cabin waiting for Sandra to ready herself for the day. As he waited he looked through the cabin's rear window. The Sukapha was now a few hundred yards further down the river. From its new mooring Brian could no longer see a jumble of rust buckets but just a nondescript bank edged with nondescript buildings – and some people. He could see a number of Guhawati's poorer residents going about their early-morning ablutions in the river. After scrambling down its muddy banks they would stand in the water, soap themselves, rinse themselves and then clean their teeth and finally wash out their mouths with a mouthful of the river itself. Then they would scramble back up the bank, dress themselves and amble away with their towel and the remains of their soap.

As he watched he began to feel like a voyeur. But he couldn't help himself. Everything about this communal washing scene was just so fascinating. Here were men and women bathing together, and not for any other reason than necessity; there were clearly a limited number of accessible and suitable bathing sites within the city itself and this was one such site. They had very little choice. But they were bathing discreetly; there was the minimum amount of flesh on display, and how the women bathed themselves thoroughly whilst still modestly clothed was a revelation in itself. So there was good here: men and women sharing a common space for the conduct of a fairly intimate task without any embarrassment or discomfort and without any of them being overcome with lust. Men in Guhawati, it appeared, weren't inevitably roused into passion by the sight of a woman rubbing herself, and the women didn't need to be protected from their gaze. Indeed everybody seemed simply to ignore each other, and a man only looked at a woman when he was looking to avoid her as he left the river. All in all it was a very instructive display of people's desire to behave decently and, of course, of their desire to keep themselves clean.

However, as well as these encouragingly positive aspects, there was what in Brian's eyes was a ruddy great negative: these people were bathing in (and cleaning their teeth in) a body of water that was quite obviously filthy. This was in the middle of a city. The river was abused. It had things floating on it. It inevitably had a great many more things floating in it, things that one couldn't see but things that would make sick or even kill a western softy such as himself. But these people had to endure this. To keep clean, each day they not only had to expose themselves to public view while they bathed, but they also had to expose themselves to the dangers of any number of water-borne diseases. Brian began to wonder how any of them survived into old age.

He also wondered what all these bathers would make of the bathroom in his cabin and the shower there. How they would react to crystal clear water at just the right temperature – and the privacy and the convenience of your very own shower cubicle. No bothers about a rogue bit of bare flesh and no climbing back up an eight-foot bank of mud when you've rinsed yourself off. It made him feel guilty about his thoughts of yesterday all over again.

But now Sandra had announced it was time to go. He was awoken from his reverie and was now required to apply himself to the duties of a Nature-seeker once again. For now they were off to make their last excursion from the Sukapha, their last Brahmaputra outing: a visit to another temple.

It began with a walk over the nondescript bank (with no life-jackets) to the waiting pair of minibuses. This is when it became apparent that the nondescript bank was in fact part of a freight terminal. Just beyond the minibuses was a newish looking warehouse, an even newer looking wharf, and a sign announcing that together these two constructions constituted Guhawati's latest publicly owned freight terminal.

It also became apparent that the only users of this terminal were the bathing party, which was now much smaller, and a troop of children, which having been alerted to the presence of aliens, was now much bigger. There were no boats anywhere and no workers anywhere. There were not even any workers on a rail track to the warehouse, a rail track that currently had no rails and very little in the way of track, and that Brian suspected might remain in that state indefinitely.

There were, however, some guards. The minibuses were now approaching a pair of enormous gates at the exit to the inert freight terminal, and opening them for their passage were a couple of uniformed security guards. They seemed not to care that, despite the grandeur of their gates, the freight terminal was not in the least bit secure, and that anybody who wanted a wash and any child who wanted to stare at visiting Brits could quite happily enter the terminal's grounds through its entirely permeable perimeter wherever and whenever he or she chose.

But at least they wouldn't enter through the gates. That wasn't allowed!

Brian's minibus was now through the gates and into the metropolis of Guhawati. He turned to Sandra and imparted some advice.

'Keep a look out for the hillocks,' he said. 'They rise above the smog.'

'What?'

'The hillocks. You remember. The green hillocks that rise curiously above the noisy smog…'

Sandra looked bemused.

'You can't have noisy smog,' she observed. 'That's ridiculous. You might as well talk about a smelly anthem.'

'A smelly anthem?'

'Yes. If a band plays an anthem next to a sewerage works, it doesn't make it a smelly anthem, in the same way that noisy traffic in a smoggy city doesn't make it a noisy smog. Get it?'

Brian did get it. He smiled.

'You're right. I must write to "*Lonely Planet*". As soon as I get back.'

'You might ask them where the hillocks are while you're at it. All I can see is shops.'

Sandra was right. They were in the middle of an infinite market, an unbroken huddle of tiny booths and shabby emporia through which there was a linear space just large enough to allow their bus to pass. On quieter days this space might just qualify as a road, but today it was no more than a passage through the chaos of a bustling bazaar, and the Nature-seekers' progress was slow to the point of being almost sedate.

Brian didn't mind this in the least. If they hit anything at their current speed he would not be killed.

This happy state of affairs eventually came to an end. The minibus was now on a discernibly main road. There was traffic everywhere and the traffic was travelling at speed – wherever the road or that new dimension allowed. Brian was in the middle of the bus on its right hand side. This gave him a very good view of the three nearly-dead-pedestrian incidents when on three separate occasions a local inhabitant of this town had rushed across the road from the right to test the effective operation of the new dimension by not being crushed beneath the wheels of the bus when he quite clearly should have been. The last guy, in particular, who was rushing towards the front of Brian's carriage with an empty wheelbarrow, proved without an iota of doubt that all was in order on the new dimension front and that no matter how inevitable a collision might appear, today in Guhawati, it would not happen. Brian, however, was not completely reassured and was more than a little relieved when his minibus pulled into the side of the road. They were stationary. It was his favourite in-bus situation.

They were not, however, at their destination. They were parked by a high wall in which there was a pair of huge gates, and in front of the gates were some guards. Brian wondered whether rather than visiting a temple, it had been decided that instead they should embark on a guard-crawl. There being no pubs in Guhawati, but clearly a surfeit of guarded gates, maybe Sujan had made this switch in plans. But no. It wasn't the guards they had stopped to observe, it was the foxes.

Ron had expressed his disappointment at not having seen any Indian flying foxes on the trip so far. Accordingly, the minibuses had made a small detour on their way to the temple to take in a flying fox roost – which was obviously just as dependable as an adjutant stork rubbish dump. They were always here – at this time of day. Ron was suitably delighted, as were the rest of the party. There were hundreds of foxes hanging in the tops of a dozen or so trees, looking like giant brown cocoons beneath the feathery foliage. Brian wondered how they coped with the noisy smog.

Back onto the bus and on to the temple.

'Look,' said Sandra. 'A hillock.'

'Yes, and there's another one there,' added Brian. 'And look at this one here. That's not a hillock; that's a fully grown hill.'

It was also where they were going. Sujan had told them that the temple was on a high point in the city, and this was it. The minibuses had now turned off the main thoroughfare and were heading up a narrow winding road that presumably took them all the way to the temple. At least Brian hoped it did. He had no wish to climb any part of this urban mini-mountain, and certainly not in what was now turning into a fiercely hot day.

He looked out of the bus's window. He now had a remarkable view of Guhawati below. Not all of it, but enough to see where the "*Lonely Planet*" author had found his words. There it was: a messy sprawl bathed in smog with hillocks in it. None of which was quite as high as the hillock they were on themselves. Or quite as congested at its summit. For they had now arrived, not at the temple proper, but at the temple car park with its temple guards. Or maybe they were regular police. Brian hadn't yet sorted out the various uniforms. But whoever they were, they were valiantly trying to bring a degree of order to the chaos of the temple approach and its teeming droves of visitors. They were having only limited success.

The minibuses stopped and disgorged their cargo of Nature-seekers. It was now as hot as hell and there was still some way to go to the temple. Uphill and on foot. Brian began to think of the sundeck of the Sukapha and a dishonourably early beer.

'Put your hat on,' commanded Sandra.

Brian scowled. He hated wearing hats, and especially sun-hats. He only ever did so if the sun's intensity made it unavoidable – and he was in a "field" situation where his companions had been made to look as ridiculous as himself. But this was urban India where there were lots of urban Indians to observe his appearance, and so a hat was out of the question.

'I'll be OK,' he responded. 'It can't be that far.'

'Well, it's up to you. But don't complain later.'

'I won't.'

And so the official warning had been delivered and the official acknowledgement made. The walk to the temple could now commence.

It began with a stroll past a number of open-fronted shops selling trinkets and offerings for the temple. It then continued past more shops selling trinkets and offerings and ended in a narrow, gently rising alley running through yet more shops selling trinkets and offerings. Brian thought it must be like this at Lourdes, albeit Lourdes was probably not quite so colourful but probably a great deal tidier. The alley, for example, was a blaze of colour at eye level, but above this level it was the usual mix of faded paint, unfinished concrete, corrugated iron and a tangle of wires. The alley was also heaving with people, all of whom, save for the Nature-seekers, would have looked very out of place at Lourdes. They were all very obviously Indian. Even in this "gateway city" to Assam (at one of its "interesting temples") there were no other Europeans. 'Maybe,' thought Brian, 'they've all read that "Lonely Planet" advice and "moved swiftly on"'.

But for whatever reason, the Nature-seekers were very much the out of the ordinary species here, as was evidenced by the reaction of many of the Indians. Some stared at them, some smiled at them, and some even took their photos... Brian could scarcely believe it. Wasn't it the role of the Nature-seekers to take pictures of them? But then it occurred to him. This reaction was in no way different to what they'd already experienced in rural Assam. However, there the locals didn't have quite the confidence (or the equipment) to turn their gaze on the gazers as was happening now. But why shouldn't they, he thought? After all, it was their city and their temple. And it was also good fun – for all concerned. Brian couldn't remember the last time a stranger had pointed a camera at him. And he quickly realised it was delightful. Indeed, it was so delightful it almost took his mind off the incline of the alley and the stifling heat.

Almost, but not quite. So when he arrived at the shoe repository at the top of the alley he was more aware than ever of the ambient temperature and his body's inability to deal with it. He was now glowing, and as he struggled to remove his shoes in the crush of visitors, the glow was running down his face and streaming down his back. He again thought of an early beer on the sundeck.

The temple itself was... well, temple-ish. It had domes on its roof, carvings on its side and lots of flags around it. It also had some temple-goats, some temple-pigeons, a few ex-temple-pigeons and lots of temple pilgrims. They were everywhere and so was the sound of their exhausted and overheated children. It was all a bit chaotic. Which may have been the reason for the cage.

On one side of the temple was a caged corridor. In this elongated cage were more pilgrims, but quiet, passive pilgrims, who were queuing up to enter the temple and visit its inner sanctum. Sujan informed Brian that the queuing time was five hours – unless you paid a premium to the temple authorities, when you were then given the business–class treatment and a fast-track admission. But that was not the norm. For most, it was this five hour wait – in a cage with no facilities and in the awful heat. 'How,' thought Brian, 'can so many people be so religious – or so desperate?' He just couldn't understand.

Needless to say, none of the Nature-seekers joined this queue and therefore none of them saw the inside of the temple. Few of them appeared to want to, with the notable exception of Pam and Julian, for whom this display of caged dedication was clearly nothing less than an enthralling manifestation of real Indian culture.

Brian was just happy to get his shoes back. Given how many items of footwear had been stacked in the shoe repository, he was relieved as well. There were hundreds and hundreds and they all seemed to end up back on the feet of their owners, which either said something about order in chaos or the karmic consequences of walking away from a temple in somebody else's shoes, or possibly both. Putting his back on proved more difficult than taking them off. Such was the density of the throng that he couldn't sit down to do it, and by the time he'd grappled with the task standing up he was well and truly dripping and interested only in getting back to the Sukapha and its air-conditioned cabins. And maybe a beer.

But he would have to wait. First they had to make it back to the minibuses. Then the minibuses had to extract themselves from the mêlée of other traffic around the temple approach… and then the minibuses drove not down the hillock, but around it – to a "*point de vue*". Quite understandably, Sujan had taken the opportunity to give the Nature-seekers a panoramic view of the Brahmaputra that was available just a short way from the temple. And who wouldn't have welcomed a last wonderful view of the river they'd sailed down for the last ten days before they were obliged to leave it? Even Brian, in his still damp shirt, was eager to leave the comparative coolness of his minibus to see the view on offer. And whilst it wasn't up there with the view of Toledo from that Parador or the vista one enjoys from the top of Mont Ventoux, it was still pretty impressive. The huge Brahmaputra flowed below, green hillocks rose curiously from the smog – and black kites wheeled around in the sky. It was a lot better than the temple.

But now it was time to return to the boat. They set off again and Brian occupied his mind with thoughts of beer all the way back as a distraction from the traffic. It worked, and ultimately his minibus made the safety of the cramped market where it was immediately reduced to an almost walking pace and Brian could relax. Julian, however, was still very much alert and spotted from the minibus a vendor of buckets. The bus was stopped, he disembarked with Sujan, and two minutes later he re-boarded the bus holding in triumph a small galvanised bucket. It was needed, he explained, for his new boat back in England. This size was apparently difficult to find in the UK, although Brian thought it might be an even more difficult size to pack into one's luggage. But he didn't say anything. At least not until he spotted that this splendid example of vernacular manufacture was in fact made by the monolithic Tata; it said so on the side. He then said something about it being a "*pail* imitation" of local craftsmanship. But he wasn't sure Julian recognised the pun. And probably just as well. It wasn't one of his best.

However, they were now at those guarded gates again, then through the gates and enjoying the greeting from the massed ranks of the freight terminal urchins. And then they were on the boat. Time was now getting on. So for Brian, it was a rapid shower, a quick beer and a prompt lunch. And then it was time to leave the Sukapha for the very last time.

Brian thanked everybody he could thank as profusely as he possibly could. Their cruise on the Brahmaputra hadn't been a luxury cruise but it had been a fabulous cruise. It had been a series of memorable expeditions from the simple comfort of a floating guesthouse, the sort of guesthouse that provides impeccable service with style but without pretention. Whatever faults Brian had found with India so far, they stopped at the gangplank to the Sukapha. Indeed, there was many a hostelry in Britain which would do very well to study how they did it on this boat. Attitude and attention to detail were, he believed, far more important than opulence and excess.

Brian was on that nondescript bank again. Cases were being taken to the minibuses and the Nature-seekers were being organised into a huddle for a final group photo. This meant Brian's six-foot-two frame was required to station itself at the back of this huddle, and he now stood there attempting to smile rather than grin and wondering whether a letter to the "*Lonely Planet*" publishers was really worth the trouble.

The trip to Guhawati Airport was uneventful. As earlier predicted, no collisions occurred – and no more buckets were purchased. Guhawati maintained its unexceptional, untidy demeanour all the way and eventually they arrived in the airport car park. It was now very hot. So Brian was more than usually gratified that there was somebody else to manhandle all the luggage onto some trolleys and to push these trolleys to the terminal building. His unencumbered state even gave him ample opportunity to study some sizeable cockroaches scurrying around a drain cover at the entrance to this building. He trusted they were not allowed inside.

The Nature-seekers were. They were deposited in a lounge area beneath a single fan while Sujan, Rajan and Tika went off to sort out all the check-in stuff. Travelling in a guided group could render one completely dependent. Nevertheless, one was inevitably thrown back onto one's own resources when it came to the security check. Brian had a small holdall in which he carried his binoculars, his camera and his other precious pieces. When it went through the X-ray machine, the machine's operator thought it contained something rather more dubious. It was put through again. Dubious had moved up to plainly suspicious and one of the security guys insisted on making a search. He removed the camera and its spare batteries and the bag was put through the machine again. Now it was highly suspicious. There was something in there that was causing all sorts of consternation. So the bag was relieved of more of its contents and went for a further encounter with the X-rays. Still a problem. Which is when Brian remembered that in a small side pocket of his bag, was his house-key, a chunky lump of British brass. He extracted it, showed it to the security guy, who then returned the bag for yet another jaunt through the innards of the machine. Success! The key was the culprit, and as it was decided that it did not constitute an offensive weapon it was allowed to proceed with its owner to the departure lounge where waiting for them both were Sandra and Tika.

Brian explained the reason for the delay and presented the troublesome key for their joint inspection. Tika sympathised and Sandra told him not to lose it. She didn't want to have to break a window when they got back home. Brian informed her that neither did he and then a truce was called as it was time to go – and time to leave Tika. He was on his way back to Nepal and to his home there near the Chitwan National Park. Brian shook his hand and Sandra gave him a hug. He had been the epitome of a brilliant guide and a splendid companion. Both made their feelings about him as clear as possible without it getting too embarrassing, and then the rest of the party did the same. It proved a lengthy procedure.

But finally it was onto a tube of "Jetlite". Brian, Sandra, their house-key and all the other Nature-seekers were soon airborne with this local carrier and soon estranged from Assam. In what seemed like just minutes they had abandoned an adventure and were now on their way to the humdrum, back to the modernity of a city and to the normality of life.

This, of course, was rubbish. They were on their way back to Kolkata and half of them would then be on their way to another adventure. Modernity and normality wouldn't get a look-in for some time.

The flight back took them over Bangladesh. From twenty thousand feet it looked very crowded. Kolkata domestic airport was also crowded, but in a different sense; it was full of people waiting for their luggage, the luggage handling system and the number of luggage carousels having been overtaken some time ago by the number of luggage-bearing arrivals. The luggage handling system was also a bit brutal; it violated the integrity of Karen's case. Nothing was missing, but it was now in no fit state to cope with its imminent onward journey to Heathrow. This was a problem. Karen and Tim, with Sujan in attendance, would now have to report this to an airline representative. For it was the airline's responsibility. But this meant they would have to engage with the airline's unavoidable bureaucracy.

While this was underway, all the other Nature-seekers were parked in their coach just outside the arrivals hall. There they enjoyed a great view of a whole army of yellow Hindustan taxis – and an example of Indian humour: a sleeping rickshaw driver being relieved of his shoes. He had taken his shoes off, not to visit a temple, but to secure some further comfort while he invested in an extended doze on his rickshaw. This allowed two of his colleagues to sneak towards him, liberate his shoes, and leave him to wake to the surprise of disappeared footwear. Unfortunately Tim and Karen returned with Sujan before he woke, so Brian was unable to establish whether the rickshaw driver, on discovering his shoeless state, thought what his friends had done was a great wheeze which he only wished he'd thought of himself or whether the shock at the loss of his prized and probably valuable possessions killed him on the spot. However, the damaged-case case had been sorted. The airline had offered about a tenth of the value of the damaged item (on the basis that a similar (looking) item could be purchased for this amount from any street vendor in Kolkata) or alternatively the prospect of a large set of forms to fill in and the outside chance that there might be a better compensation deal sometime in the future. As there were only three hours to go to dinner and Tim and Karen were aware of the plight of their colleagues on the coach, they had accepted the former offer. And the coach was now ready to make its way into the centre of the city.

The Nature-seekers had made this same journey when they'd first arrived in India. Their trip to Assam had started with an overnight in Kolkata, and so this was the second time that they had travelled from the airport complex into the middle of "that great city". So now there wasn't so much a sense of shock on board the coach as a sense of horror and dismay. Kolkata unfortunately is not a great city but it is a terrible warning of what the whole world will turn into if more and more people consume more and more of its resources.

Brian tried to see it some other way, but he just couldn't. Kolkata was crowded, dirty, decrepit, squalid and above all desperately ugly. Even at the beginning of their route there was ugliness. This was an area where huge blocks of apartments were now being built to accommodate the upwardly mobile young of Kolkata, and whilst the individual apartments might very well be excellently appointed on the inside, from the outside the blocks themselves looked like something out of "*1984*". Brian imagined Winston Smith making his way over the bleak and dreary wasteland that surrounded these buildings, wrapped up in a raincoat despite the searing Kolkata heat and wishing he was somewhere else. Not, however, in the city itself. For after this bleak "affluent" suburb comes the real Kolkata, a Kolkata of unfinished buildings, dilapidated buildings, ramshackle buildings, abandoned buildings and buildings that look like prisons. These latter are amongst the worse: squat, neglected blocks of apartments with balconies protected from the attentions of the ubiquitous house crows by heavy lattice metal work or concrete screening – which must make their interiors studies in stifling claustrophobia. Brian could not imagine spending a day in them let alone a lifetime. Nor could he live with the rubbish dumps, the ever-present litter, the filthy open urinals, the starving "sacred" cows, the wretched looking dogs, the wretched looking beggars – and the constant noise and the constant demented traffic… For as in Jorhat and Guhawati, vehicles in Kolkata are all driven as if they are trying to outrun a tsunami and as if there is some prize to be had for whoever first wears out his horn. Brian even wondered whether there was a driving test system in India, and if there was, whether to pass the test one had only to demonstrate a competence in horn-craft, and in particular an ability to sound a horn at least ten times per minute whether it was warranted or not.

Life is lived on the roads of Kolkata – on its pavements and in its vehicles – and in such a manic and congested manner that Brian knew he could never cope with it. Such a frenetic existence in the midst of such unremitting ugliness would be simply intolerable, and for once he was unequivocal and unforgiving in his views. Whether Mumbai and Delhi and other Indian cities were quite like this place he did not know. But as far as Kolkata was concerned, it was one of the most horrible and most distressing places he had ever visited. He had seen poverty before all over the world, and neglect and "unpleasantness", but he had never before seen anything quite like this place, and never anywhere that was so unbelievably ugly. It made him feel so thoroughly dismayed that he hardly noticed the risk to his own life in the rush of traffic – held at bay only by a super-sized helping of that magical new dimension. Had he thought about it more, he may have concluded that this agent of salvation was the only thing in Kolkata that was either magical or new – or that seemed to work as was intended.

That conclusion, however, would not have been accurate. It would have ignored the Oberoi Grand Hotel. This was the Nature-seekers' destination and the hotel in which they had spent their first night in India. It was in the very middle of Kolkata, it had been built by the British in the Nineteenth Century, and whilst therefore not new, it was magical in the extreme and it worked not only as a grand hotel should work but as a great hotel should work.

It was a five-star establishment and the best place to stay in Kolkata by a long way. It had not been the original choice for the Nature-seekers, but after the attack on the hotels in Mumbai, one of which was its sister hotel, the Oberoi Trident, it had clearly experienced a dramatic fall in its own bookings. Hence a deal had been secured that meant that the twenty-three Nature-seekers could rest their weary heads in its sumptuous surroundings for presumably the same cost as that of their more modest initial hostelry. Furthermore they had to share the hotel's three hundred rooms with no more than twenty other guests. The Oberoi, despite its obvious attractions, was being avoided. Maybe after the national elections and when the Mumbai attack had become a distant recollection, its business would return to normal. But for now it was virtually at the exclusive disposal of the Nature-seekers, and Brian for one couldn't wait to get back there.

He had to wait no longer. The coach had just pulled up to the frontage of the hotel – protected from the thoroughfare itself by a series of barriers and a squad of guards – and the Nature-seekers were now disembarking – and knew what to expect next. This was an initial greeting by more guards who were stationed behind large elaborate gates (it really was a guard-crawl today) and equipped with metal detectors that they used to check that none of the Nature-seekers was armed. This was all performed with the maximum of grace and the minimum of offence, after which the new visitors to the hotel were allowed to approach its entrance. This was across a handsome courtyard, in one corner of which was a sand-banked machine-gun post manned by two regular soldiers. The authorities were taking people's security very seriously indeed. As was the management of the hotel. For now there were more guards and more metal detectors at the hotel entrance, more body sweeps, and now a search of hand luggage, accompanied with the same degree of charm and deference as was on display at the gate.

And then you were in! The glass doors opened, the traffic din outside disappeared in an instant, and you were standing there in an air-conditioned sanctuary with Mendelssohn soothing your travel-weary self as you came to terms with your new surroundings. In the middle of all that ugliness out there was this haven of absolute elegance. There were chandeliers with muslin-wrapped hangings; there were beautiful flower displays and beautiful *objets d'art*; there were rich carpets and intricately carved woodwork. Indeed there was everything to make you think that you had just been transported from purgatory to a rather well-appointed heaven. Even if you didn't believe in heaven and didn't deserve to go there if you were wrong.

Brian bathed himself in his new situation. Opulence really wasn't at the top of his wish list and he was still very conscious of the sea of deprivation that swirled around the outside of this establishment. In many ways it was rather obscene that such an establishment could even exist in such a place. But it did. And whether he felt decently guilty about this or whether he just cast his conscience to one side and simply enjoyed it while he could, he would not change that fact. So, no contest really.

First up was a laze on an over-sized bed, second was a leisurely ablution in a marbled bathroom, third was a change into some respectable clothing, and then fourth was a sally forth – to the bar. Here, in what could have been the lounge of one of the more thoughtfully appointed gentlemen's clubs in London, he and Sandra both demolished a pair of gin and tonics and chatted for the last time to those of the party who were finishing their holiday. There was now something to say to all of them, even Jim. They had spent only a few days together, but they had shared a lot. And Brian had formed an opinion of them all. Just, as he was sure, they had formed an opinion of him.

Tim and Karen, he'd decided, were Mr Un-fashionable and Mrs Very-fashionable.

Karen was very fashionable in every sense. She was fashionable in her choice of clothes, in her hairstyle – and indeed, in her entire demeanour. She "moved" fashionably. And she was also fashionably thoughtful and fashionably just a little bit mischievous.

This last fashion accessory in her make-up may have been a result of her having Tim as a husband. Because here was the clear winner of the "most-unfashionable" contest on this trip – albeit not in terms of his appearance or his demeanour. No, Tim had earned this title by being the most unfashionable member of the group in terms of his character. Everything about his nature had been out of fashion for years. Because here was a man who was staid, restrained, sober, deeply honest, hard-working, diligent, careful and conscientious. This combination of qualities might have made him just a little bit dull, but they were all qualities that Brian admired greatly and qualities that in many aspects of life were now entirely passé or simply the subject of others' derision. Fortunately, Brian thought, Tim would remain out of fashion for the rest of his life.

Then there was Rosamunde and Judy, the heterosexual pair of ladies from the Home Counties with whom Brian had shared some time but not much and to little effect. He always thought that everybody with whom he engaged would have an impact on his life, some a significant impact and others barely an impact at all. Rosamunde was in this latter category. Whereas some people he had met had virtually bent his chassis, Rosamunde had not even put a dent in his paintwork. He was already having trouble remembering what she looked like, and all he could recollect of her as a person was that she was a physiotherapist who had met Prince Charles. Or was that Pam? No, Rosamunde hadn't even scratched his wing mirror.

Judy, however, had put a small chip in his windscreen. For how could he ever forget the impact of that flying pebble that was her discourse on real tennis? He would never forget it. And whilst it might not change the direction of his life, he would always be aware of it, as if out of the corner of his eye. So that every time, for the rest of his life, whenever the subject of real tennis cropped up, he would think of Judy – even though she didn't play it herself and probably thought her husband, who played it all the time, was a bit of a saddo. Brian wondered how they reconciled their level of interest in the sport – and whether they ever admitted the existence of fantasy tennis (as played at Wimbledon). And if they did, whether they ever questioned why it was about a million times more popular than their own real variety. He suspected they conveniently ignored it.

And so to Ron and Irene. Ron, Brian considered, was a little like a new flavour of ice cream, which initially is so tasty that you can't get enough of it, but which soon loses its magic and leaves you desperate for just vanilla. At the beginning of the tour this most uncomplicated of individuals had been one of the more open and more affable of all the Nature-seekers and was never at a loss for something to say. He was a welcome and "easy" companion. Unfortunately, however, his ability never to be at a loss for something to say was unbounded, even when all he could assemble to say was either irrelevant, barely interesting, positively tedious or a combination of all three. And so the desire for that vanilla, somebody with a few less stories about their offspring and their holiday in Fuerteventura. That said, he was a good-hearted sort of chap. And Brian knew that if he was looking for anyone to accuse of being a bore, he might start by taking a look in a mirror. Irrelevance and tedium weren't quite his stock in trade – but he was well aware that he would often supply them as a special offer whenever he'd run out of everything else…

Irene was not a bore. She had less to say than Ron, but what she did have to say was often thought-provoking and revealing. She was the antithesis of a self-absorbed liberal and therefore very good company.

The same could not be said for Pamela and Julian. Whilst they were similarly thought-provoking, the thoughts they provoked in Brian's head were ones only of frustration and exasperation. They were the most "culturally inclined" of all those in the party. They were in their element in the temples and in the rural villages and appeared to look at every aspect of Indian life through a pair of cultural spectacles that blinded them to everything else. In particular they appeared blind to the very real and often very negative consequences of the culture that so fascinated them, and Brian was constantly bewildered by their "intellectual denial" of its detrimental impact. Many people in India were living miserable lives and much of this suffering could be laid at the door of an unreformed way of life held back from reform by traditional beliefs, the sort of beliefs that they found so "culturally stimulating". They exemplified the very soft and very hazardous approach of many liberally minded intellectuals that pays far too much respect to the conventions of the past at the expense of the reality of the present. Brian couldn't really dislike them; they were a very pleasant couple. But he could never empathise with their outlook on the world. It was silly and it contained within it everything that was needed to frustrate real progress and with this progress, real enlightenment and real liberation.

No such criticism could be levelled at John and Vivien. In Brian's mind these two were heroes. Two people who had devoted themselves to science (and to enlightenment), two people who were civilised, amiable and cogent, and two people whose intellect shone through everything they did. Indeed, in many ways, they were everything that Jerry and Edith were not...

And that is probably all that needs to be said – or should be said – about this last pair of leavers. Except to say that Brian had now convinced himself that this Donald McGill pair really were on the wrong holiday – by mistake. He just hoped that they'd make it back to Britain without finding themselves in Mali or North Korea on the way.

Jim would have no such problems. For all his peculiarities, he was very well organised. Most civil servants are – especially when it comes to looking after their terms of employment and their pension arrangements. In fact Brian was constantly worried that one day they'd manage to negotiate themselves not just an indefinite guaranteed income, but also an indefinite guaranteed life. That they'd all become bloody immortal. And that really would be the end...

But now another end... The end of the group of twenty-three and their trip down the Brahmaputra. Tomorrow thirteen of them would be gone and the group would be reduced to just ten – plus one other: Sujan. It would be his job to make the next few days as rewarding as the past ten, and maybe even to find for the rump of his charges, a tiger – in the killing zone of the Sundarbans! It wasn't likely. Indeed Brian thought it was no more likely than his finding a cure for coughing. His was worse, Sandra had developed a dose of her own, and all the remaining males in the party, other than Sujan, had now succumbed to the curse of "the hack". It didn't come with any other of the usual cold symptoms, but it didn't need to. A constant sore throat and a dry, barking cough were quite bad enough on their own. Brian just hoped they'd all leave it behind in Kolkata.

After all, if they did find a tiger, they wouldn't want to scare it away...

11.

anging by its drawstring from the handle of the door was a white linen sack. Brian had known it would be there from his earlier visit to the Oberoi and that it would contain his complimentary newspaper. He collected it, walked back into his room, withdrew and discarded the newspaper and then studied the sack. It was like the drawstring sack he'd kept his pumps in at primary school. Although not exactly like it. His footwear holder from all those years ago, he thought, was made of cotton not linen, and it was a cotton printed with pale peppermint stripes and therefore lacking the monochrome elegance of the receptacle he now held.

He considered imparting this riveting piece of personal history to his companions at the breakfast table. But he'd already told Sandra, who had been less than captivated by his tale, and he judged that Derek and Yvonne might be similarly unimpressed. Why, after all, would a retired Concorde pilot and his wife have the slightest interest in anything to do with drawstring sacks, particularly when they had on their minds an imminent trip to the Sundarbans and all that was on offer there? Furthermore, this was the first time that Brian and Sandra had Derek and Yvonne to themselves; they were normally fastened to their permanent travelling companions, Dennis and Pauline.

So Brian was eager not to make a blunder and thereby prejudice his relationship with a couple with whom he would now be in close contact for the next five days. He therefore asked them about their children instead. Experience told him this was always safer ground. It was never especially interesting, but as his own contribution to the topic was normally just nodding his head in agreement at the appropriate times, it was virtually impossible to make a faux pas.

Accordingly, when the team of ten plus one boarded their transport outside the hotel, relations were unsullied on the Derek and Yvonne front – and promising on all other fronts. For now, despite the coughing epidemic, which was still in full swing, there seemed to be a renewed sense of bonhomie in the group, something no doubt to do with its reduced number but also with the prospect in everybody's minds of a new adventure – in the company of people who were no longer complete strangers. There wouldn't be all that unavoidable evaluation going on, all that gauging whether he or she was even worth talking to, and if they were, whether there were any topics to avoid – like cultural myopia or seaside postcards. That had all been done, and what had been learnt could now be built on, and that would be easy. Heck, even Sujan was now a known quantity. It was going to be a good time for all. Brian was sure of it. And he couldn't wait to get started.

He had expected a minibus. The group and its luggage would have fitted into one almost comfortably. What there was instead though was an enormous coach. And not only was it enormous but it was also luxurious, with a really good air-conditioning system, well-upholstered seats, tinted windows and a copious amount of curtaining. It was, in fact, nothing less than an exercise in insulation against the outside world, a lesson in how to hold at bay the reality of the heat out there, the state of the roads out there, and the sight of the squalor out there. It worked well for the heat and as well as it could for the potholes, but even the best of curtain-framed tinted glass was no match for the scenery. Kolkata in all its horror still made its way into the coach and nothing could stop it.

The coach was so large everybody had selected for themselves a window seat. Brian was no different. He was in the centre of the bus (and thereby emotionally a long way from the consequences of a head-on impact or even a back-of-the-bus crumpling incident) and sitting in a window seat on its right hand side. He therefore had a grandstand seat for all the sights on show on their way out of Kolkata and for all those new ones that came into view in the countryside beyond.

The Kolkata sights were as dismal and demoralising as ever. They even included his first visual encounter with a rubbish dump and its population of rubbish sorters. This one had no complement of storks on it but it did have its full quota of criminally demeaning behaviour. It was just wrong. No society, no matter how poor, should commit any of its citizens to such an abominable occupation.

It didn't get much better in the "countryside". This turned out to be a string of scrappy looking vegetable plots interspersed with what looked like some forgotten and very unpleasant precursor to the industrial revolution. These were expansive yards within each of which was a vast brown "boiling pot" set above a rudimentary furnace, and surrounded by what looked like piles of rags and beyond these swathes of greyish ash. And amidst the haze of smoke and steam that swirled around the pot were the workers, the benighted individuals whose lives were devoted to the production of fertilizer from off-cuts of leather.

For that is what these yards were all about. They took the spoil from Kolkata's tanneries and by boiling it up (maybe with some other ingredients) they produced a cheap but phosphate-rich compost for use on the adjoining fields. The work must have been hot, hard, smelly and degrading – but presumably a step up from working on a rubbish dump.

The distance to the Sundarbans was about eighty kilometres. The trip was scheduled to take two and a half hours – before the coach was abandoned in favour of a boat – and it was advertised as passing through several "dusty" villages. In this part of West Bengal, Brian was now learning that "dusty" meant "rural-squalid". There were more than several of these villages and they were not noticeably dusty at all, just filthy and decrepit, like mini versions of Kolkata and a million miles from the elegance and cleanliness of all those fishing villages back in Assam. What was it about extreme poverty that seemed to spawn a certain pride and almost an innate sense of aesthetics as against urban or semi-urban "mild" poverty that seemed to generate nothing more than neglect and abject ugliness? For it was clear; these semi-urban village dwellers had far more in material terms than their counterparts on the Brahmaputra (there were well stocked shops and all sorts of simple machinery here), but they lived in settlements that were little more than shanty towns, with none of the order and dignity that comes from having barely anything at all. And maybe that was it, thought Brian. It was that simple. If you haven't got anything, you haven't got anything with which to foul up your environment. But once you do have something, no matter how little that something is, you can use it to make a mess. There again, that was a terrible thought. It undervalued people's pride and their natural dignity. So Brian rejected it and instead turned his mind to people's level of activity.

The coach had now reached an area where, on each side of the road, there were huge man-made lagoons and on the few pieces of actual dry land, a number of brickworks. What was going on here, as far as Brian could understand, was fish farming, or at least fish-fry farming, and in the brickworks, the useful conversion of excavated mud (from the lagoons) into a product that was much in demand in the Sundarbans (as would soon become apparent). And what struck Brian about these enterprises – and the fertilizer production and the market gardening before – and the "dusty" villages – was people's level of activity.

Feeding and tending a boiling pot of tannery waste is clearly hard work. So is working in the fields and digging out and maintaining fish lagoons. Even harder must be working in a brickworks. Everything in these places appeared to be being done by hand – with no machinery of any sort visible anywhere. So all in all, the inhabitants of this part of West Bengal were very active indeed; they worked their socks off and then some more – except if they were in those villages. Then they were not active in the slightest. They were instead like those fabled Assamese, indolent and indeed largely immobile, content merely to sit on the doorstep of a shop or on a sack of rice looking at the traffic or at nothing in particular and staying well out of the way of anything that could be construed as any sort of work or any sort of effort.

There was an activity apartheid here; one was either overactive or entirely inactive, and Brian could not decide why. How in the face of so much hard work to be done could so many appear to avoid work completely? And what did they do? And how did they support themselves? They couldn't all be shopkeepers. And they couldn't all be simply unemployed. Or maybe they were. Maybe work, no matter how demanding or how degrading, was a real prize here in a way it no longer was in Britain, and the village-idles were all the unfortunates. But they didn't look too distressed, and most of them seemed to be thriving on their idleness. It couldn't be that simple. And then Brian had a thought. It was a thought about the caste system. Then he aborted the thought. It was probably wrong, but even if it wasn't he had no way to pursue it. He might know Sujan pretty well now, but quizzing him on that topic was definitely a non starter. In any event, there was now a new circumstance demanding Brian's attention. The coach had stopped. After two and a half hours on the move it had eventually come to a halt (in the middle of a dusty village) and the Nature-seekers were being invited to disembark.

Brian's first thought was that they appeared to have completed their coach ride without the coach colliding with anything. This was good news. Judging from the continuous use of the horn by the coach driver, the occasional swerve and the occasional sharp braking, there had been plenty to collide with. So this was excellent. The other members of the party seemed similarly elated. All for their own reasons no doubt. Indeed, the only small flies in the ointment were not knowing where they were or what was now going to happen, and from some of the ladies in the group, the beginnings of mumblings about their apparent remoteness from any toilet facilities. There had been those two and a half hours on the road, and for some, their bladder capacity was now at its limit.

'This way,' announced Sujan. 'The luggage will come.'

'Where are we going?' asked Pauline.

'To the water.'

'Ah,' she acknowledged, and then clearly chose not to

pursue the subject of toilets. But Brian expected her to broach it when they eventually found this "water" – which he hoped was not too far away. It was now exceedingly hot, and nowhere was there any shade.

It wasn't far. No more than two hundred yards and there was the promised aqueous medium, a stretch of water that could have been a wide river or a small bit of the sea with a big island in it forming the far bank. Brian had no real concept of the Sundarbans at this stage, and he couldn't tell which it was. Nor could he tell how they were going to travel on the water. There was no tin boat in sight and just a virtually empty quayside (surfaced with bricks) and neither were there any public conveniences. Pauline spoke again. She had Yvonne and Tina in attendance, both looking concerned.

'Sujan,' she started, 'are there any toilets... before we set off... It's just...'

'On the boat,' replied Sujan. 'There.'

He was now pointing to a vessel that was moored a little way along the quayside. It was not a tin boat and it had clearly been discounted by everybody in the party as being much, much bigger than they had expected.

'On that?' questioned Pauline. 'We're going on that?'

'Yes,' confirmed Sujan. 'That's our boat for the next few days. It's called the "M B Sundari", and it has two lavatories.'

People looked stunned – either by the size of the boat or by the incredible news that they would never be more than seconds away from a water closet. It was a lot to take in.

Brian's surprise was not at the availability of lavatories but at the size – and the style – of the boat.

It was about thirty feet long, constructed of wood (anything up to a century ago), had a top deck with a wheelhouse at its centre, and below this deck and running virtually its full length, a line of square portholes. The below-deck cabin was clearly capacious and well able to accommodate a pair of convenience-type pedestals. As became apparent later, there was even a galley down there as well – and the master's living and sleeping arrangements. This was a serious boat.

The luggage was now with them, so it was now time to examine the boat at closer quarters. They all moved along the quayside, Sujan in the lead, the Nature-seekers following, and in the rear, a couple of young kids and their baggage tricycles. They were clearly the village stevedores, dependent for a few rupees on the tiny stream of traffic that used this quayside, and eager to earn a few more rupees by loading the baggage onto the boat themselves. This was not allowed. Sujan held them back and invited the Nature-seekers to board while the boat's own crew tackled the luggage.

This boarding was achieved by way of the boat's narrow prow. One stepped carefully onto this, and then two steps later, one climbed a tiny set of stairs to the side of the cabin entrance, to find oneself in the "passenger area". This was the space on the top deck, in front of the wheelhouse and covered by a blue awning. It was also equipped with ten brown plastic chairs that were arranged in a rough U shape facing out over the front of the boat. For the next few days the reduced band of Nature-seekers were to become forward-facing mariners whose duties would be restricted to those of lookouts – for anything that showed itself before the progress of their craft. It didn't sound like too arduous a task.

Soon the luggage had been stowed, the facilities had been utilised, and the Nature-seekers were ensconced on their plastic seats. It was time to cast off. For Brian this was a wonderful experience. Not only was the nastiness of urban and "rural" West Bengal now behind him, but he was about to embark on a journey across water unhindered and unencumbered by any sort of life-jacket! In complete contrast to his experience on the country boat on the Brahmaputra, where each expedition entailed his being constricted in an awful orange strait-jacket, here there was nothing. Health and Safety had simply not got here, a fact that was reinforced beyond doubt by the state of the boat's life-belts. There were six of these, all within easy reach of the Nature-seekers. But whilst easily reachable they were certainly not easily deployable. All of them were on the rather decorative railings that surrounded the upper deck, and they were tied to these railings – with lots of string and lots of knots. Brian reckoned that it would take ten minutes and three broken finger nails to release any of them. By which time whoever was in the water would either be full of this water or alternatively inside a crocodile and full of just terminal trepidation. They were clearly simply for show and not ever to be used. Brian was delighted.

They were now under way. The M B Sundari was floating down the placid waters of what had now been confirmed as a river – and tea was being served. Brian was delighted all over again.

The "cook's assistant" had appeared from the cabin beneath with two large trays on which there were cups and saucers, spoons and two big tea pots – and for those who did not imbibe of this beverage, a coffee pot as well. There was even a plate of biscuits. Sujan then took control. He had seated himself on a plastic chair just by the cabin door. So he could now stand on the foredeck below the upper deck and play mother. He poured out the teas and coffees, added milk and sugar as requested and then handed round the cups – while Dennis handed round the biscuits. It was all unavoidably charming and at the same time all rather surreal. This wasn't the Norfolk Broads. This was the Sundarbans – where tigers roam – and where the concept of an English late-morning tea was probably less than firmly rooted – especially when one was "afloat".

Brian thought all this, and then he thought about the Norfolk Broads. Because, so far, that was his only frame of reference. He had sailed on those beautiful waters when he was a child, and where they were now was not entirely dissimilar. They were on a broad waterway (albeit much broader than any of those in Norfolk) and the waterway flowed through the flattest of landscapes. There were other vessels on this water, although not many, and there were various signs of habitation along its length. It all had the air of settled occupation about it – in a rather pleasant and ordered environment. Just like the Broads back home. But this was where the similarities ended. This gateway into the Sundarbans might have displayed some superficial likeness to the Broads, but that's all it was; very superficial. And the scale was all wrong. As the boat proceeded down the river, Brian began to see that the Sundarbans were on a phenomenally larger scale – and that their inhabitants lived rather more risky lives.

The sides of the river were man-made embankments, some made of just earth reinforced with a palisade of stakes, and many more of earth that had been surfaced with a skin of bricks (no doubt from all those brickworks up the road). Beyond these raised ramparts were trees, palms – and the thatched roofs of houses. But just the roofs. The walls were often not visible. Brian quickly realised that people lived in houses here, which if they were not just at sea level were often just below sea level. They were conducting their lives behind the shelter of a man-made defence, which if it failed would mean the end of their lives. It sounded dramatic but it was true. The Sundarbans environment was not a safe one. Just like those who had carved out a life on the edge of the wayward and unpredictable Brahmaputra, the people who had chosen this place to live had also to accept that their lives were on the edge in more than just a literal sense. The Sundarbans might not be susceptible to flood like the Brahmaputra, but they were even more susceptible to the direct effects of the Monsoon – and to the potentially disastrous effects of cyclones. This was the top of the Bay of Bengal where cyclones were endemic, and the Sundarbans were in reality no more than low-lying specks of land parked in the way of these cyclones, some of them populated by people whose defences against these excesses of nature were just those they could construct by hand – surfaced with some hand-made bricks if they could afford it. It was a very scary thought.

Presently, however, it just seemed very peaceful. The sun shone, a small breeze blew through the boat, and the world sailed past, a world of more and more embankments and more and more water. The river had now joined another, and the waterway had become more like an inland sea – which in many ways it was. The Nature-seekers were now entering the Sundarbans proper, a network of huge mangrove-covered islands separated by channels that were more saltwater sea than they were freshwater rivers – and where wildlife took over from hard life...

Here was an example of it: a whiskered tern sitting on a buoy in the middle of the flow. And there was another: a collared kingfisher. And yet another: a lesser adjutant stork taking to the air from the side of the river – and looking like he had never taken to the air before.

And so it went on. Until at last, after two hours of enforced but pleasant idleness, the Nature-seekers had their first view of their very own island, the place where they would now be based and from where, over the next few days, they would sail out in their oversized boat to find whatever they could find. It was clearly a very large island; it looked like an infinite stretch of land along the waterway and could have been the mainland itself. But it wasn't. It was "Bali Island". No, not that one, just this rather less well known one off the coast of India. It looked very inviting. It was green and in some places there were natural mangrove beaches rather than embankments. And facing it, across the channel, there was another infinitely long island, upon which there were no embankments at all, just uninterrupted mangroves. Presumably that was part of the reserve, as opposed to Bali Island, which was home to a number of people. Brian didn't know how many, but then Lynn asked Sujan whether he knew. And he did.

'Forty thousand,' he replied immediately.

'Forty thousand!' shrieked Lynn. 'Did you say forty thousand?'

'Well, it may be a little more now. You know how it is.'

There then followed a classic stunned silence. All the Nature-seekers knew their destination was an island in the Sundarbans, and clearly all of them had developed a vague mental picture of this island. It would be green, hot, small, and isolated – just like most of the other islands Nature-seekers tended to visit. And it would have a few villages on it maybe, in which would live a few people. But just a few. No way would there be forty thousand of them. Hell, that was as many people as lived in Droitwich. And Nature-seekers never went there...

Then it struck Brian. He had just about realised that the

Sundarbans easily dwarfed the Norfolk Broads, but he now realised just how pygmy this English attraction was in comparison to this vast expanse of mangroves and water. This place was truly gigantic, and it was a place made up of islands many of which were large enough on their own to accommodate the whole of the English Broads if not most of the rest of Norfolk as well. They were certainly large enough to accommodate thousands of people – and a handful of visiting Nature-seekers. And these Nature-seekers would need more than a small tin boat to explore them. They would need a much bigger boat, one with plenty of room, one with shelter and with refreshment facilities – and one with loos. In fact, just like the one they were on now. How fortunate they were.

Fortunate also that they had arrived at Bali Island at high tide. This seemed to make the master's job of bringing his boat into the landing-stage that much easier, a landing-stage that looked a little like a low Mayan mound. It was more of the ubiquitous embankment, but this time surfaced in sloping paving stones with a very creditable imitation of a Mayan staircase running up its centre. As the Nature-seekers disembarked their craft and climbed this staircase, it became apparent that the top of the embankment was paved with bricks and that it provided a view of the rice fields beyond – and of a few simple homes. This was mud and cow dung territory again. And by the looks of it, a territory with a fairly desperate degree of poverty. There was no ugliness here, just order and elegance. Brian was delighted, although he suspected that the locals might have settled for a little less charm and a little more wealth.

The party of visitors now followed Sujan along the embankment for about two hundred yards until he stopped at a set of steps leading down its land-side to a simple wooden gate. This, he explained, with an almost straight face, was the entrance to their camp and the gate was to keep the tigers out. It would, of course, not. Brian could have stepped over it with a bit of an effort; a tiger would not even have noticed it. Everybody laughed, but Brian was more intent on those steps than the gate. Looking here, from the top of the embankment, down into the grounds of their camp on one side and to the waters of the Bay of Bengal on the other, it was quite clear that there was no difference whatsoever in their levels. If this embankment failed during the night they would need floats on their beds.

But that was unlikely. Indeed Brian quickly convinced himself that such an event was in the realms not just of the unlikely but of the highly unlikely, and he now turned his attention to his immediate surroundings. Everyone was now in the camp, being greeted by its manager and having a good look round. It wasn't a very large place. There was a central, open-sided dining room built of bamboo, mud and thatch, and on the other side of a small concrete-lined pond, three small huts of similar construction, albeit closed-sided and with solar panels. Beyond the dining room was a concrete water tower, a kitchen and the manager's and guides' accommodation, and on its far side was a large oblong-shaped lagoon crossed by a bamboo bridge. This was the route to two further huts and not much else. The Nature-seekers therefore filled the camp completely: two to a hut and ten to a dining room. Brian had wanted it no other way, and whilst it was exactly what he had expected, he was still relieved. He would have detested the idea of any "strangers" spoiling the integrity of his group – and providing all sorts of concerns at meal times. As it was there was no such warping of his karma, and he was able to sit down for his first lunch on Bali Island confident in the knowledge that everybody around the single long table was of a sufficiently known status to provide just company and no serious concerns whatsoever.

The meal was simple. It was a relative of those enjoyed on the Sukapha: rice, vegetable curry, fish curry and some watery dahl. It was perfect. And even though the heat of the day was now intense, Brian had no trouble in finishing it. Or the beer he had with it. And he was now ready for the afternoon.

This started in his and Sandra's room, where a modicum of unpacking was achieved and where the controls to the lights and the ceiling fan were investigated. The fan was essential. The room was pretty small and without the fan on, pretty stifling. So was the bathroom. This was large-phone-booth size, and with only a very small window for ventilation it became very sweat-inducing very quickly. It also induced the arrival of a certain sort of insect into Brian's holiday; on the wall behind its door were two mosquitoes! Yes, here were the first mosquitoes he had seen in India and the first he was now keen to deal with. He retreated into the bedroom of the cabin and took from the bedside table a red can. It was the can that claimed it brought death to cockroaches and was therefore not very good news for mosquitoes or indeed humans either. Brian would use it with care, a quick squirt into the bathroom, an even quicker closing of the bathroom door and then a rapid exit from the hut – and then from Bali Island itself. For conveniently, all the Nature-seekers were now required to board the boat again and set out for the Sundarbans Tiger Reserve's "Office of the Reserve Officer" to register their presence in this sensitive and protected area. Albeit no one was interested in protecting mosquitoes.

The trip to the Reserve Officer's Office took about forty

minutes. For most of this time their boat was skirting the island opposite Bali Island, which was indeed part of the much larger reserve area and which was therefore lacking in any sort of embankment work, houses or other constructions, and indeed any sign of humanity at all – other than a stretch of insubstantial netting along the mangroves on its shores. This apparently was to deter tigers. Whilst they were very welcome to go wherever they wanted to in the reserve itself, here or anywhere else where an island in the reserve faced a populated island across a channel, there was a very firm consensus that they should be discouraged from "paying a visit". This netting was a deterrent, a low-tech attempt to dissuade them from swimming across the channel and into the lives of the locals. And as they could swim very well, this wasn't necessarily a bad idea. Indeed, Sujan believed they could swim up to twenty kilometres, based on the recent observation of a Sundarbans tiger midway across a channel of this width and still going strong. This made Brian think of the less than one kilometre channel between this netted island and their own island of Bali – and that small wooden gate. Perhaps Sujan's earlier comments shouldn't have been regarded as entirely humorous, especially when one observed how often the netting petered out when it encountered the entrance to a creek on the island – which presumably would have made an ideal launch-point for any self-respecting swimming man-eater...

Brian's reservations (concerning the proximity of the reservation) stayed firmly in place when he then spotted the location of the Reserve Officer's Office. This was on the bank of the next island along, across a channel between the two, and its single outstanding feature from the vantage point of the boat was its twelve-foot high chain-link fencing. There was a small landing-stage and a protected walkway leading into what could only be described as a caged area, where, unlike in normal cage situations, it was the humans on the inside and the animals outside. They clearly took these tigers very seriously indeed.

Brian was now on the landing-stage – looking at oysters. The boat had been secured to its mooring and the Nature-seekers had been warned to mind their step on the slippery landing (it was now low tide and much of the landing that had been underwater was now exposed) and to make sure they had a look at the oysters that lived on the landing's concrete legs and that were now similarly exposed. Brian had his look and was suitably impressed. The legs were covered in oysters. There must have been thousands of them – which presumably meant they were either inedible or they fell within the protection of the reserve. More likely the latter, Brian decided. After all, who's ever heard of inedible oysters?

Inside the cage there was a little shrine, some faded posters on some notice boards to tell you what birds and animals you might see (other than tigers) and there were some nondescript buildings, one of which must have been the Office of the Reserve Officer. Brian didn't know. One of the boat's crew had disappeared with everyone's passports and was now taking care of the registration – whilst Sujan took care of the party.

He was clearly keen to show them the Sundarbans reserve – in miniature. This was a concrete model of the Indian Sundarbans in their entirety sitting in a fifteen-foot concrete square. At the top of the square, which was painted blue on its base to represent the sea, were raised irregular blocks of white. These represented the Indian and Bangladeshi mainlands and the (non-reserve) populated islands off their shores. Below these white blocks, and representing the reserve proper, were island-shaped blocks in yellow, green and red, packed very closely together with blue channels running between them. It looked like a massive jigsaw where the jigsaw pieces had been moved just a little way apart – as there was a great deal more land in the Sundarbans reserve, and therefore more colourful blocks, than there was sea and therefore blue-painted channels. The yellow and green blocks were near the white blocks (one of which was Bali Island) and were the islands in the reserve which were "open" to visitors. That is to say one could sail around them and stop off at one of these cage arrangements wherever they were situated. The red blocks, which were in a majority, were towards the bottom of the square, well away from the white, and these represented those parts of the reserve that were completely out of bounds and where only scientists and professional naturalists were allowed. Brian was reassured at the size of their majority.

It was now time to move on – still within the cage. This soon became an exercise in utilising any available shade (it was now simply scorching), seeing very little in terms of wildlife through the cage sides, and seeing just a canopy of various mangrove trees from the top of a lookout. There was, however, something to see at its base: a group of puzzled looking Indians who had gathered to see some whities. This Office of the Officer compound was also the site of the government-run "hostel" in the Sundarbans, where a dribble of visitors from Kolkata came to… well, Brian wasn't sure why they came. Maybe to see tigers. But certainly not to enjoy the experience of the hostel itself. This was constructed out of brick, wood and corrugated iron and had the air of "condemned, dangerous, keep out" about it, and it really did look as though it might collapse at any moment. Thank God, thought Brian, for a mud and thatch hut with a ceiling-fan.

Everybody was now clearly knackered, with barely enough energy left to cough. So it was decided to return to the boat and drift back to camp. This was a good decision. They were just in time for some late-afternoon tea (with a different variety of sweet biscuits) and well in time for their first view of a Sundarbans sunset. This was all pink and grey and completely fabulous. Brian and most of the others took endless photos of it, and Dennis and Derek's video cameras were soon in danger of overheating.

There was also a special sighting as the light was failing: an Irrawaddy river dolphin. It slipped out of the surface of the water. But only just. This new species of cetacean for the Nature-seekers was even more reserved than its Gangetic cousin and restricted itself to just the slightest emergence from the depths; a brief glimpse of the top of its shiny back as it broke the surface and that was it. Show over. Needless to say, even such a fleeting view was exciting. This chap was a rarity. And not just because he was a long way from the Irrawaddy. He was rare full stop. So rare that a full stop might be what his whole species would soon come to. So not just exciting but really upsetting as well.

Indeed, it wasn't until they were back in camp that Brian's mood was restored to its normal good health. He and Sandra had returned to their hut and had examined their bathroom. And success! There, on the floor, were two dead mosquitoes – and no other live ones in sight. There was also an enormous dead cockroach, which could have been regarded as a bonus or as a bit of regrettable collateral damage. Brian's view lent towards the latter, Sandra's to the former. But they didn't fall out about it. Instead they showered and changed as quickly as they could so that they could adjourn to the dining area and slake their sore throats as soon as possible.

The agent of slaking was gin and soda. This wasn't their agent of choice. But the camp only had a licence for beer. So the gin had been acquired in Kolkata by Sujan on their behalf – together with a supply of soda – as tonic, quite remarkably, could not be obtained there. No wonder, thought Brian, that the Empire hadn't lasted; mosquitoes in bathrooms, no Imperial aerosols – and no easily digestible quinine. It was probably all a plot. It was also the ruination of good gin. Soda might be a happy companion for Campari, but when it came to the juniper juice, only tonic would do.

Nevertheless, both Brian and Sandra managed with the soda surprisingly well. It was, after all, wet and cold and ideal for throats which were dry and bodies which were hot. It also left room for some beer, which was secured just in time to accompany the evening meal. This was curry as usual – but with the addition of a bowl of chips to supply some necessary ballast to the meal – and a bowl of salt – for tomorrow's sweat. The day had been roasting. The Nature-seekers had been sweltering – profusely. And they would be again tomorrow. The salt was essential and it proved a popular choice.

So too did an early night. Coaching, boating, coughing and sweating are together exhausting, especially for middle-aged people. By ten, the camp was in darkness, its occupants were in their beds, and for all Brian knew, a tiger was sniffing at the gate.

Although he suspected it wasn't.

12.

rian awoke wanting a shower. No tigers had disturbed his night but the heat certainly had. He had slept on and off within a mosquito net, a device that may or may not have been necessary, but one that certainly added to the airless nature of the cabin. He was now lying on his bed slicked with sweat, and he longed for a sluice in the bathroom. Sandra had suffered similarly, and it was she who made it to the waterfall first. This wasn't a problem. It just made Brian appreciate the water-borne relief even more when it came. Although the relief was short-lived. As soon as he started to dress, even though he did this under the fan with the power full on, the perspiration returned immediately. He needed to finish his toilet and exit the cabin as soon as possible. It was still only 5.30 in the morning and it had to be cooler outside.

It was, but only marginally so. The Sundarbans, at this time of year at least, were clearly never cool. And how much hotter would it get?

Brian thought about this as he consumed his breakfast, an Indian concoction with a plain omelette. It was completely delicious and soon extinguished any concerns he had about the heat. Or maybe it was the discussion at the breakfast table, the talk about noises in the night and the sighting of a snake in the lagoon – and the unguarded chit-chat in general that had now taken root in the group. There was a very good feeling in the air and everybody was clearly intent on enjoying themselves, but not on their own. This holiday had now turned into a properly "joint and several" expedition where all the members of the party were eager that their companions enjoyed it as much as they did themselves. It was a good way to start the day.

This began in earnest at 6.30 when their boat cast off. They had boarded it via the Mayan steps at low tide. This had entailed a transit across their lower reaches and therefore an encounter with the dangers of slime. All had succeeded without mishap in this endeavour other than Lynn. She, as one of the last to make the transit, had taken it upon herself to demonstrate the perils of slippery surfaces to the rest of the group by losing her footing and descending onto her bum parts with an almost theatrical thud. Her bum parts, it has to be said, being significantly younger than those of most of the others in the party, were a little better designed for this opening gambit. But nevertheless, her gesture was still appreciated by all her companions. From now on, everybody would be more careful than ever as they tackled these treacherous landing-stage surfaces. And all thanks to Lynn. And to her bum. It said everything there was to say about how selfless people had now become in their desire to act for the group. To enhance the experience of all its members – to the point of protecting them from harm – even if this was at a cost to themselves. It made Brian feel really English for the first time since he'd been in India.

The boat proceeded slowly. Brian doubted it could do otherwise. But this was fine. It gave all the Nature-seekers not just a great view of the Sundarbans and their ubiquitous mangroves, but it also gave them all the time they needed to attune themselves to the pace of this place, a pace that was somewhere between dead slow and stop. Nothing moved. The water was smooth. The mangroves were still. And even the breeze through the boat seemed hardly to stir. It was peaceful and then some more. They were sailing past some of the Sundarbans reserve proper where no people came and where little happened – in human terms. There was just the growth of the trees and the life of those creatures that lived off them and in them, and of these there were few. Mangrove forests are very different to tropical rain forests. Only a handful of animals can thrive within them and even the birds that can prosper here are limited, not just in their numbers but also in the number of their species. The Sundarbans, it was becoming apparent, were an experience but not a wildlife hotspot.

Brian minded this not in the least. He reckoned he could have sat on the front of this boat for days just looking at what was around him. And what was around him was a series of vast islands, all covered in those famous mangroves, with at their edges, smooth banks of mud studded with mangrove "knees". These were the strange spiky excrescences of the "front-line" mangroves, the handful of mangrove species out of the forty or so mangrove types that lived here, which could withstand this very on-the-edge existence, and whose muddy roots formed an eerie intertwined backdrop to the banks themselves. These roots also provided a home – for a number of crabs, for the occasional adventurous mud-skipper and for the even more occasional wader. For birds here were certainly not common, and minutes could pass on the boat without any at all being seen.

Again, this wasn't a problem for Brian, or for most of the group. The very infrequency of bird sightings made them all the more rewarding when they were made. And they provided a real challenge for everybody – and a real opportunity. For we are now back to those "group dynamics", everybody's desire to enhance his or her neighbours' enjoyment. And what better way than to announce that in the distance, along the bank of the channel, there was a white-bellied sea eagle. So by the time it came into full view, Derek and Dennis would already be in record-mode with their videos, Pauline and Yvonne would have selected the right camera or the right lens or whatever, and everyone else would know where to point their binoculars.

This worked very well. There were soon constant sightings being announced on board the boat, with the "one o'clock", "eleven o'clock" and so on directions becoming almost reliable, even when offered by the less spatially aware members of the party. And no matter of what gender, everybody was bloody good at spotting things. This was a well seasoned group, made up of amateur naturalists who between them had spent literally thousands of hours looking for the slightest movement of the smallest creature in order to satisfy their desire to see a particular bird or a particular small critter, and who almost without fail could be relied upon to distinguish between the motion of a fluttering leaf and that of a passerine's tail. They were good, and with the stimulation of this mutual society of literal Nature-seekers, they were very good indeed.

In fact, they were so good they reinforced Brian's long-held belief that if the authorities in Britain insisted on retaining the ridiculous jury system there, then they should at least have the decency to draw the juries from the ranks of just bird watchers. His reasoning was along these lines:

The jury system was an overhang from the times when a peasant population had to be given confidence in a new legal system by their own involvement in it. And as they all knew what a pig was and what stealing was, there was a fairly good chance that they'd be able to get their heads round a charge of pig stealing and some sort of real justice might be achieved. Sadly those times have long since passed and the jury system is now nothing more than a very inefficient and very unreliable machine, the principal purpose of which is not to secure justice but instead to enrich lawyers.

Brian had never forgotten that old exam question; 'Either I get better justice by paying Sir Timothy Arbuthnot twenty guineas than by paying Mr Bunk two guineas, or I do not. If I do, justice is bought, contrary to Magna Carta. If I do not, the legal profession is obtaining its money under false pretences. Discuss.' He had also never forgotten the answer: 'Justice is bought (contrary to Magna Carta) because Sir Timothy Arbuthnot can confuse, mislead and cajole a jury more ably than can Mr Bunk – and that's why he is paid so much more.' He could not, however, if he did not have a jury. Or if he had a jury made up only of bird watchers...

Then, his advocacy could be ignored. The bird watchers, rather than being duped by his words, would instead focus on the impact of these words on the accused and on the witnesses. They would study these various players in the courtroom, and they would observe their very smallest movements... They would watch their faces and their bodies and they would be on the lookout for the slightest tick, the slightest flicker of doubt, the slightest flutter of eyes. Or even a discreet shift in buttocks. Or anything at all that might indicate where the truth might lie and who was and who wasn't telling it. In this way they would establish an individual's guilt or innocence free from the distortion of advocacy and all through their highly developed sense of observation and their ability to spot that tiniest of movements.

The Nature-seekers aboard this boat would be ideal. They were all intelligent, they were all (common) sensible, and they were all mature without being senile – a combination of qualities which in themselves would put them at the pinnacle of jury quality. But on top of this, and critical to their role as an "observing jury", it would be difficult to find a collection of other souls who would be quite so proficient in the art of micro-surveillance. There were twenty eyes here that would be able to see the truth in a courtroom within no time at all, and that might prove as much a problem for the earning power of the legal profession as they would for those other miscreants in the dock.

But for now it was not the truth they were seeking, just the whereabouts of avian wildlife, and Brian's new criminal justice system would have to wait for another day. In any event, who would want to serve in it? Better to use those skills in the field than in the so-called halls of justice. Far more sensible and far more rewarding. For example, one might see a little egret, like the one up that creek there. 'Or how about that rose-ringed parakeet there? And isn't that a pied kingfisher on that branch? And look, just behind him, it's a white-throated... And actually isn't that a pair of them?'

And so it went on until Tina, who was sitting immediately in front of the wheelhouse, announced that she had spotted a new landing-stage. It was their destination, another caged-in lookout where they would disembark (carefully) to scan the forest for other wildlife.

However, it all turned out to be rather disappointing. The lookout was not in the caged area itself but at the end of a very long raised walkway leading off this area and protected on both sides by more amazingly high chain-link. It was so hot now that nothing was stirring. The walk to the lookout therefore proved fruitless, as did the view from the top of its tower. The only point of interest was the tower itself. It tilted. It had been built with concrete, presumably vertically, but like the leaning tower of Pisa, it was vertical no more. The weight of the concrete had clearly been far too great for the earth on which it rested, and the tower was now in slow-motion toppling-over mode; slow enough, Brian hoped, that it would not have fallen to the ground before they'd left it. It didn't. But it did provide a very strange sensation as one climbed its stairs – and an unmistakeable sensation of intense heat on one's head as one gazed from its top. The sun was now fiery. It beat down with an almost vindictive intensity. So much so, in fact, that most of the party soon sought refuge from its rays in a small patch of shade at the tower's base, and there they stood sweating profusely. Brian was clearly not alone in having lost interest in the invisible fauna – and having instead developed a longing for the relief of some liquid refreshment.

Sujan got the message and soon he was leading his charges back to the boat and to a welcome round of tea and coffee. Much revived, the party settled down for the return journey. Dennis had a doze, Alan applied sun lotion to his exposed knees and almost everybody else indulged in some serious coughing. Whatever they had all caught was not to be relieved by caffeine or tannin or by the heat of the day. In fact the heat seemed to make things worse. Maybe all that throat lubrication was leaking out through their skins, and their throats were suffering more than ever.

Nevertheless nobody succumbed to the affliction with terminal consequences, and the full party was still intact as the boat pulled up to the Mayan steps again. It was now nearly full tide, so disembarkation was not fraught with quite the degree of danger they'd experienced on the way out. Nevertheless Lynn's demonstration had been taken to heart, and the Nature-seekers didn't so much walk up the staircase in one single action as plod up it in a series of slow and deliberate steps. Nobody wanted to injure him or herself before lunch.

This meal proved as agreeable as ever; curry under powerful fans and with beer. What more could one ask for? Well, in this heat, a post-prandial period of complete inactivity under another fan. All the Nature-seekers retired to their cabins, and if they had any sense they did exactly what Brian and Sandra did, which was to put the room fan on to full blast, take off all their clothes and lie as still as possible on the bed not even thinking about England. It really was the only thing to do in what was turning out to be the hottest day so far on their Indian odyssey. And they needed the rest. Nature-seeking was due to kick off again at 3.30 sharp. There was another lookout to visit.

On the way to this one Brian thought he saw a crocodile. It was no more than a glimpse of not even a small movement, but just something that caught his attention in the shadows of a small creek. But he'd called it. It's what everybody did now. And the master of the boat began to turn his vessel around to make another pass of the creek's entrance and so confirm the spot. Brian immediately felt exposed and nervous. Had he really seen anything at all?

Initially it appeared he hadn't. The mangrove bank had a number of small creeks along its length, and he couldn't even remember in which one he'd seen his croc. But then there it was; not a big one but a real one and the first they'd seen. Bill made a point of congratulating him. Brian's indiscretions on the subject of snipes had clearly been completely forgotten and he was therefore free to bathe himself in what was now the unanimous gratitude of the company. He was unduly delighted and now keener than ever to spot a tiger as well…

That achievement wasn't forthcoming. Instead he had to console himself with the sight of a water monitor – spotted first by Sujan as they approached the landing-stage of the next lookout location. It was brown, about five feet long, and it was creeping along the muddy bank. Maybe, thought Brian, it was a good omen for this new destination.

He was right. Where the previous lookout had furnished them with only potential heatstroke and not even scraps of wildlife, this one furnished them with a veritable banquet of the stuff. It overlooked a large excavated lagoon beyond its cage perimeter, and as soon as they arrived there so too did the animals and the birds. There were three more monitors waddling their way towards the lagoon's water along a cleared path, and there, just within the cover of the forest, were some deer. Then they emerged into full view, three beautiful spotted deer, grazing unconcernedly at the water's edge and, in the sunlight of the late afternoon, looking more beautiful than was possible. They were truly exquisite, and Brian thought, truly exposed. If there was a tiger about, one of them might not be grazing for much longer. And as much as Brian wanted to see a tiger, he knew very well that he didn't want to see one in action. Especially if it involved one of these gorgeous creatures. He knew how he was and how he'd reacted to a leopard kill in Botswana. The cat had taken an adult baboon. He hadn't seen the kill itself, just the post-kill feeding at close quarters. And to see the butchering in such bloody detail was, he had to admit, fascinating, but it was also a little stomach-churning. In particular there were the sounds of the butchering, the sounds you never hear on a wildlife programme on the telly, the sounds of teeth on bone and teeth through bone. No, tigers could wait. Indefinitely if they liked. Brian was quite content with these grazers, and with what else was on show...

For the trees around the lookout were full of birds. There were oriental magpie-robins, jungle mynahs, a rare forest wagtail – and a fabulous orange-breasted green pigeon.

How these pigeon types did so well around the world, Brian had never been able to understand. They seemed so unwieldy and so dim, as though they were just meals on wings for any other bird or animal that had a taste for flesh. But despite this they thrived – in all sorts of forms in all sorts of environments. And even here in these inhospitable mangrove forests. And not just any old pigeon either, but an awkwardly and inadequately named orange-breasted green one. Its name just didn't do it justice. It was stunning. All in all, thought Brian, wasn't it a fact that nature was simply totally and unbelievably splendid?

The journey back to camp proved uneventful. But it made Brian think. For after another round of biscuits and a brief exchange on the subject of forest wagtails, the company of Nature-seekers subsided into near silence. This was partly due to exhaustion and partly the result of there being ever fewer birds about and therefore fewer opportunities to call them. It wasn't quite dusk yet, but at this time of day the Sundarbans seemed more deserted than ever.

People dealt with this hiatus in various ways. Brian was still content to scour the banks and to examine every creek in the vain hope of catching sight of a tiger. Lynn and Derek seemed similarly disposed. But other members of the group appeared to become withdrawn or even tharn. And Dennis nodded off again and Alan resorted to a crossword. There was definitely some empty time here – for at least some of the party – just as there'd been empty time during the hottest part of the day, when everybody had retreated to their cabins. Furthermore, this empty time would be with them tomorrow and again the next day. They would be spending a lot more time on the boat, some of it without the stimulus of wildlife. And they would have to retire from the heat of the day at the beginning of each afternoon. And it was this prospect of more "redundant" time that triggered Brian's thoughts – his thoughts about his books…

Unbeknownst to anyone in the party other than Sandra, Brian was an amateur author. Since retiring, like many other poor souls, he had poured his heart into writing, and like the vast majority of these poor souls, he had failed to arouse the interest of a single publisher with the end results of his efforts. He had therefore become more bloody minded than ever and had used some of his own money to publish his own work. Needless to say, his publishing role consisted of little more than organising the printing process for his books and then their post-printing storage – in his garage. The world had not cried out for his works. Possibly because, aside from any questions about their merits, the world didn't know about them. Even though he'd constructed a perfectly serviceable website on the internet thingy, where not only could you read a synopsis of each work, but you could even order the works and pay for them using Paypal. So anyway, Brian had capitulated. He'd long ago accepted that his writings could not be converted into a commercial success and that the only way to empty his garage was to enter the arena of literary munificence. That is to say, Brian gave his books away – to anyone who would take them. And whilst most of those who were on the receiving end of this generosity failed to read them, some did and some even expressed some delight in them. So Brian continued with his giving. And if there were people around with time on their hands, he would continue it now…

He had a number of his titles with him. They made up half the weight of his bag. A few were his full length novels (all three of them). But most were copies of his short works. There were just two of these: "*Crats*", which was set on a South Sea island and dealt with the ruination of its civilisation by bureaucracy (It was a parody of the same process underway in Britain within the European Union), and "*Eggshell in Scrambled Eggs*", which was a set of essays and poems on some of Brian's pet hates. This latter one was intended to be humorous.

So, tonight, during drinks before dinner, Brian would do the deed. He would throw caution to the wind and he would deliver a copy of "*Crats*" and a copy of "*Eggshell*" to each of the other four couples and the same to Sujan.

When he got back to camp, he made his preparations. He unpacked the required number of works and he had a quick flick through them to assure himself that they contained within their pages nothing that might offend or affront a native of India and in particular a native like Sujan. And with Jim no longer in the party, he had already decided that he was on pretty safe ground with all the Nature-seekers as well. So he was now ready to go.

When he then finally made his unscheduled literary delivery in the dining room, there was mild surprise and a degree of confusion. He'd handed them round whilst explaining that they could be used as an antidote against tedium – in the early afternoon or during a "flat" phase on the boat. But he had failed to make it clear that he had written them himself. This lot were on first name terms only, so his surname on the cover meant nothing to them. It was only when Sujan made the connection with his knowledge of the passenger list that all was made clear, and then the Nature-seekers looked more confused than ever. Or was that alarm on their faces? In the light of the dining room it was difficult to tell.

It was also difficult to discuss the books further. How could they? Nobody had read them. So it was now imperative that Brian dealt with what could be mounting discomfort for the whole party by leading them somewhere else. And where better than into some bird-listing?

'OK, Sujan,' he started. 'Why don't we do some listing? I need to sort out my kingfishers.'

He didn't really. But it sounded a plausible sort of opener, and it did the trick. His masterpieces were laid aside and the Nature-seekers began to address their notes and their lists – while Brian addressed his aperitif. He was now feeling rather abashed, as was to be expected, and he was wondering how one turned back time. If he could somehow manage that, not only could he not hand out the books, but he could also not have left Kolkata without some tonic. There must have been some there. And he wouldn't now be having to cope with this soda and gin compromise. Mind, it was still wet and it was beginning to taste almost pleasant.

The bird listing over, another curry arrived. It was scrumptious, as were the chips on the side and the salt, both of which proved as popular as ever with Dennis. Maybe it was his overconsumption of this staple and this condiment that was making him doze all the time. And maybe for the others, it was the salt that was bringing out their right-wing tendencies. For the conversation this evening around the dining table revealed a number of illiberal prejudices. Nothing that was actually fascist, but just the sort of beliefs held by many "mature and world-weary" thinkers.

It had started with Sujan's concerns about the tiger population, here and in Assam, and how he suspected that their reported numbers were now more a matter of politics than of science. Essentially they were now disappearing at such an alarming rate that their decline could not be officially acknowledged. Instead there was a "conspiracy of optimism", which apart from being dishonest was positively dangerous for their survival as a species. This debate then led on to the threats they faced from poaching and the degree of "robustness" that should be adopted in tackling the poachers, and whether this was currently anywhere near what was needed to deter them effectively. Nobody had much to say in favour of a "light touch" approach.

Dwindling tiger numbers then led on to dwindling personal wealth and the culpability of the financial services industry for this calamity. Here there was a similar reluctance to speak out on behalf of the bankers or the regulators or the responsible politicians, and one or two around the table made some suggestions concerning the bankers that would have seen them meeting a similar fate to those who poached tigers, and it didn't involve anything to do with community service.

The subject of politics was then raised. First of all politics in West Bengal, where the party in power was the Communist Party, and where after the forthcoming elections, Sujan believed it would still be the Communist Party. He explained how it now had such a tight grip on power that it would be almost impossible to dislodge, and how the exercise of this power was now costing this part of the country dear. Why, if you were an international business looking to establish yourself in India, would you choose Kolkata or some other town in a Marxist province, with all that meant in terms of restrictions and corruption, when instead you could set up shop in the more liberal locations of Mumbai or Delhi – or in any one of another thousand locations anywhere outside West Bengal? It was a no-brainer. You didn't come here. And all the Nature-seekers had seen the results of this reluctance to come here: a gruesome capital and an impoverished society within it and around it.

Then it was the turn of British politics, and as everybody in the group clearly held such similar views about their government back home, there was barely any food for serious debate. Instead Alan suggested that there should be a discussion about who might qualify as the very worst British politician of them all. This suggestion was quickly adopted and the initial front runners were soon identified as Blair and Brown. However Bill, on a point of order, succeeded in eliminating Blair. It was wrong, he argued, to regard a man who was now undergoing a process of self-sanctification allied to a quest for unlimited wealth, still to be regarded as any sort of politician. Yvonne then argued that Brown should be similarly barred from the competition. A politician, she claimed, is a person who is versed in the theory of government or the art of government. So how could a man, who had shown himself incapable in every aspect of government, possibly be considered a legitimate politician? He couldn't be, and therefore he was eliminated too.

That left the field open for three other hopefuls: Margaret Beckett who was judged to be pompous and useless, Peter Hain who was considered to be annoying and useless, and Jack Straw who was seen to be simply unprincipled and useless. Hain was dropped quickly; all politicians are annoying and useless to varying degrees, and whilst it was pointed out that he was unnaturally tanned as well, he had to be dumped. There were stronger contenders. Straw looked to be gaining ground, but Pauline made the very obvious case that any politician who submits him or herself to the party system has to be prepared to discard any principles he or she might hold quicker than you can say 'a three line whip'. So he went too. Leaving as the winner of the worst politician of all, the delightful Margaret Beckett, loved by farmers and freedom of information campaigners in equal measure, and someone whose pomposity wasn't only unique in terms of its scale but also remarkable in terms of its lack of justification.

Brian thought Sujan was a little left out of this discussion. How could he know all the names – and what they did in the government? Nevertheless he seemed to be paying close attention and he seemed also to be deriving a great deal of enjoyment from seeing a group of grown-up English people behaving like schoolchildren. Then he spoke.

'Where has that sense of respect for authority gone?' he asked. 'I thought all English people were proud of their institutions and looked up to all those who ran them.'

This produced a look of confusion on the faces of all those present which was on a par with those apparent after Brian's surprise distribution of books. But then Sujan smiled.

'The next thing you'll be telling me is that you don't like Peter Mandelson.'

Brian then realised that Sujan knew infinitely more about British politics and British politicians than any of the rest of them knew about West Bengali politics or even Indian politics. He felt suitably humbled, and then when he remembered that he'd given this erudite man two of his stupid books he felt simply embarrassed. Was there no way he could turn back time?

13.

t had been a marginally cooler night. Brian and Sandra had decided to risk a little more ventilation in their cabin. They had opened all the windows and had relied upon the mosquito screens within them to keep out not just mosquitoes but also any itinerant tigers. This had apparently worked. There was no evidence of tiger intrusion anywhere. And whilst it was just about conceivable that a very dextrous tiger might have made it inside by peeling back the Velcro that held the screens in place, it was certainly not conceivable that he or she would then have been able to reattach it on his or her way out. The chance of that happening was about as high as Sir Alex Ferguson running out of chewing gum or the Queen running out of clean underwear. So effectively no chance at all. Their room really had remained tiger free.

Breakfast, however, was accompanied by animals. The camp dogs had apparently overcome their initial reticence and were now in attendance around the dining table. This, of course, earned them some pieces of omelette and some affectionate stroking. After all, Brits come to India not to carve out an empire anymore, but instead to enjoy India in whatever way they choose – and, if it seems safe, to make friends with dogs. Brian was surprised that this pack of mutts had been so slow off the mark, and that they hadn't exploited this well-known British foible as soon as they'd seen the Nature-seekers arriving in camp. Maybe they'd somehow mistaken them for Koreans. However, he was also sure that they now knew the score and this meant that the Nature-seekers would now have a canine complement whenever and wherever they were in camp. This companion party would be made up of the permanent contingent of one adult bitch and two male puppies and whichever other dogs might be visiting at the time. The camp's own trio were all small and all under-exuberant – although the puppies did occasionally indulge themselves in a slow roil or even a half-hearted run. But one could very easily see that they had already learnt everything there was to know about the enervating effects of extreme heat and the importance of conserving energy. Sundarbans dogs were all destined to be lazy.

Bill didn't join in any of this newly initiated dog-bonding. He'd already explained how he'd once had a less than cuddly experience with a rabid dog in Kenya, and how this had made him wary of all dogs he met abroad. Brian thought that Bill would only have had to give even a rabid dog one of his more belligerent expressions and it would have reconsidered its actions immediately – and would then have run a mile. But at the same time he understood his reservations. Not too many air ambulances had passed overhead and there was always a risk. (That said, the chance of catching anything off these charmers was so infinitesimally small, we are back to the realms of Alex Ferguson's chewing gum and the Queen's drawers again.)

Breakfast, this day, was notable not just for the emergence of the dogs, but it was also notable for the emergence of comments on Brian's books. Yes, some of them had already been opened! Sujan made a reference to one of the characters in

"*Crats*". Lynn admitted she'd dipped into "*Eggshell*" and had been rebuked by Alan for keeping him awake with her laughing. And most incredible of all, Bill said how much he'd enjoyed the item in "*Eggshell*" dealing with macadamia nuts (which reveals how they are an Australian joke on the rest of the world, and are not nuts at all but just bleached kangaroo poo – served up as a delicacy to all those unsuspecting Pomms). Brian was amazed; they hadn't even reached an "empty time" yet, and here were some of his companions reading his works when they should have been getting to sleep. Of course, he was also hugely delighted.

But now it was time for Nature-seeking again, and the day would begin with another visit to the lookout that had proved so fruitful the day before. Before it became too hot again.

The party arrived there after an hour or so of drifting along the channels and an hour or so of not spotting tigers. Instead there were just birds, crabs, mud-skippers – and a solitary dolphin. It was quite enough for Brian, who, if the truth were known, was still more absorbed in his books and their initial reception. But he didn't let it show. He still maintained a careful watch on the mangroves and called out everything and anything he saw, including quite a few mud-skippers.

Now, however, there was a chance of seeing something more, maybe something none of them had seen before. And indeed, immediately there was a new sighting; not of a tiger but of *the* Tiger. They had landed at the lookout's other landing-stage, where parked above the level of the water, and clearly never intended to have any further dealings with the water, was a derelict catamaran with painted on its stern the word: "Tiger".

Sujan explained how this vessel had been commissioned by the reserve authorities (at an astronomical cost) as a patrol boat for the whole of the Sundarbans, capable of deterring poachers and at the same time gathering all sorts of important scientific information necessary for the maintenance of the reserve's World Heritage status. Unfortunately this capability was never tested as it lacked two further capabilities: the capability of functioning like a real boat and the capability of taking to the water at all without making a measurable addition to global warming. It was essentially unseaworthy and did little more than float, and for the short time it was afloat, it ate more diesel than a pair of Ark Royals did. It had therefore been withdrawn from service before its service had really started, and it now had a new role: that of the most expensive reserve warden's office in India. For that is what it had become – in addition, of course, to its use as a laundry aid. The rigging above its rusting superstructure, as was apparent this morning, now served only as a drying place for the reserve warden's washing. Which meant that if one discounted the office function (on the grounds that it must have been far too hot inside that lump of metal for most of the day to be anywhere near tolerable), that worked out at about a million rupees per foot of clothes line – which must have been some sort of record. Sujan thought that it was probably the worst financial investment ever made in West Bengal, and Brian could only agree. It had to be up there with putting money into a Bernie Madoff fund or into the Sinclair C5. No doubt about it.

Fortunately this wasn't the only new sighting the Nature-seekers made. For when they'd stationed themselves on the lookout tower, they were treated to a variety of new pleasures – and something very special indeed. Because in addition to the appearance of white-breasted waterhens, spotted doves, a common hawk-cuckoo and a greater coucal, there was genuine slice of magic...

Derek had spotted it first. He had been filming a large tree about forty yards from the tower, when something at its base had caught his attention. It was the very slightest of movements. He then forsook his camcorder and instead trained his binoculars on the tree, focusing on where it met the ground and where it was surrounded by leaf litter. He could see nothing. Maybe he'd been mistaken. But no, he knew he'd seen something. It was time to call in Sujan.

Sujan appeared and with Derek's guidance trained his own binoculars on the base of tree. Within seconds he made an announcement, and the announcement was just one word. 'Wryneck,' he said.

This had a remarkable effect. Within just a few more seconds all the Nature-seekers were surrounding him and were studying the foot of the tree with their own binoculars. He had told them where to look and what they were looking for. And as first one and then another of the Nature-seekers located their prize there were gasps and exclamations, and from those who had yet to be successful, groans of desperation. This was time for a truly mutual effort, and all those who had already found the wryneck's exact position were now helping all those who hadn't – until everybody had. There then followed a long period of sustained, ecstatic viewing, where binoculars were only ever renounced in favour of cameras with adequate zooms. Brian had a crack at a few photographs himself, but the tree was a long way away, and his subject was so small and so discreet that it was almost impossible to identify it in the viewfinder. It was more a case of pointing his camera at where he'd thought he'd seen the bird with his binoculars and just hoping that one of the most cryptic birds in the world was still within its scope when he pressed the button. It was. But none of his photos was quite up to publishing standard. He knew that straightaway. He also knew that this sighting would be the highlight of the day. Certainly for him and for Sandra, and, he suspected, for most of the party. Because a wryneck is a quite exceptional creature.

Many people like birds. Even those who are not that interested in them find them pleasing. They are often colourful, they sing, and they are a very visible manifestation of that thing we call nature – as they fly around in the sky or perch on branches. Who could not like them – even accepting that sometimes they might crap on your car or steal your ice-cream? But those are just little wrinkles in what is otherwise a generally very welcome phenomenon: the presence of birds in our environment.

Of course, if the birds are not colourful, they might not attract so much positive attention. Nor will they if they are quiet or if they are difficult to see when in flight or at rest. And if they combine all this visual and behavioural discretion with a small size, an innate shyness, a tendency to move only slowly when on the ground and what can only be described as Grade-A camouflage, they might be overlooked completely, especially if they are few in number. Indeed most people might pass through life without even knowing that they exist, even most people in Britain where the wryneck is found. Conversely, however, for those people who *are* interested in birds, all these characteristics manifesting themselves in a single species is what makes the wryneck such a marvel and such a triumph when they find one. Brian and Sandra had never before seen one, and never in a million years had they expected to see one in a mangrove forest in India, not here in the Sundarbans. But there it was, still pecking around in the leaf litter and still being almost impossible to see.

The wryneck, or to give it its wonderful Latin name: "Jynx Torquilla", is just 16 centimetres long, has a small head, a slim body and grey-brown plumage. It spends much of its time feeding on the ground and when threatened will raise a small crest on its head, spread out its tail and twist its neck from side to side like a snake. And this last action is key to understanding what a wryneck looks like – when viewed from somewhere like a lookout tower in the Sundarbans; it looks like a reptile. This is what had foxed Derek. He had been looking for a bird at the base of that tree, not something which appeared more reptilian than avian. And it had taken Sujan's professional skills to see what it was.

So this is why Brian and all his colleagues were quite so excited. They had within their view a bird, which if not very rare, was still extremely uncommon and extremely difficult to find – anywhere – but also a bird which was discreetly beautiful, superbly cryptic and probably more like a reptile in its movements and it its appearance than any other bird in the world. Their spotting of it wouldn't make the front page of the "*Indian Times*", nor would it be a cause for celebration by the locals, but for Brian and his companions this extended sighting of this remarkable creature was a genuine high point of the whole holiday. In Brian's own mind, it was no less an event than the sighting of that Bengal florican back in Assam or those views of a pied harrier in flight. All three episodes he would remember forever.

There again, he would probably never forget the ants either.

They lived on the boat. They were small and highly opportunistic, and they would appear in large numbers from cracks in the decking whenever food was around. So now, on their way back from the lookout to the camp, Brian had a cup of coffee in one hand, a biscuit in the other, and around his feet, a multitude of insects. They didn't appear to want to bite; they were more interested in biscuit crumbs. But that wasn't entirely correct according to Sujan. The master of the boat lived on his boat – and they bit him in bed at night. For years apparently he'd been trying to get rid of them, but without success, and probably because he carried too many careless and sentimental Brits on his boat, people who would always provide them with food but who would never willingly kill them. Hey, ants have to make a living as well. And if the master was really concerned he'd long ago have banned the biscuits. Such was Brian's thinking on the matter.

The ants remained on the boat as the Nature-seekers left it at the Mayan steps. There they were greeted by the camp bitch. She had so understood the soppy nature of the camp's current residents that she had awaited their return and was now going to provide them with an escort. Having identified Brian as the soppiest of them all, it was he who had her in close attendance all the way back – and he who had to stop her from joining him in his cabin. Even soppy Brits have their limits.

This rejection didn't stop her from joining them again at the lunch table. She stationed herself under it while the two puppies crowded around Brian's chair. How the hell did they know? And they even knew when to call it a day, which this lunchtime was near its conclusion when a bowl of mangoes was placed on the table. This fruit was clearly not to their liking. They withdrew to the threshold of the dining room and fell asleep. Or maybe they were just closing their eyes to the sight of a group of English people grappling with the challenge of whole fresh mangoes. Because even for those of a barely squeamish disposition, this is not a sight to be welcomed.

Brian didn't join in. He was only ever prepared to tackle any sort of food when there was a half reasonable chance that a majority of it would end up in his mouth and not on his hands and his face. However there were apparently no such concerns for most of the ladies in the party. And it was just as well that, for these plainly more reckless individuals, there was a generously sized sink at the end of the dining room. It had clearly been installed by the camp's management as a result of their observation of similar tussles between the English and their mangoes in the past. Brian could only think that for an ex-colonial race, it was all rather embarrassing, and might even border on the shameful. Or did he mean comic?

Nothing more had been mentioned on the subject of books. So Brian suggested to Sandra that they retire to their room again. It was time for more nudity beneath the fan – and for Brian to remind himself of what he'd actually written in those books. If they were mentioned again, he thought it might be useful to know what people were talking about.

In the event, it wasn't necessary. Even though, as soon as they'd set off in the boat again an hour or so later, Alan had pulled out a copy of "*Crats*". He proceeded to read it but not to challenge Brian on any of its contents. Instead he just made Brian feel a little unsettled… For it was one thing to know that people were reading your books; it was quite another to be in their company when they were doing this. Brian tried not to notice and instead occupied himself with some active spotting. If there was anything out there, he intended to call it – and to be seen to be calling it, rather than to be suspected of listening for any reactions from Alan. But it was difficult. They were heading south, to that part of the Sundarbans well away from human settlement where the islands are no bigger but the channels between them become wider all the time. And this meant that because the boat was now keeping to the safety of mid-channel, away from hidden sand banks, the land was more distant than ever – and the prospect of spotting wildlife had become remote. Alan had known this was going to happen and it was why he had brought the book with him and was now reading it – in favour of staring into the distance or attempting another crossword. He had known he was unlikely to add to his bird list on this voyage and he had therefore wanted to add to his reading list instead. Even if it was just the work of an unknown and untested wordsmith.

He had made a good choice. The boat was now "at sea" and land was distant in all directions. In fact Brian began to consider the sea-worthiness of their vessel. They weren't gliding on smooth water anymore; they were cutting through a choppy main, with flecks of foam around, and occasionally a drift of spray across the upper deck. He just hoped that those ants hadn't been hungry enough to chew through too much of the boat itself.

It seemed they hadn't. The boat ploughed on and it soon became clear that enough of it remained un-eaten. Brian was reassured – right up to the point where the master of the boat began to execute a turn. Because in conducting this manoeuvre, he appeared to be taking a risk – and the risk was of capsizing his vessel. Well, maybe it wasn't leaning that much. But it was now sailing across the direction of the waves – and there were waves now. And it was doing this close to what Brian could only think of as a maelstrom. There was a huge patch of turbulent water that the master clearly wanted to skirt in making his turn, but that threatened to engulf them at any second – with or without the help of those worrying waves…

Then, as quickly as it had begun, it was over – and the boat was approaching some land and the mouth of a more modest-sized channel. Brian indulged himself in a sigh of relief – as Alan put his book down and the photographers and cinematographers in the party readied their equipment. They were now getting close enough to the mangroves to stand a chance of seeing something.

They did, but it wasn't too many birds. Instead their first encounter was with another boat. This was of a similar design to their own, but bigger, and it had on board not a party of bird-watchers but a party of partygoers. This apparently was still the major use to which visiting Indians put the Sundarbans: as an exotic backdrop to their floating and often very noisy celebrations. Why party in crowded Kolkata when you can party at the top of your voice in the middle of the deserted and romantic-looking Sundarbans? And who knows what regulations were recognised on these boats compared to those enforced on the mainland? It seemed like a good idea, even if it didn't seem to be utilising the Sundarbans for the purpose for which they were now being maintained.

Anyway, the Nature-seekers exchanged waves with the partygoers as their boat passed them in the other direction, and then some of the Nature-seekers, including Brian, realised that there wasn't just waving going on there, but that there was also some pointing. A number of the revellers were pointing down the channel towards something they must have seen, and that would soon provide the Nature-seekers with their second encounter. The master of the Sundari spotted it first. It was a salt water crocodile on the bank, and it was enormous.

The boat turned towards it and cameras and camcorders were primed for action. Then the boat was virtually alongside it, and everybody on board must have been thinking what Brian was thinking: that the crocodile he'd spotted yesterday and which he'd taken such pride in, was to this crocodile what a midget is to a giant. This chap must have been fifteen feet long – and about half of that wide. He looked as though he'd just eaten a couple of cows and then John Prescott for afters. Brian was humbled and he was impressed, and he took as many photos as he could before they moved on. Then he had a thought, and the thought was that it was a good idea that nobody lived here. It was a very dangerous place. For everybody. And not just for John Prescott.

Then they had their third encounter, and Brian was reminded that although nobody lived on these reserve islands, some people, other than scientists and naturalists, did visit them. For a long-standing aspect of Sundarbans culture is the collection of honey from the wild. Or more specifically the almost lunatic expeditions into the mangrove forests that are still made by a number of licensed honey-collectors, and that frequently get them killed.

No, this third encounter in the channel wasn't the floating body of a honey-collector, but it was still horrifying nonetheless. It was a scrappy looking flag on the end of a scrappy looking stick, and it told all the living honey-collectors that this was where one of their number had become a departed honey-collector. This was where some poor unfortunate had been taken by a tiger and it was therefore not a good place to search for the sweet stuff. Better to sail a little further up the channel and risk your life there. God, it was terrible. We put up accident black-spot signs when there's a one in a million chance that we'll prang our car and even injure ourselves in the process. Here they put up death-spot signs when there's every chance in the world that even if you take notice of them you'll still be the cause of a new one yourself – no matter where you try your luck. Pity the tigers but pity the honey-collectors too. How poor do you have to be to run that sort of risk?

Probably about as poor as the workers the Nature-seekers saw next to the camp when they'd finally returned home.

The return trip had been uneventful other than for a dramatic fly-past of literally thousands of yellow wagtails returning south to their roosts – and an upsurge in coughing. It sounded like a barber-shop chorus gone wrong. But now they were back and being escorted by all the camp dogs along the dyke to the camp. And there they were: a dozen or so men defying the scale of their task. For these men were not just digging out a new lagoon, they were digging out an Olympic-size lagoon – without any machinery whatsoever. And they had already made incredible progress. They were at the bottom of a very big oblong hole – which had been there when the Nature-seekers had first arrived, but which was now noticeably deeper at its centre where the labourers were gathered. And here, some of them were carving out more chunks of clay from the Earth with their mattocks and loading these into what looked like big, straw fruit bowls. Others were then lifting the filled bowls onto the heads of porters, who themselves would then make their way up the side of the excavation to the head of a dyke. This earthwork ran at right angles to the dyke that carried the path to the camp, and it was being broadened at its top by all the bowls of mud being dumped there and shaped into the flat and regular crest common to all the local dykes. But again by hand. There wasn't a machine to be seen.

All the Nature-seekers stopped and gawped. They couldn't not. It was such a splendid and, at the same time, such a truly dreadful illustration of human perseverance and maybe human desperation as well. How long they'd already spent on this work, Brian couldn't tell. Nor could he estimate how much longer they needed to spend, how many more thousands of fruit bowls of mud they still needed to cart to the top of the dyke before their lagoon hole was finished and it could be filled with water – presumably for raising fish-fry. But he could still be amazed and horrified at what they were doing – and at their lack of resentment. For work had now stopped and they were all lining up for a group photo. There they were, working their proverbial whatsits off, and along come these lazy rich foreigners who have probably never wielded a mattock in their life, let alone carried far too many kilos of mud on their heads, and rather than cursing and shaking their fists in disgust, they go and line up for them – with huge smiles on their faces and not even a hint of annoyance.

Brian was flabbergasted. Why weren't they indignant? Why weren't they resentful? How could they be so friendly to these idle strangers? He couldn't answer these questions, but he suspected it was something to do with absolute poverty and a complete ignorance of how other people lived. It was to become a suspicion that was reinforced in the strongest possible way just the following day.

First, however, there was a shower to attend to, a gin and soda to deal with, and a dinner to enjoy with his companions. It was a good one; the food was excellent, the beer was cool and the dogs were peaceful – as they always were. Furthermore, there were two more references to his books and an indication that Alan wanted more. He had digested the whole of "*Crats*", and as Lynn had yet to finish their copy of "*Eggshell*", he needed something else. This was all that Brian needed – to fetch a copy of "*Ticklers*", one of his full-length books, which was a brilliant (or so Brian thought) parody of his career as an accountant – set of course in the context of an intergalactic band of adventurers. This was a risky strategy on Brian's part, but he had already risked a lot, so why not some more? And tomorrow, they had a very long trip in store. Sujan had told them. So Alan would need a demanding sort of novel – in terms of word-count, if nothing else.

Then, just before they retired to their rooms, Brian had a final thought on this risk he was running – of embarrassment or rejection or even ridicule. Alan might think he was a prat. But so what, he thought? Because that sort of risk pales into insignificance when you compare it with other sorts of risks. Like the sorts of risks that can earn you a flag at the end of a stick. It was a sobering end to his evening oday there was to be a "full day's sailing". Sujan would be taking his charges to a heronry on a distant island, and that meant that the Nature-seekers would be onboard their boat for most of the day, with even lunch being served whilst afloat. Maybe this is why he thought it would be a good idea to give them all some exercise before they plonked their bottoms on those plastic chairs for several hours. And what better exercise than an early-morning walk to find an owl nest? Yes, before they set out on their vessel, the whole party would process through the village next to the camp and seek out the nest of two barn owls which had apparently been discovered on its far side.

This was a good idea in theory, but in practice it proved less than ideal. To start with the weather had turned unbelievably sultry. Even before they set out it was not only ridiculously hot but also absurdly humid. And as soon as the walking got underway so did the sweating. Brian's pre-breakfast shower was soon overtaken by a new shower of perspiration and his clothes became disgustingly clammy. Then there was the dawdling. Everyone was interested in everything, whether it was the small schoolroom next to their path, or the lentil-picking going on in the fields – or even the ubiquitous discs of cow dung drying in courtyards and on roofs – for their subsequent use as fuel. It was all fascinating and it all had to be filmed or photographed. And as often as not from an exposed vantage-point in the full blaze of the sun. And the perspiration continued to flow…

Brian wouldn't have included this excursion in his list of the most cherished events of the holiday, but even he was captivated by the sights around him and he tried to take them all in. There were the houses, for example, all constructed from mud and cow dung with thatched roofs (as was to be expected) but all slightly different and all constructed with an eye to their appearance. They were sculptured – beautifully. They had little sculptured window openings and sculptured door frames and even sculptured seats on their outside walls. There was something "hobbit" about them, and although they were a product of acute poverty they were also a statement of the dignity and pride that this total absence of wealth seems to inspire and that Brian had observed in every poor village they'd visited. Then there was the path they were using, the brick-surfaced dyke that ran all through the village, and for all Brian knew, all the way around the island. It was attractive in its own right, and well-maintained. Even though it was in constant use by any number of pedestrians, scores of bicyclists (each with a working bell) and a host of village dogs. Every house, it appeared, had at least two hounds, and their job was to bark at anything that moved, to run out and challenge their neighbours' hounds when they'd run out to challenge the Nature-seekers, and generally to be as boisterous as the heat would allow. In fact, it was now so hot that the camp's own dog, the adult bitch who had started off with the Nature-seekers, had called it a day herself and trotted back home. Very sensible. Why would any animal or anybody exert themselves on a day like today? Well, only if they had to, thought Brian. If they had to pick those lentils. Or if they had to unload a boat-full of bricks.

And this is where the dawdling ground to a complete stop. At a point on the paved dyke where, sitting next to it, in the low-tide mud of a now almost empty channel, were two "brick boats". At least that's what they were today; two fat, black cargo boats, each with an open hull (save for a small cabin area in the stern), and these hulls packed tight with bricks. Brian could scarcely believe that these vessels could have floated; they seemed preposterously overloaded. But clearly they had floated – all the way from one of those brick works he'd seen. And here they were now being unloaded – in presumably the same way they'd been loaded in the first place: by hand – and by head. For here, in this crippling heat, were a number of men using the very same method to transfer the bricks from boat to shore as that used by those cheerful chappies who'd been digging that lagoon by the camp. Indeed maybe they were the very same men. Mornings as dockers, afternoons as diggers. And if they were, how the hell did they not just waste away? They must have been burning more calories every day than they were consuming in a week.

Brian was stunned. These guys were carrying on their heads the same fruit-bowl baskets he'd seen in use yesterday, but now not full of mud but instead full of at least fourteen full-size house bricks. He recalled the day when as a student labourer he had attempted to emulate the actions of a professional hod-carrier on a building site (in the days when hods still existed). He'd loaded it with probably no more than ten bricks, and had managed to walk a few paces with the hod over his shoulder. But then he had come to ascend the ladder to where the bricks were needed, and he'd found he couldn't even raise himself past the first rung. Fourteen bricks, he knew, constituted a very big weight for anyone to carry. For a slightly-built Indian, walking along a very wobbly gangplank, this number of bricks – on his head – constituted a virtual impossibility, especially when one took into account the temperature and the number of times he would have to bear such a load.

Well, that was it. So many minutes were spent marvelling at these heroes that the Nature-seekers ran out of time. They had dawdled and now they had ceased moving at all, and they would therefore have to forego their viewing of the barn owls and return to the camp. Back there, there might just be time for a further quick shower, a change of clothes and a drink – before their full-day's voyage got underway and they could get hot and sweaty all over again.

Their journey would take them a little way north and then a long way east. For most of the way, the populated Sundarbans would be on their left and the unpopulated tiger-reserve Sundarbans on their right. And should all go to plan, they would then arrive at the most easterly populated island within the Indian Sundarbans, beyond which was Bangladesh, but on which was the promised heronry and their ultimate destination. And the journey would take three and a half hours – each way.

Fortunately there was plenty to occupy most of the group (although Alan soon resorted to "*Ticklers*"). The populated islands were all protected by more dykes, but there were local variations in their design and big variations in their well being. Some were recently dressed with bricks and looked capable of withstanding just about anything. Others looked rather more tired and potentially fragile. And others were in pieces; they had been half washed away and new dykes were being constructed beyond their remains. The people here had been forced to retreat and forced to rebuild their defences to stop their retreat becoming a complete rout – with the loss of their homes and their livelihoods. As in so much of the Sundarbans, the houses and the peoples' farmed land was at or below sea level, and in Brian's view the word "precarious" seemed almost inadequate in describing their existence.

Precarious too was the future of the tiger. For despite the huge expanses of pristine mangrove on the unpopulated islands, there were very few of them, and far too few for Brian ever to have a chance of seeing one. But he kept on trying, looking up every creek and peering through the netting and the tangled mangroves whenever he ran out of creeks. But nothing – other than the occasional bird. And then they were often the birds one associates with human habitation: little cormorants, little egrets, collared doves, spotted doves and house crows and drongos. Rarely was there anything more interesting. And it was therefore just as well that there was also a constant flow of river traffic – as this provided a whole host of distractions.

The Sundarbans, as far as Brian could tell, boasted no roads. At least no roads that might carry four-wheeled traffic. Instead, commerce and people looked to the water for their practical means of transport, and the channel the Nature-seekers were now using was clearly one of their principal thoroughfares. It was the Sundarbans M25, full of small passenger ferries, small fishing boats and all sorts of freight hulks, built to the same basic design as those they'd seen earlier full of bricks.

They didn't see any others with bricks. Maybe, Brian thought, they really weren't capable of floating with a cargo of bricks after all, and what they'd witnessed earlier was not the unloading of a pair of brick boats but the withdrawal of stock from a pair of brick stores. But no. Here was a cargo boat, not loaded with bricks, but hopelessly overloaded with rice-sacks, so much so that the boat seemed hardly to be above the water, and the lower sacks at the side were intermittently not. As the vessel ploughed its way along, saltwater was washing over its lower line of cargo, and as this was rice, that didn't seem to Brian to be a very good idea. Not if you cooked your rice without salt anyway. Then there was another big black hulk – carrying nothing but watermelons, thousands of them, sitting in the hulk's open hull – which, for this cargo, had been lined with straw as a cushion. It made it look like the nest of some fabled giant bird, a bird that not only laid giant green eggs but a bird that also had a case of giant and rampant fecundity. It was just as well it was only fruit. Had they really been eggs, the whole world would soon have been up to its neck in fabled giant birds.

The last boat Brian took an interest in was one a little like their own – but scruffier – and with a gentleman in its lower cabin who was bailing it out constantly. He'd either spilt a lot of something inside the boat or he was trying to prevent the boat from sinking. Brian suspected it wasn't a spillage problem and he hoped that the gentleman and the guy upstairs driving the boat made it back to a quayside before they sank. And that's when Brian's boat made it to a quayside. They had finally arrived on "Heronry Island".

It then transpired that although they were now on the island, they were nowhere near the heronry. This was on the far side of the island some miles away and their journey was not yet complete. There was still some way to go. At first sight this appeared to be something of a problem; it was obviously too far to walk and there were clearly no motor vehicles available. But Sujan was already smiling. He knew it wasn't a problem at all. Because, as on many of the lived-on islands in the Sundarbans, there were always the "cycle vans"!

To give them their full description they were "kerosene-driven three-wheel cycle vans", but even this more expansive moniker doesn't really describe them completely. For these "vans" were not much more than motorised platforms built out of floorboards and scrap – and they were just about to provide the Nature-seekers with the sort of experience that they would never forget.

Each of them looked like a generously-sized tricycle, but the sort of tricycle that could have been an unsuccessful prototype of a machine never put into production by BSA in the Fifties. And each was surmounted by a square of wood, on top of which was a simple metal frame which supported a blue fabric roof. They all had a driver's seat at the very front and a kerosene fuelled "motor" beneath it, but they were all marginally different, their exact specifications having been dictated by whatever scrap was available for their construction at the time. Nevertheless these subtle differences in their appearance and in their construction did not detract from one feature they all shared in common. Yes, they all looked like nothing less than a potential death trap.

This didn't seem to faze Sujan in the least. He selected two of their number and invited the Nature-seekers to board. This process had to be seen to be believed. For with ten Nature-seekers, Sujan, three "assistants" from the boat and two drivers, that was eight people per van, seven of whom had to share the four-foot square of floorboards which now constituted the van's passenger accommodation. It was incredible. Two daredevils seated themselves on the leading edge of the floorboards, with their legs dangling to either side of the kerosene power-plant, two seated themselves on the trailing edge with their legs dangling over the back, and the remaining three took the side positions and arranged themselves according to size. That is to say, Sujan, for example, had a side to himself. And without seat-belts, a safety video or even a prayer, the kerosene was ignited and the vans were ready for the off.

Brian and Sandra had the trailing edge of the first vehicle. This wasn't a good choice. For as it moved off and then gathered speed, they had a terrible view of the speed that it had gathered but no view at all of what disaster that speed might lead to. If they were going to hit anything, they would be the last to know about it and the last to be able to take any evasive action. Sandra actually began to feel a little sick and Brian found that he was gripping the metal frame supporting the van's roof as though he never wanted to let go of it. And he really didn't. The van was now rocketing along at such a speed that should it have come to an unscheduled stop as it hit a bicycle or another van, there would almost certainly be a record death toll in the annals of accompanied bird-watching. It wasn't just that there weren't any safety features on this machine; it was also that safety didn't appear to be a locally known concept. The driver was clearly pushing his machine to the limit to get his passengers to their destination as quickly as possible. (If they made it to their destination.) And if something horrible happened on the way, then so be it. 'And what the hell's safety anyway?'

It made Brian think. All those times on the country boat on the Brahmaputra when they insisted on those stupid life-jackets, and now this: an excursion into the realms of extreme sport, Indian style, without so much as a gum-shield.

Brian tried to concentrate on other things: on the local houses, the local flora – and the weather – which was now looking a little threatening. But he was failing. All he was really aware of was the following van, with a subdued looking Alan and Lynn sitting either side of its driver – and bouncing a lot – and the locals, for whom the sight of two racing tricycles full of funny white people must have been a sight to behold. As they passed them, the local inhabitants would stand with hands on hips or with hands on heads (it was obviously a local custom) and either wave, gaze in disbelief, smile or actually burst into laughter. Brian even began to wonder whether the Nature-seekers were the first ever humans to be carried by these machines. Maybe normally they were reserved for rice-sacks or bricks. They certainly had the right suspension for rice-sacks or bricks, a view with which his bum would now wholeheartedly agree. Just as it would not dispute that it had become airborne for a second.

This happened when the leading van left what was a reasonably level road for a side road that was no more than a path of bricks, and that started at a few important inches below the road. Brian and Sandra had known nothing about its arrival – until it arrived. And then they were both jolted upwards from the surface of the floorboards. Had they not both been holding on for dear life, they would now have been on the brick path and just about to be run over by the second van. And what a way to go: mangled to death by a kerosene-smelling tricycle. Not exactly up there with being killed in the Isle of Man TT or dying from a sky-diving accident, is it?

Nevertheless, Brian was still alive and still able to see his own discomfort mirrored in the faces of Alan and Lynn, who were now being bounced about on the yellow brick road just as violently as he was. And he was still able to draw some comfort from the fact that he didn't have a side seat. Because those poor unfortunates didn't have to cope with just the acute bumping, but they were also faced with the threat of instant limb removal at any time. Their route ran through a series of little settlements, and in many of these there were hedges of sorts and various fences that abutted the path itself. And as the path was not much wider than the wheelbase of the tricycles, this meant that the side-passengers' dangling legs were often no more than centimetres from these barriers. And Brian could not believe that sooner or later they would not be closer than this – and that an amputation below the knee would become an odds-on certainty. It never did on this outward trip, but its possibility made Brian decide that he and Sandra would avoid that position at any cost for the ride back. Even if it meant walking, missing the boat and having to learn Bengali to allow them to spend the rest of their lives on this island.

Then, eventually, the van drew to a halt. It had been half an hour of excitement and terror – and astonishment. But now it was over, at least for a little while, and Brian could enjoy some herons.

Or so he thought. The heronry was on the far side of a channel from a linear village that nestled behind the protection of a rather weatherworn and un-surfaced dyke. But it appeared it was too early in the season and the heronry was deficient in one very important ingredient: the presence of herons. There were absolutely none of them there. Which meant that the Nature-seekers had sailed for three and a half hours and then put their lives on the line for a further half an hour to see precisely nothing at all in the heron department, and would now have to invest a further four hours of their lives to get back.

Brian took all this in his stride. As he kept telling himself, birding holidays were as much about experiences as they were about birds. And who could have asked for a more genuine experience? He would remember it forever. Or for as long as he survived on the way back. And there was the village as well. This was fascinating in itself. For not only was it full of beehives, and therefore presumably some very sensible fellows who had abandoned bee-hunting with all its perils in favour of bee-keeping with none, but it also had a flaming water pump. Yes, quite incredibly, there was a water pump at the edge of the village that didn't need pumping because the water was constantly being forced to the surface by dissolved gas – which, with the application of a cigarette lighter, could be made to ignite. One was then presented with the sight of a spout of (drinkable) water on top of which was a healthy looking flame. It must, thought Brian, be methane, but to have so much of this dissolved in the ground water that it pushes the water to the surface without the need for pumps and then burns there so freely, was quite remarkable and well worth a photo. Although at the time Brian didn't notice the presence of this water-source pun.

What he did notice, however, was the intense interest being shown by the villagers in the presence of such odd-looking strangers, this band of weird and wonderful folk who dressed like aliens and who were draped about with all manner of even weirder looking machines, some of which they held to their eyes as if to shade them. It was pretty damn clear that these local inhabitants hadn't seen too many outsiders before, and if the heronry was so bloody unreliable Brian could well understand why. But he hadn't yet learnt just how infrequently the outside world impinged on this community. And when he did, and when he learnt what the villagers actually thought about the Nature-seekers, he found the revelation even more fascinating than the burning well – and a reinforcement in spades of his suspicions about the locals' ignorance about how others lived.

Sujan told him. When they'd been in the village, a number of the villagers had approached him to ask him (in Bengali) who the Nature-seekers were and in particular where they were from. Now, to understand the remainder of this tale, it is necessary to be reminded of some Indian geography, and how the state of West Bengal, of which the southern edge is the Sundarbans, is bordered to its north by the state of Bihar. From this island in the Sundarbans to the nearest point of Bihar is probably no more than two hundred miles. But for the inhabitants of this island that is a long way indeed. And not just in distance terms, but in imagination terms as well. For when Sujan told them that his companions were from England – which was a very long way away – their response was at first puzzlement and then a realisation.

'Ah!' they would say. 'You mean Bihar!'

'No,' he would reply. 'They're from England... a long way away.'

'Yes,' they would agree. 'Bihar... a long way away.'

'No, England... a very long way away.'

'Yes, Bihar... a very long way away. These people are Biharians.'

'No, they're from England.'

'Yes, Biharians...'

'Yes,' conceded Sujan eventually. 'These people are Biharians...'

He could not convince them otherwise. So he gave up. He knew that they lived such isolated lives and had such little education, that they knew nothing about England, had no concept of where it was – or that anything could be that far away – on a globe shaped object. And they could only countenance somewhere far away as being Bihar, a place they

237

had heard of which they knew to be distant but which they had never visited and never would visit. And this incredibly narrow view of the world enabled them to accept a band of white bird watchers as a delegation of their fellow Indians from an adjacent state, always assuming, of course, that they had a concept of the nation of India. This was by no means certain, and it was quite obvious that they had no concept whatsoever of any England being involved in its creation as a nation.

For Brian, this insight into the lives of these people made the boat trip and even the tricycle trip very well worth it. He found it completely astonishing that there could be people living within just a few hours' travelling of Kolkata, in a supposedly modern nation like India, who knew next to nothing about their place in the world or even about their place in their own country. It was appalling yet at the same time almost reassuring. Ignorance as a concept is terrible. But in practice it does at least allow you to live a life which may not be that much worse than those lived by others who have all the knowledge in the world – and in some ways it might even make that life better. How, for example, can you worry about North Korea or Iran if you've never heard about them, and how can you yearn to be somewhere other than your own village if you have only a very vague idea of where somewhere else is?

India, even at the nub-end of this holiday, was continuing to provide surprises. Brian just hoped that the tricycles didn't do the same on the way back. They didn't. Partly because Brian and Sandra had secured the forward-facing "seats" on the leading van for the trip and partly because there were no unforeseen incidents. In fact the only incident worthy of mention at all was the interruption to the ride when the two tricycles attempted to rejoin the road. For not only was the road a few inches above the level of the path, it was also at the top of a slope. Not a steep slope, just a very gradual slope. But, for a kerosene-powered tricycle, a slope too much – when it is carrying anything. So all the passengers had to dismount while the empty tricycles struggled their way to the top of the slope, and they were allowed to remount them only when the road had been regained. From then on it was simply a mix of plain sailing and plain terrifying. For example, several cyclists approaching the vans seemed so entranced by the sight they were witnessing that they forgot to steer their machines, and the leading van had to undertake a number of swerves. But at least Brian and Sandra could see what was happening now, so only a manageable amount of plain terrifying, and Brian was even almost sorry when the ride came to an end. But only almost.

Then it was aboard the Sundari again and for most of the Nature-seekers a visit to one of its loos. It had not only been a long time, but it had also been a very bumpy time, and bumpiness has its consequences. So too does a very long morning without food. Everybody was very hungry.

It was just as well then that, directly after the relief session and when the boat was underway, the refreshment session arrived – in the form of a wonderful kedgeree with all the trimmings, including some wonderful dahl. The boat's master had been cooking this while they had been doing their tour de island and he now presented it just as the weather was getting even more threatening than before and as the water they were sailing on was becoming rougher by the minute. Then it began to rain. So another new experience for Brian, and for all of them, he imagined: a kedgeree lunch aboard a small boat being assailed by worsening weather. And then a new twist to the new experience; Sujan asked the assembled company to move their plastic chairs back as far as possible within the confines of the upper deck. In setting off from the camp that morning, the boat had apparently engaged with the Mayan steps a little too vigorously and had sustained a small hole in its prow. The master had applied some sticky tape as the kedgeree was cooking, but he was not entirely confident in his work. He therefore wished to raise the prow as far as possible out of the increasingly restless water, and he was seeking to achieve this by pulling the weight of the passengers from the front of his craft. That way there was a much better chance that the sticky tape wouldn't be tested beyond its capability and that therefore his boat wouldn't sink. Everybody moved back willingly and Brian thought of that chap in the other boat on the way out who had been bailing all the time. Maybe he could empty out the remains of the kedgeree dish and use that for the job. Or maybe he should just have a look at those knots on the life-belts instead.

Inevitably, disaster didn't overtake them, and soon most people had forgotten about the lack of total integrity in their craft and were doing what they'd done on the way out. Derek was scanning for tigers, Bill was frowning, Dennis was sleeping, and Alan was sniggering; he was still reading "*Ticklers*" and to Brian's delight and amazement, really enjoying it. At one point he even leaned over to Brian and complimented him on his writing. This was astounding. In fact it was a first. Life would not be the same for Brian ever again.

For now though he had to ignore his new-found fan base and join Derek and the ladies in the party in the general watch for tigers and other wildlife. He also had to give some thought to the existence of God.

He was pretty well convinced there wasn't one. But he was now experiencing a phenomenon, which taken on its own, was nothing less than proof positive that this greater being could in no way exist and had certainly never had a hand in the creation of man. And what this phenomenon was was the inevitable consequences of digesting an Indian lunch and the manner in which one coped with these consequences in the company of others. For there was no doubt about it; if there really was an all-seeing and all-powerful god-being, then to start with he would have foreseen the arrival of curries. He (or she) would then also have foreseen the action of curries on a human metabolism and how this action is not without its gaseous ramifications. He would also have known that other than in the case of recluses, these gaseous ramifications would very often be experienced in a group situation, and sometimes in a group situation that could not be avoided – as on the deck of a small boat sailing through the Sundarbans. So why then would he provide a system to deal with these ramifications that was not only malodorous in the extreme (for here we are talking about curries) but that also stood a very good chance of announcing its employment by means of sound? And that was assuming, of course, that one was able to overcome the restraints imposed on the system by the seats of those plastic chairs.

It was hopeless. A real God would have allowed us to pass wind out of somewhere like the back of our neck. And he would have engineered some sort of organic catalytic converter that would render that wind odourless before it was released into the atmosphere – and a silencer arrangement to make it noiseless as well. Indeed, the neck could have had a permanently open vent in it. So one didn't have to fart in discrete pulses but instead one could have discharged one's vapours constantly – but entirely unnoticeably. And certainly a lot less noticeably than was likely now.

No. Brian was certain. The present arrangements were the product of evolution. After all, flatulence, as it was currently dealt with, wasn't a threat to survival and it didn't even get in the way of sustaining the species through reproduction. It had obviously evolved as far as it needed to – and would only evolve further, over countless future generations, when either the social or the curry imperatives had finally required it to do so. But it was nothing to do with intelligent design and therefore nothing to do with God. Therefore God didn't exist. QED. Hell, it was such an elegant proof Brian wondered why Richard Dawkins hadn't alighted upon it himself. Maybe when he got back to England, he would write to him. But meanwhile he would wait for a change in the wind and be ultra careful. It was all he could do.

This strategy worked and nobody appeared to notice. The sticky tape and chairs-far-back strategy worked as well, and eventually the boat made it home. The weather was now sultry but windy, and Sujan told them for the first time that there was a cyclone in the vicinity. This didn't fill Brian with confidence, but he did think that the camp might be a safer place to be than on a small boat if the cyclone arrived, and he was pleased to be back. Furthermore, the gin had to be finished on this, their last evening in the camp. So, if something awful did happen, he'd not be anything like so bothered as he would be if he were sober. But he'd better start drinking early.

He had to. The meal was to be served more promptly than usual because after the meal the Nature-seekers were to be treated to a show! Yes, a party of locals were to arrive after the meal and act out a play about the tigers in the Sundarbans – and how they needed to be appeased...

Brian had reservations. He'd seen "local culture" for the

benefit of tourists before. But he need not have been concerned. For when the dining table had been pulled away from one end of the dining room to create an impromptu stage, what then followed was a revelation and a delight.

To begin with, four musicians arrived, one with some symbols and castanet devices, one with a row of drums, one with a squeeze-box and one with a voice box. It turned out that this last chap was a singer and a remarkable one at that. Then the actors began to appear, and the first thing Brian noticed about them was their appearance, and in particular their costumes. They were stunning. They were colourful, rich, highly embellished and just downright splendid. But where had they come from? These were all very local actors – from the adjacent village – who spent their lives picking lentils or carrying bricks and they dressed like proverbial peasants. Because that's what they were: poor peasants who didn't waste the very little they had on fripperies like fine clothes. But these costumes! Well, they were finer than anything Brian had in his wardrobe back home – and far more elaborate than anything he'd ever worn in his life, even when he'd been a student. 'And where do they keep them?' he thought. 'Where in their small mud and thatch huts, can they store them and keep them so clean and so smart?'

He couldn't supply answers to these questions, but he soon became distracted by the play itself and the enthusiasm and quality of the acting. It was all in Bengali, so he couldn't understand a word. But he didn't need to. The plot was easy to follow: essentially the depositing of a boy in the mangrove forest as a required offering to the tiger – with various other good guys and bad guys. And it wasn't about the plot anyway; it was about some real people getting involved with some real culture and enjoying themselves immensely.

The boy was played by a youth of only twelve, who had the acting ability of someone twice his age and a powdered face that was as haunting as it was expressive. The "female lead" could easily have been his sister; she had the same almost gaunt looks and the most accusing eyes Brian had seen in years. It made him feel guilty just looking at her. Then there was the principal bad guy, armed with a wooden sword and his features hidden behind a gruesomely painted face. He snarled a lot and rolled his eyes a lot. But he was good. So too were the "council of elders" who, much to Brian's surprise, appeared to be made up as Muslims. They all had big, stick-on beards and not so big, stick-on-the-top-of-your-head hats. Maybe it was something to do with the plot that he hadn't understood, because otherwise it was quite peculiar. This community was Hindu; it was inconceivable that they'd include a Muslim element in their play just for the hell of it. There had to be a purpose. Nevertheless, it simply added to the charm and to the impact of the whole thing. As did the appearance of the tiger...

Brian had come to India never expecting to see a tiger anywhere, and especially not here in the Sundarbans, where even if one is around (and that's not very probable) it's far more likely that the tiger will see you than that you will see the tiger. They are not just rare, they are also very secretive, and there are millions of mangroves out there in which they can be as secretive as they choose. So it wasn't a great disappointment that he hadn't seen one of these incredible animals; he had seen so much else. But now, on this last evening in this fantastic place, here was a genuine Sundarbans tiger. OK, there was a villager inside his skin and it wasn't a real skin; it was just some sort of fabric shaped and painted to look like a skin. But nevertheless, it was a tiger; there was no doubt about it. And it was a tiger in a play about a Sundarbans tiger – which made it a fully paid-up, entirely legitimate, no arguing about it, Sundarbans tiger. And even when its "operator" approached the Nature-seekers after the performance to sneakily tell them that it had been him inside it, for Brian it still remained the genuine article.

It had been a great end to their stay at the camp, and Brian felt moved enough to make a generous contribution to the theatre company's coffers. For this, the boy in the play offered him some sweets from a basket. Brian took one, but as he was holding his camera in his right hand, he used his left hand for the sweet. Sujan, behind him, made a sharp intake of breath. Brian had just done the equivalent of mooning at the Queen – on her official birthday – in the middle of Horseguards. And he felt like a prat. Nearly three weeks in India, and he couldn't even get that right. Nevertheless, the boy with the sweets didn't seem to mind. Maybe he had his own views on customs and traditions, and looked beyond the gesture to the intent. And good for him if he did. It was what India needed more of.

What Brian needed more of was gin. There was still some left, and he needed to finish it – with the help of the remaining audience. This achieved, he went to bed. It had been a long day and an intriguing day. After all, it isn't that often that you come across Indians who think you are an Indian yourself, you then establish the proof of the non-existence of God, and then on top of all that, you see a Sundarbans tiger…

15.

Most of the Nature-seekers went off to find the owl nest they'd failed to reach the previous day. Brian, however, remained in his cabin to finalise his speech to Sujan. He had been volunteered by Derek and Alan to offer the group's thanks to their guide and to hand over his tip. He didn't mind doing this, but he wanted to get it right. He also wanted to avoid another sweat-inducing walk through the village before they commenced their journey back to Kolkata. So this little preparation session under the cabin's fan was ideal.

The presentation was a success. At least to the extent that Brian didn't forget what he wanted to say. And he was also able to get in a bit about writing another book. He told the assembled company that if its subject matter was a birding holiday to India, then the likeness of any of its characters to themselves would be purely coincidental, and that he would argue this fact in the courts if necessary. This "warning" met with their approval and it even prompted Alan to say further nice things about "*Ticklers*". This, in turn, prompted Brian to give Alan another book. This was "*Lollipop*". It contained the same main characters as those in "*Ticklers*", but in this work they were exploring the foolishness of mankind – via an adventure on a giant spaceship, the business of which was everything and anything to do with sex. So it was more profound and more lewd than "*Ticklers*", but in Brian's mind, almost as humorous. He thought Alan would enjoy it.

Then, with the owl nest found and the presentation concluded, it was time to go. Further tips were proffered, many hands were shaken, profuse thanks were rendered, all the available dogs were stroked for the very last time – and the Nature-seekers were finally on their way. They boarded the Sundari, and as it pulled away from the Mayan steps most of the village had turned out to wave them off, and the Nature-seekers waved back for as long as they could. And then Brian began to feel quite miserable. Bali Island had been such a wonderful place to spend a little of his life, and now he was leaving it forever. The prospect of his coming back here, he knew, was remote, and that sort of finality always made him sad.

Nevertheless, this sadness didn't last. It was soon overtaken by mild alarm. A wind had been blowing all morning, and whilst this had done little to alleviate the heat, it was now more noticeable than ever and it was churning up the water. This, announced Sujan, was the edge of that cyclone he'd mentioned, and it wasn't done yet. Indeed, it was still so potentially dangerous (if it moved towards them) that the decision had already been made to make for a closer landfall. They would not retrace the route they had taken to get here initially, but another one that would see them arriving back on mainland India as soon as possible. Brian thought this involved their sailing north-west rather than directly north, but he wasn't sure. What he was sure of, however, was that this seemed like a good decision. It was getting almost stormy now, and he had no idea whether that sticky tape on the prow had been replaced with anything rather more normally nautical. The chairs were still pushed back as far as they would go.

In less than an hour they had arrived at their destination, a scruffy little village full of scruffy looking cycle-vans. Fortunately these were not their chosen means of transport for the ride back to Kolkata. That was to be another coach – just as soon as it arrived. Quite some time passed before it did, and when it was finally with them it was immediately obvious that it wasn't the coach they'd enjoyed on the outward trip. It was older and smaller. When it started to move off, it then became apparent that its suspension was as well. It felt as though it was well past its use by date and not up to the job anyway. Maybe it had once been on a car. Because now, on this coach, it just couldn't manage, and every pothole and every bump in the road became an intimate experience for all those on board. The coach also had a terribly loud horn that was soon in constant use and an air-conditioning system that circulated outside odours as well as cool air. This, in particular, was very bad news. The road back to Kolkata ran beside a river that was no more than an open sewer. Its smell was disgusting.

So this return journey was not going to be a repeat of their luxurious experience on the way down. It was going to be purgatory. Or it would have been had it not been for the intervention of Alan and Lynn. For Alan and Lynn had an idea, something they'd mentioned in passing the previous evening, and something that was now ripe for application. And the idea was a quiz…

It was a simple quiz. Some might say a moronic quiz. But in Brian's opinion it was an inspired quiz, a daft competition that would keep a coach-load of birders fully occupied and fully amused for over an hour, and most importantly of all, fully distracted from all those smells, bumps and horn-blasts for a large slice of the journey.

Everybody other than Alan and Lynn, as adjudicators and scorers, joined in. They competed as married-couple pairs or, in the case of Sujan, as a willing if slightly bemused solo contestant. And what they had to do, every ten minutes, was to compile a list of birds. But not just any birds. No, each list had to be a collection of birds that met a certain ridiculous criterion. So, for example, the first list required as many birds as possible, from anywhere in the world, that had in their name a reference to something that might be found in a kitchen. Birds such as an "*oven* bird", a "*spoon*bill", a "*pot*oo", a "trago*pan*", or even a "*fork*-tailed drongo". This was completely stupid but also ingenious and very demanding. It also called for imagination, and for Brian, as much stretching of the rules as he could manage. Although on this round Alan and Lynn decided that "*kettle* egret" was a stretch too far, and this cheeky suggestion was not allowed to stand.

Other rounds involved birds in song titles – such as "Rockin' *Robin*" and "The Ugly *Duckling*", and birds with a food reference in their name – such as a "mag*pie*", a "*macaroni* penguin" and a "*honey*creeper". But the best round of all, which really saw people pulling out all the stops, was the round which called for birds that included a body-part in their name. So as well as the respectable "wry*neck*", "black-*nap*ed oriole" and "short-*toe*d tree-creeper" there was also a "black-*rump*ed flameback" and, of course, a "blue *tit*". That appeared to be the extent of the crudity on board the coach until Brian reported that he and Sandra had included in their list a "*willy* wagtail" (from New Zealand) and any sort of "wood*pecker*" you care to choose. Willy wagtail made it, woodpecker didn't. And it wasn't until the following day that anyone thought of "*cock* of the rock".

It was a hard fought contest. Derek and Yvonne and Dennis and Pauline did their best, but it wasn't good enough, and the competition was really between Brian and Sandra, Bill and Tina and the solitary Sujan. Ultimately Sujan lost out from being on his own and not knowing as much about world birds as the two well-travelled duos against him. Then it was down to the final round, when Bill and Tina's encyclopaedic knowledge of birds just pipped Brian and Sandra's combination of not quite so comprehensive knowledge and their superior "imagination". Bill and Tina won by just one point. Their combined lists had included just one more bird than those of Brian and Sandra's. (Although Brian was convinced that their Madagascan "*elephant bird*" – in the "birds with an animal in their name" round – was a bird that was somewhat stretching the rules. After all, there aren't any – and there haven't been any for over four hundred years. Ever since we killed them all off. He didn't mount an official challenge or anything. It wasn't that sort of contest. But in Brian's mind, for him and Sandra, it was a draw not a defeat, and he felt suitably proud.)

He also felt fortunate. Outside the coach it was getting grimmer than ever as they approached Kolkata. People were leading pretty miserable lives out there, whilst here, inside this coach, he and his companions could indulge themselves in a session of nonsense and could now dream about another appointment with the comfort of the Oberoi Grand. For that was where they were heading again; through the ugliness and bustle of Kolkata to its principal haven of beauty and calm – assuming, that is, that it hadn't been burnt to the ground by a raiding party of Pakistanis. But Brian thought that was unlikely. Sujan would have known, but he'd said nothing. So Brian could continue to anticipate his rendezvous with luxury – while all those people outside the windows, struggling to make a living of any sort at all, could anticipate only more of the same. Maybe he should have felt guilty as well as fortunate, but that, he argued with himself, was to drift into pity, and that was not a good place to go. So just stick with the "fortunate" and hope that the driver of the coach doesn't switch it to the "terminally unfortunate" by making contact with the back of the lorry from which he's now only inches away. With the quiz over, Brian had become aware not just of the discomfort of this vehicle but also of its repeated dependence on that Indian other dimension. The driver appeared to have a death wish, which was currently being frustrated only by the magic of that impossible new space. But how long would the magic last? Might it finally run out?

Well, if it did, it was after the driver had deposited his English cargo at the gates of the Oberoi Grand. They had made it back and the hotel was still there. So too were the charming guards, the intense security procedures and the machine-gun post – and after this gauntlet of protection, the serene interior of the hotel itself. It was as fabulous as before but even more so, for now the management and staff gathered in reception greeted the Nature-seekers with the words 'welcome back'. Brian didn't think that this was a contrived sop to their egos. He thought it was the genuine recognition of a rather out of the ordinary contingent of Brits in what was clearly still an almost deserted hotel. The elections had still to take place and the Mumbai attacks were still very much in everybody's mind.

This continued absence of guests and the "frequent-stayer" status of the Nature-seekers probably accounted for the scale of Brian and Sandra's room. It was even bigger than those they'd been allocated on their previous stays, and whilst still technically a room, obviously had pretentions of becoming a junior suite.

It had its own corridor, a bedroom that could have accommodated their entire cabin in the Sundarbans probably twice over, a generous washroom with his and her wash basins, and off this, not just a bath and shower room, but also a walk-in wardrobe-cum-dressing room. It was stupendous and so were its furnishings. There were elegant cabinets, a desk, a suite of rather rococo chairs and a couch – and a four-poster bed. This was grand living and grand style, even by British standards, and Brian found himself wondering again. 'What would people outside this place think if they were let inside? Would they be overwhelmed? Would they be angry? Or would they just not believe it? Would they simply not be able to comprehend the existence of something that was so far outside their normal experience – a bit like those villagers in the Sundarbans who could come to terms with people from England only if they believed they were from Bihar?'

Brian couldn't make his mind up, but many weeks after the holiday he was given a clue as to how many of the poor people in the subcontinent might react to the interior of the Oberoi. It was in a documentary programme about the Mumbai atrocities, which included security camera footage from within both the Taj hotel and the Oberoi Trident there – and recordings of the terrorists' phone-calls with their handlers. It was all understandably obscene. But what caught Brian's attention in particular was the film of two of the attackers walking around a landing of the Taj and at the same time telling their handlers all about the "large windows" and the "big-screen TVs" and the general grandeur of the place. Even while they were busy booking themselves a ticket to Nirvana by murdering innocent people, they could still not avoid being mesmerised by the opulence of the place. But not because the inside of the

Taj, like the inside of the Oberois, was so splendid, but because it was so unknown. These were hicks from the back end of beyond in Pakistan. Not only had they never in their lives come close to reason, but they had also never come close to what might be described as splendour or elegance – or even a big pane of glass in a big window. Brian knew that a typical inhabitant of Kolkata almost certainly had a more sophisticated view of the world than that of a young Pakistani assassin, but he still thought that the reaction of those terrorists at least indicated how anybody who had not experienced sumptuous surroundings might react. And, of course, if they were mesmerised, that's where most would stop. He was confident that all normal people wouldn't then go on and murder those enjoying the opulence. But this thought then led to another question in his mind concerning those who did go on to murder:'Would it be opulent in this promised heaven they were going to, and if so would they be mesmerised all over again or just a little disappointed that it was no better than what they had finally realised existed back on Earth?'This was a question to which he never expected to get an answer.

However, that was all in the future. The present was still about exploring the room – and inevitably looking out of the window – a big one with a big pane of glass. Outside, across the street, there was a substantially-built pay-to-use lavatory, a sort of private convenience for those who could afford it. To both sides of this, and crammed right up to its doors, were drifts of luggage and handbags. For this was "leather alley" or maybe "simulated leather alley", where those in Kolkata who needed a carrying container for their clothes or their make-up could satisfy their need. There were cases and holdalls of all shapes and sizes and more handbags dangling from towering display boards than Brian had ever seen in his life. Why Victoria Beckham wasn't down there he couldn't work out. But maybe price trumps choice, and he doubted that there was anything down there that could be described as even marginally expensive. This was Kolkata, not Beverly Hills.

Having tired of the view after just thirty seconds, Brian suggested to Sandra that they should probably get some lunch. It was now quite late and he was hungry as well as thirsty.

'Where do you want to eat?' asked Sandra.

'Well, I don't fancy changing yet,' he replied. 'So how about the bar? They must do some food there.'

'Do they?'

'Well, if they don't they don't. But I fancy a drink first anyway. So I vote for the bar. And we can find out whether they do any food when we're there.'

This was the sort of critical-path analysis on which Britain had once built an empire.

'Wither do you want to sail, captain?'

'Well, I don't fancy that Cape Horn stuff. So how about south and then east? There must be some land there.'

'Is there?'

'Well, if there isn't there isn't. But I fancy a voyage first anyway. So I vote for an easterly course. And we can find out whether there's any land there when we're there.'

This probably wasn't historically correct or anywhere near the truth, but Brian was sure that it was just this sort of pragmatism and just this sort of confident single-mindedness that had served Britain well in the past. However, Sandra didn't seem entirely convinced.

'Uhmm... I'm not sure we won't miss lunch altogether,' she offered. But then she bowed to the inevitable and accompanied her (still shorts-wearing) husband to the bar. He wasn't the only one who wanted a drink.

All was well. In the bar they were able to indulge themselves in a pair of gin and tonics (not gin and sodas) – and they were also able to secure for themselves that ultimate in international dining: a generously accessorised club sandwich. There was not only an edible helping of salad with the speared delicacy but also a bountiful supply of wonderfully cooked chips. It was not very Indian and not very healthy, but it was thoroughly enjoyable. Brian finished his completely and even polished off Sandra's remaining chips. Then as they rose to leave the bar at the conclusion of this delightful repast, their waiter approached the table. He was a very pleasant and very deferential member of the Oberoi's staff, and he very pleasantly and very deferentially informed Brian that: 'Sir, excuse me and I wish to cause you no offence, but I have to tell you that there is a dress code in this bar, and that it precludes the wearing of shorts by its gentlemen patrons.'

His English was better than most that is spoken in Britain, and Brian attempted to respond as concisely and as grammatically as he could.

'Oh, I am sorry,' he said, 'but we've just returned from the Sundarbans and I hadn't taken the opportunity to change. Clearly, had I known of the code I would have done so, and you can rest assured that when I return to your establishment this evening it shall be in suitably long trousers. You have my word.'

This was received by the waiter with a nod of his head and a smile.

'Of course, sir. It's just that I wished you to avoid any embarrassment.'

'Thank you,' responded Brian, and then he nodded and smiled too. For he knew that the waiter meant exactly what he'd said. He also knew that he and Sandra had been allowed to spend their money on a drink and lunch before they'd received this advice. This was possibly something to do with the fact that they were the only customers in the bar, but more likely it was to do with a practised ability on the part of the Oberoi's staff to balance genuine civility with commercial considerations. Why frighten off paying customers with a premature piece of advice when this could be just as well delivered after the conduct of some lucrative business? The drinks and the club sandwiches were expensive, and there were so few residents in this hotel at the moment that everything helped...

Brian thought that the waiter's approach had been impeccable and liked to think that it was exactly the way he would have done it himself. He was therefore not offended in the slightest and, on the contrary, saw it as a wonderful demonstration of how to secure a necessary outcome – in this case the communication of a rather admirable dress code – in the most respectful and pragmatic manner possible. Just like his forbears had built that empire. Only with rather more respect.

So now there was the prospect of an afternoon at leisure – and free from dress codes. Brian and Sandra exploited this in the only way they could; they took themselves to the swimming pool. Despite all the water that had surrounded them on the Brahmaputra and then in the Sundarbans, recreational immersion had not been a possibility. So now they wanted to put that to rights. And where better than in the palm-fringed courtyard of the Oberoi Grand and in its expansive and virtually empty bathing pool? It was superb. A bottle of water and a bottle of sun-tan lotion as one settled onto one's padded sunlounger and the delivery to one's side of some Oberoi style towels made to Oberoi size dimensions. Greed might never be good, but just occasionally outrageous self-indulgence has its place.

This excursion into pampered indolence lasted into mid-afternoon. Brian and Sandra then learnt from Derek that the Oberoi had a "special" visitor, someone who had just returned from Guhawati where he'd been doing some cooking or something. Yes, Gordon Ramsey was in residence. Well, of course, both of them so wanted to meet him, they had no choice but to retire to their room immediately, put up the "do not disturb" sign and double lock the door.

So now they were not only safe from a real-life celebrity, but they were also free to do what all Brits do at the fag-end of a holiday; they turned on and tuned into telly.

Brian soon discovered (for it was he who did most of the tuning) that Indian television was just as dire as any other television in the world. It had the usual mix of the incomprehensible, the banal, the frenetic and the downright dull. But it had something else that marked it out from any other national telly he had ever experienced: a gigantic overload of cricket and an almost sickening concentration on the sport's local stars. There were just so many channels that were full of various sorts of cricket-mania that one couldn't help thinking that it was no longer simply a sport in this country but that it had now gained the rank of "religion".

There were matches, bits of matches, excerpts from other matches, lots of different coloured cricket outfits, lots of sunglasses, lots of lingering shots of batters and bowlers – and very little of what Brian would have recognised as traditional cricket or traditional cricket coverage. It was all manic, and in his eyes, entirely nonsensical. Whatever was on screen at any time, on any one of these so-called cricket channels, it had as much in common with real cricket, where people wear whites and take days to avoid a result, as "*King Lear*" does with "*Mother Goose*". Both of these, the Shakespearian production and the pantomime, might use the same tools and the same techniques (in their case, actors and acting) but they are hardly comparable. In the same way, floodlit, hysterical, limited-over, limited-attention-span and dressed-in-green-pyjamas quickie-cricket might use a bat and a ball and the basic rules of cricket, but it has less to do with proper cricket than it does with something you'd find on a Play Station. And Brian liked it just as much as he liked the idea of a Play Station, which was not at all. 'Poor old India,' he thought. 'Just as it might be ridding itself of some of the nonsense of the past it goes and lumbers itself with this. Talk about losing the plot.'

Then there were the adverts. And Brian was convinced that they'd lost the plot. Because so many of these adverts were for skin-whitening products.

'God,' he thought, 'they change their cricket whites for darker clobber, and they then go and change their darker skins for white ones. What the hell's that all about? And isn't it a bit... well, weird? Why in a country of dark-skinned people would you want to stand out as being pale – and being... well, dishonest about your heritage? After all, this country has so many problems already that it could do with a "colour problem" about as much as it could do with an upsurge in its birth-rate... or getting its own Gordon Ramsey.'

Brian finally switched off the telly. He could stand it no more, and anyway he fancied a doze before he went to the bar again, this time in long trousers.

There, he and Sandra met all their fellow Nature-seekers, some of whom had not swum or dozed, but who had ventured into the big city. This experience had, for most of them, been either exhausting or harassing. It had been very hot in the afternoon, and as white people on the streets of Kolkata they had been very obvious and therefore very attractive to any number of sellers and hawkers. 'This way please. My shop is just round the corner. I have much in it that will interest you.' This and other encouragements were offered every few yards along the road, and as Brian knew from similar experiences in the past, even if you want to buy something, this is the last way to attract your attention successfully. If the other Nature-seekers were anything like him, in the face of this sort of continuous bombardment, they wouldn't have bought a thing. And this was largely the result. Only essential gifts for grandchildren had been acquired and very little else. And whether the grandchildren in question would appreciate the sacrifice that had been made on their behalf was open to question. What could one buy for little Nigel in Kolkata that would interest him if he couldn't play it on his I-pod or rig it up on his perishing Play Station? Answer: nothing that wouldn't be a problem with British Customs.

Brian was aware that he was becoming a little jaundiced in his views. It must have been all that kiddy-cricket on the telly. But now it was time to eat. Maybe his mood would improve.

It didn't. The Nature-seeker's real last meal had been last night – when they'd still been on their expedition and when they'd all been together. But now they were back in "civilisation", and as seductive as this manifestation of civilisation was, it was not the same. Furthermore Sujan wasn't there; he was spending the evening with his family, of whom he'd seen far too little in the past three weeks. Then Alan and

Lynn announced that they intended to try the Thai restaurant in the hotel. So only eight Nature-seekers remained to share a meal in the main restaurant. It wasn't very enjoyable. There was too much of a sense of the party being over and of the balloons having already been deflated, and this mood could not be raised by either the conversation or by the food. Brian had a Goan prawn curry, which although tasty was strangely unappetising. The wine also was a let-down. It was another Bangalore Sauvignon Blanc. But unlike the commendable "Riviera" tipples that he'd enjoyed on the Sukapha, this stuff was flat and it may even have been off. It didn't stop him drinking it, of course, but when he had he wished he hadn't. And he also wished he'd asked the waiter to taste it. Even at the risk of being told very pleasantly and very deferentially by the waiter that: 'No sir, this wine has not corked. Bangalore Sauvignon Blanc is meant to taste like this.'

Everybody went to bed early. Brian and Sandra were no exception. They tumbled into the four poster, Sandra with a book and Brian with a small bar of Toblerone that he'd taken from the room's mini-bar. When he opened it he found that its surface was more white than brown. It may well have been in the mini-bar for as long as the mini-bar had been in the room. Nevertheless it still tasted OK and Brian consumed it with relish. As he did so he had a thought.

'Skin-whitening,' he mused. 'I wonder whether chocolate-whitening holds the key. And if it does, how might I exploit it?'

Then he was asleep, and by the morning the thought had been lost.

16.

The wine *had* been off. When Brian awoke he could not believe that there was any other explanation for the state of his head. 'Great,' he said to himself. 'My last day in India and the prospect of hours in the air, and I start the day with a hangover. Pathetic!'

And so was the sight of Brian's attempt at dealing with a full English breakfast. He'd thought this might help his condition, but all it did was add a feeling of nausea to his headache. He needed some fresh air. He needed a walk outside the confines of the hotel. That is to say, he needed to confront the city of Kolkata outside the cocoon of the Oberoi.

He went on his own. Sandra had no taste for a taste of urban life and chose to stay behind. Brian thought this was a good idea. Apart from anything else, there was a half-reasonable chance that a single white individual might not be quite as conspicuous as a white couple. He might be able to undertake his recuperative constitutional unheeded by the teeming masses. Just walk around a block or two of this city without being too much bothered.

His view proved optimistic. He was fifteen paces from the gates of the hotel when his first "companion" arrived and began to walk with him. This gentleman, it transpired, knew somebody in England, wanted to visit there himself, and just happened to have a shop around the corner that was bursting with irresistibly attractive goods, and that Brian simply had to peruse. The second gentleman, who took over companion duties at the first corner also knew someone in England, didn't express an interest in going there, but also had a well-stocked emporium that quite clearly could not be ignored by any European visiting Kolkata. Gentlemen three and four were clones of one and two, but had some sort of stall in the "New Supermarket", a large building at the back of the Oberoi that looked as though it could have been newly built in Bolton sometime in the Thirties.

Brian reacted to all these approaches with politeness. One could not do otherwise; they were all such exercises in politeness themselves. And Brian even had the impression that all his suitors knew their task was futile in the first place and that they were merely going through the motions of a "retail enticement" for form's sake. It was all a charade – but a civilised charade. And that's how Brian would conduct proceedings himself – with a smile and a polite and almost apologetic rejection of their kind supplications. This always worked. But, of course, it then left the ground free for the next entreaty and the next rejection, and so on and so on. Which is why Brian cut short his promenade and simply made a circuit of the hotel. This made a city-block all on its own, and it was quite enough in the heat and noise of this Indian ant-hill to satisfy Brian's need for "fresh air" – in the metaphorical sense of the term – and he was soon back inside the real fresh air of the hotel. His head was still not very good.

It was just as well that he and Sandra had notified Sujan the previous day that they would not be participating in the very last excursion of the holiday. This was a visit to a flower market, to another temple and to the famous Victoria Memorial. There was no way that either of them had wished to expose themselves to the delights of a flower market or another temple, although they had wavered a little on the Victoria Memorial option. It was, after all, the most obvious and most popular tourist attraction in the city. But they hadn't wavered long. It was soon decided that the Victoria Memorial would have to join that long list of other famous must-sees around the world which they'd been very close to but for which they'd had too little interest to visit. It would join such eminently un-missable attractions as St George's Cathedral in Georgetown, the world's tallest wooden building, a Maori cultural evening in Rotarua, Victoria Falls, the Eiffel Tower and Raffles, all wonderful things to see, Brian was sure, but just not quite worth the effort. Especially if one had a headache.

So when the Nature-seekers went off for one last time, Brian and Sandra were able to remain in the hotel, and Brian was able to cosset his head by laying it on one of those beautifully soft towels on one of those beautifully comfortable loungers by the pool. This helped his head a little. But in the end it demanded an early siesta back in a real bed, and ultimately it began to behave itself only just in time for their departure from the Oberoi and the start of their journey home.

This cheered Brian up immensely. He had no appetite for travelling whilst in pain, and especially when the travelling kicked off in the middle of Kolkata. For then it meant one last engagement with the traffic of Kolkata – which was quite enough pain on its own.

For some unknown reason, the trip to the airport was to be made, not in a coach, but in two cars and a small minibus. Brian and Sandra shared one of the cars with Lynn and Alan. The other six Nature-seekers were stowed into the minibus.

And the second car was packed with Sujan and all the luggage. When everybody and everything was in, the little convoy then set off, with Sujan's vehicle in the rear to ensure that nobody got lost. Unfortunately this arrangement didn't ensure that Sujan didn't get lost…

It had started out as just the normal gamble played out on the edge of eternity, where one's life might easily slip into the void of non-existence by the arrival of some sudden unforeseen event. Not, of course, an event such as a careless turn of a lorry's steering wheel or a failure on the part of your driver to see an oncoming bus – but by a special event. By nothing less than a lapse in that Indian magic. By a hole in that unique Indian dimension that allows two or more vehicles to occupy the very same space at the very same time and thereby keep their occupants unharmed. It was possible. Brian knew it. He had seen the evidence of collisions everywhere. And this had to mean that sometimes the magic failed. So it was a gamble, and on this last trip out of Kolkata it felt more like a gamble than ever. After all, it was the very last throw of the dice. But when the journey was approaching its conclusion and they were virtually in sight of the airport, the nature of the gamble changed. Because Brian and his companions were now not in the middle of a tangle of threatening traffic but on a virtually clear dual carriageway on the outskirts of Kolkata, where a respectable speed was achievable – and was being achieved by the drivers of other vehicles – whilst the driver of their own vehicle was managing just two miles per hour.

This chap didn't speak English. It was therefore very difficult for a quartet of non-Bengali-speaking Britons to communicate with him and to establish what he was up to and whether he appreciated the dangers of being at a virtual standstill on a road that was carrying fast-moving traffic. Ultimately, however, an explanation was forthcoming. Thanks to the invention of the mobile phone and Alan's use of the driver's to talk to Sujan, it was discovered that this driver and the driver of the minibus had adopted their extreme-crawl practice to allow Sujan's car to catch up. It had been delayed. When it did catch up it was then discovered why it had been delayed. It appeared that a policeman had stopped Sujan's car because he thought he wasn't wearing his seat-belt! In fact he was, but Sujan's offended and possibly abrasive reaction had caused the policeman to introduce some of his colleagues into the proceedings and then to demand all sorts of "papers". There was then the prospect of the Nature-seekers' luggage making it to the airport at about the same time that its owners were landing at another airport somewhere near the M4. So Sujan offered to pay a "fine" (of one hundred rupees) and the policemen's interest in his papers evaporated as suddenly as it had crystallised. Almost sublimely, one might say – if one remembered one's O-level chemistry. Anyway, this chemistry had worked: add ten grams of paper currency to a heated gathering of insistent constabulary, and one gets an instant reaction and then the required ideal solution – in this case the ability to reunite some luggage with its owners before they leave the country.

So Brian had survived his last road excursion in India; he had made it to the airport – with his wife and his luggage in tow. And now all that remained was to bid a fond farewell to Sujan and to say his goodbyes to his Nature-seeker companions. They were all taking various routes back to England and this would probably be the last time they'd all be together. So there were lots of hugs and handshakes, lots of thanks and best wishes, and after that there were two long flights back to Britain. They were, of course, nothing to do with the Brahmaputra or the Sundarbans and will not be reported on here – other than in terms of what they allowed Brian to think about his holiday. What he would take home with him as his principal thoughts and conclusions about what he'd seen in Assam and in the Sundarbans delta, and what these same thoughts and conclusions might say to him about India.

Number one in his list of impressions about the place had to be its wildlife. He had been fortunate enough to see many birds and many animals in many parts of the world, and what he had seen in the two areas of India he had visited was up there with the best. There had been dozens of new birds. He hadn't put together a count yet; that would be Sandra's job. But between them they had seen far more new species than they'd dared to hope for – many of them thanks to Tika and Sujan. And amongst this bird haul had been some really fabulous ones; the Bengal florican, the pied harrier and the wryneck being the most fabulous of them all. Then there were the animals: the one-horned rhinos, scores of them, the Indian elephants, the spotted deer, the salt water crocodiles and the water monitors. Then there'd been the Gangetic dolphins and the Irrawaddy dolphins, and some of those smaller critters, the pygmy hogs, the langurs and the gibbons. It had been an outstanding wildlife expedition, and one experienced in astonishing landscapes: first that of the mighty Brahmaputra and its surrounding lands and then that of the stunning and unique islands of the Sundarbans. Both settings had been amazing in their own way – and frightening. Both were jaw-droppingly beautiful but both were also stomach-churningly fragile, places where all life was constantly on the edge.

Then number two: the Nature-seekers' temporary homes: the Sukapha, the Oberoi and the camp in the Sundarbans. The boat had been a delight; clean, comfortable, well-organised and staffed with some of the most agreeable and most efficient people Brian had ever met. It had been a joy. As had the Oberoi Grand, albeit in a different way; wonderful surroundings, wonderful people and a wonderful insulation from the reality outside. The camp in the Sundarbans had clearly not been in the same league, but like its floating and city-centre counterparts, it had provided the Nature-seekers with a memorable stay, not least through its excellent (and supplemented) food, its fantastic entertainment and the friendliness of its people.

And it was the people of India whose turn it was to have a place on his list in their own right. For all those he'd met and with whom he'd had any sort of relationship, whether it was an extended one as with Sujan, or a transient one as with the guy at the Oberoi who had enlightened him on the intricacies of its dress code, they were all charming and genuinely amicable. Even those professional accosters in the streets outside the Oberoi had been sociable and civil – and entirely unthreatening. Nowhere had he ever felt in the slightest way intimidated or even resented. And for a white ex-colonial in a now liberated non-white nation, that was more than remarkable and something that all Indians should take pride in – even if it had never occurred to them to do so. Whatever faults might be laid at their door, the bearing of grudges, or at least the open manifestation of grudges through hostility or even a coolness of manner, did not rank amongst them.

Brian had also been impressed by the friendliness of his fellow Nature-seekers and the kindness and professionalism shown by Tika from Nepal. Maybe everybody on the expedition had been infected not only with gippy tummies and a (still lingering) chronic cough, but also with the goodwill of their Indian hosts, and this had persuaded them to show their better side themselves. Or maybe it was in part their reaction to some other aspects of India, aspects of the country that forced them to seek solace in the company of fellow foreigners and to ensure they maintained this company. These aspects of India could not be ignored and now had to feature on the second part of Brian's list.

Prominent amongst them was the flip side of that first entry concerning the richness of India's wildlife and the beauty of its wild areas. It was the fact that these wild areas are few in number, tiny in size, that they are being eroded all the time and that there is every likelihood that eventually they will be extinguished completely. And even if they are able to hang on at all, the wildlife within them might still wither, such are the pressures of poaching, illegal grazing, illegal clearance, pollution – and the scourge of corruption. All that stands in the way of all these threats is an under-resourced and de-motivated band of forest guards and a handful of people like Sujan.

This won't be enough. The vast majority of Indians, and indeed all those people who inhabit the subcontinent, still regard land as a utility, something that must always be used for farming or grazing or building, and something that should never be left idle and abandoned for just the benefit of animals and birds. Brian knew that this attitude to land-use and its associated indifference to wildlife extended to the wellbeing of even that most iconic of India's animals, the failed-to-be-seen on this trip and much endangered tiger. Many of this magical animal's so-called reserves are now no more than denuded landscapes, over-grazed grasslands, chopped-down, burnt-out woodlands, and teak-tree plantations. And the tigers themselves are on the way out. There are probably less than a thousand of them in the whole country. Soon there will be none.

Of course, Brian knew that no matter how indifferent a country's population might be to its wildlife and how careless it might be with its land use, this in itself was not the major problem. If India had a population of just one million, then that population could be as irresponsible and short-sighted as it liked and the wild parts of India and their wild inhabitants would cope very well. But India hadn't got just one million people. It had one thousand, two hundred million people, three times as many souls as it had at independence in 1947. And this was where the problem really lay. India – and Bangladesh and Pakistan – were all simply bursting with people. The cities were jammed with them, the countryside was overflowing with them – and the very last remnants of wilderness would soon be overtaken by them.

This mass of humanity, everywhere, would probably be one of the two major enduring impressions that Brian took home with him. Quite simply, there were far too many people. It was a population out of control. It might be quite disconcerting occasionally to be presented with statistics of population growth and to consider their consequences, but to see it for real, and to start to appreciate, first hand, what a burgeoning mass of humanity means in terms of degradation and suffering and squalor... Well, that was really frightening – and really demoralising. Because India was a window into the future. Look at the subcontinent and you could see what the whole world will look like later this century. How things will be when South and Central America, Africa, the Middle East, most other parts of Asia and indeed everywhere where fertility rates are now off the scale, follow India's lead. It will look wrecked, impoverished, exhausted and ugly. It will also be devoid of most of its wildlife.

The other enduring impression was the general Indian attitude to the state they were already in. They seemed blind to it. Other than those really poor people whom Brian had seen in the remoter parts of both Assam and West Bengal, they appeared not only to have lost their sense of aesthetics but also any sense of pride in their surroundings and a desire to care for their environment. Brian had seen many other "disadvantaged" people around the world, but never had he seen them living in such hideous and neglected conditions. It had been truly appalling, and no more so than in Kolkata, where there was simply no relief from the decrepit, the dirty and the disgusting. What would it take to wake them up to their situation? And what would it take to wake them up to their need to have fewer children?

It was all very depressing, not least because Brian knew that there was nothing to wake them up. Their government wouldn't do it and neither would their religions. Indeed both their temporal and their spiritual institutions were in many ways the cause of their problems. When it came to reforming their culture to give it any chance of surviving into the future (let alone giving the wildlife of India a chance), the government was either unwilling or incapable, and the religions were set against it. Religions always were.

So that was it. The holiday had been great – for the wildlife that was still around, for the accommodation and for the people Brian had met. But for what it had shown him about the condition of India now and the rest of the world in just a few years' time, it had been dispiriting in the extreme. It had been truly awful. He knew that there was much to criticise in his native country, more than was needed to fill a whole book. But at least in Britain – now – there was a sense that things can't go on the way they are, and no matter how awkward it's going to be, we can't ignore that we've got only one planet – and only one chance. The trouble, however, was that Brian was only too aware that this "we" was now in a rapidly diminishing minority, and that even with whole armies of Nature-seekers recruited to the cause, the chance of our stopping the rot had probably already past.

Nevertheless, it would be good to get home. Good to get back to what he now saw, despite all its shortcomings, as a more rational and more enlightened place than ever.

Then he was home. Their plane had landed at Heathrow and Brian's expedition was finally at an end. Strange then that the first person with whom he had dealings was an Indian. Brian was about to ask him whether he knew the Brahmaputra or the Sundarbans. But as soon as he'd inspected his passport he waved Brian on. And Brian stepped into England.